Confucian Democracy

SUNY series in Chinese Philosophy and Culture

Roger T. Ames, editor

Confucian Democracy

A Deweyan Reconstruction

Sor-hoon Tan

State University of New York Press

Published by
State University of New York Press, Albany

For information, address State University of New York Press,
90 State Street, Suite 700, Albany, NY 12207

Production by Michael Haggett
Marketing by Jennifer Giovani

Library of Congress Cataloging-in-Publication Data

Tan, Sor-hoon, 1965–
    Confucian democracy : a Deweyan reconstruction / Sor-hoon Tan.
      p. cm.—(SUNY series in Chinese philosophy and culture)
    Includes bibliographical references and index.
    ISBN 0-7914-5889-X—ISBN 0-7914-5890-3 (pbk. : alk. paper)
    1. Confucianism and state.   2. Democracy–Religious aspects–Confucianism.
  I. Title. II. Series.

BL1840.T36 2004
321.8′01—dc22

2003068666

10 9 8 7 6 5 4 3 2 1

Contents

Acknowledgments

A teacher once told me that the best way, perhaps the only way, to repay a debt of kindness is to pass it on. I think it applies equally well to debts of intellectual growth. I would like to pass on not only what I have learned, but to contribute to the task of philosophical inquiry to which my teachers have devoted themselves.

This book was first written as a doctoral dissertation at the University of Hawaii at Manoa. I am grateful to the anonymous reviewers whose comments were very helpful during the revision of the manuscript. My colleague, Jiuan Heng, read the early chapters, and Keith Wiltshire read the entire text. I appreciate very much their comments and encouragement. It is entirely my own responsibility that the final product is not any better.

I am especially grateful to all the members of my dissertation committee—Roger Ames, James Tiles, Mary Tiles, Kenneth Kipnis, and Shi Mingzheng—who gave timely and invaluable feedback on the various drafts. Shi Mingzheng, though only an external member, impressed and moved me by the seriousness and meticulousness with which he read my drafts. His enthusiasm encouraged me to believe that the results of my labor might be interesting and comprehensible even to nonphilosophers.

Kenneth Kipnis and Mary Tiles provided valuable viewpoints from outside my chosen specialization; they questioned my theses and arguments vigorously and prevented me from taking too much for granted and speaking only to specialists in Confucianism or pragmatism. Their insistence on my giving Western philosophical views equal respect rather than viewing them through Asian glasses helps make the final result more balanced than it would have been.

Joseph Grange, who conducted a graduate seminar on John Dewey during a one-year visit to the University of Hawaii, introduced me to Dewey and pragmatism. This interest was further fostered by James Tiles, whose detailed criticisms of every draft of my dissertation constantly challenged me to improve my understanding of Dewey's philosophy and helped me develop different perspectives on the Confucian texts on which I was working.

Roger Ames is not only one of the best teachers I have ever met, but he continues to be my exemplar of what a Confucian scholar should be. His ability to inspire is enhanced by his willingness to tolerate and even respect dissent from his students. He not only taught students philosophical theories but, through his own example, he also instilled in them a sense of responsibility toward the scholarly community and the wider society.

The National University of Singapore granted me study leave and sponsored my graduate studies, which enabled me to concentrate on my studies and research without any financial worries. I also wish to thank my fellow graduates and other students at the University of Hawaii, with whom I had interesting and sometimes heated discussions, and faculties, whose seminars I attended. The four and a half years in Hawaii taught me much about community in practice.

Last but not least, my family's support and belief in me made it possible for me to leave more profitable careers to pursue my philosophical interests. No words can fully express what I owe them.

Chapter 1

Confucian Democracy?

DIVINING THE FUTURE

With the end of the Cold War, many have foreseen a new world order. Have we reached "the end point of mankind's ideological evolution and the universalization of Western liberal democracy as the final form of human government"?[1] Even as Francis Fukuyama's announcement of the end of history stirred up a fierce storm of controversy in 1989, events in China moved rapidly to shatter any belief that China would become a liberal democracy any time soon. How could we talk about the "unabashed victory of economic and political liberalism" as we watched a government turn its guns and tanks against unarmed citizens in the streets of Beijing on June 4, 1989?

While not claiming the immediate end of history, Fukuyama proclaims the *inevitable* end of history.[2] He supports Alexandre Kojève's defense of Hegel's claim that the inevitable end began in 1806, but the end is not so much a point as it is a long, drawn-out process, with no terminus in sight. Quite apart from being impossible to prove, any claim of historical inevitability undermines active advocacy to work for that end: if nothing we do could change the outcome, neither do we need to do anything to ensure it.

At times Fukuyama doubts the inevitability of liberal democracy for some countries. His 1989 (17) article places the Soviet Union "at a fork in the road: it can start down the path that was staked out by Western Europe forty-five years ago, a path that most of Asia has followed, or it can realize its own uniqueness and remain stuck in history." In *The End of History and the Last Man*, Fukuyama is no longer even sure that "most of Asia" will follow that

1

path staked out by Western Europe, as he acknowledges the serious challenge some recent Asian views posed to liberal democracy. Nor is it clear that the only other alternative is to "remain stuck in history." More and more Asians are becoming convinced that economic prosperity does not require, and in some circumstances may even preclude, blindly copying Western nations, that their very different cultures are the key to economic success with political stability and protection against Western social malaise. Asian countries are looking for their own paths. Contrary to his initial claim that the end of history lies in "a universal homogeneous state," the content of which is "liberal democracy in the political sphere combined with easy access to VCRs and stereos in the economic," Fukuyama acknowledges subsequently that "the existing state system will not collapse anytime soon into a *literally* universal homogeneous state," and he even conceded that "in the end . . . the contours of Asian democracy may be very different from those of contemporary American democracy."[3]

The "end of history" claim has two parts: what will happen and what should happen. Part of the distinctiveness and power (some critics would say the "fatal flaw") of Hegel's philosophy lies in synthesizing the two. Fukuyama, despite his adoption of Hegel's teleological framework, separates them and emphasizes the latter: "at the end of history, it is not necessary that all societies become successful liberal societies, merely that they end their ideological pretensions of representing different and higher forms of human society."[4] Fukuyama's contention that liberal democracy is the only universally valid norm because it resolves fundamentally the "contradictions" involved in the human struggle for recognition by ensuring universal and equal recognition is unpersuasive. His conception of a universal human nature underlying his claim that the struggle for recognition is the basic driving force of history is open to challenge. Even if there is a general human desire for recognition, it could take many forms, some of which (e.g., the desire to be superior instead of equal to others) may find better fulfillment in an undemocratic society.

Fukuyama's claim notwithstanding, no consensus has developed in the world concerning the legitimacy and viability of liberal democracy. Instead, voices of doubt and outright challenges are getting louder. Asians have been defending their departure from the liberal democratic model on *normative* grounds. They need not lay claim to "higher forms of human society" or an alternative "universal" model; all that they need to establish, and to reject Fukuyama's thesis, is that their particular historical and cultural circumstances make Western-style liberal democracy inappropriate, even harmful, for their societies, and nonliberal alternatives offer better solutions to their problems. Such normative arguments are being advanced with increasing frequency and assertiveness as various Asian countries are enjoying unprecedented economic growth and political stability while retaining their cultural distinctiveness.

Japan and the four "little dragons" of Asia—Hong Kong, Singapore, South Korea, and Taiwan—did not start out with any conscious determination to preserve their cultures in their modernization efforts. The biggest challenges for them, as they still are for most of Asia, were poverty, disease, ignorance, and technological backwardness. In the years following World War II, Western examples offered a way out. In learning from Western countries to solve their problems, Asian countries have not, however, become completely Western but retain to different degrees their distinctive cultures. Moreover, some began to notice that other countries had tried emulating Western countries but had not had equal success in improving their economic plight, and for some time, Asian economies were doing even better than advanced Western economies themselves. In the 1980s, commentators began to suggest that their common Confucian culture was largely responsible for the economic success of these countries, and the possibility of a Confucian alternative to economic development, of an Asian development model, attracted considerable attention.[5] The luster of Asian development has since been tarnished by economic crises. Some have turned the tables on Asian exceptionalism by arguing that the troubles also were due to whatever unique factors had created the temporary success, while others, probably for equally ideological motives, argued that Asia's problems lay at the door of Western speculators.

Economic successes and failures are not due entirely to cultures, but there is a need to emphasize indigenous cultural factors in view of their frequent neglect in favor of Western contribution to Asian development.[6] The interest in Asian cultures also is fueled by Western criticism of some of the excesses of liberal democracies. Increasingly confident, some Asians hope that they can progress without repeating the mistakes of Western countries, and that their distinctive cultures can provide them ways to do so. China and other countries in and out of Asia have turned to Asian models as alternatives or complements to Western models in their continued quest for higher standards of living and political stability.[7]

Despite the economic success of some Asian countries, most of Asia is still in need of Western aid, and trade with Western countries is critical even to the successful Asian economies. Competition with the Communist bloc for political influence used to be the main consideration in aid and other trade and foreign policies; with the end of the Cold War, the United States appears to have adopted the promotion of liberal democracy as its new guide in dealing with other countries. In the midst of Asia's cultural awakening, there is consternation among some Asians at the trend of tying Western aid and other policies to compliance with liberal democratic political norms, especially human rights. At the regional meeting for Asia, held in Bangkok in March–April 1993, state representatives from Asian countries boldly criticized the prevailing conception of universal human rights as being too Western and expressed their intention to set their own "Asian standards" for human rights.

Critics of this Asian challenge to the Western conception of human rights frequently stress the lack of homogeneity among Asian cultures and view exceptionalist claims based on "Asian values" as self-interested rhetoric by governments eager to protect their policies and actions from foreign scrutiny and criticism. As a challenge to Western hegemony, Asian values need not be homogeneous or impervious to external influence and change; it suffices that the values of a majority of people in various Asian countries, despite their differences, currently share a greater affinity than they do with Western values.[8] These general similarities and differences could be important to the future of Asian societies.

While conceding that some rights are universal, supporters of Asian conceptions of human rights reject a key foundation of the Universal Declaration of Human Rights—the ideal of individual autonomy—which they argue has little meaning to Asians who emphasize the primacy of community. There is an increasingly widespread feeling that very often "universality is actually the Western approach in disguise."[9] Nor is this an exclusively Asian view. Henry Rosemont argues that the concept of human rights, for all of its important achievements, is culture specific. At an Amnesty International lecture, among other occasions, Richard Rorty drew attention to the "ethnocentrism" of human rights as a core value of liberalism, though he was unapologetic about promoting human rights from an ethnocentric position. Attempting to rid his theory of justice as fairness of metaphysical entanglements, John Rawls's political liberalism, starting from within a certain political tradition and deriving its basic ideas from the "public political culture" of a specific Western liberal democracy, also admits to cultural specificity.[10]

In 1947, when the Universal Declaration of Human Rights was being drafted, despite the participation of non-Western representatives, the American Anthropological Association rejected "the applicability of any Declaration of Human Rights to mankind as a whole. . . . The rights of man in the twentieth century cannot be circumscribed by the standards of any single culture, or be dictated by the standards of any single people." Half a century later, Wm. Theodore de Bary argues that greater political participation and freedom of expression in China depend in part on "agreement that human rights should not be understood or defined solely in Western terms; rather, they are a growing, expandable concept that will be enhanced through shared multicultural learning and experience." There is increasing support for Western and non-Western countries working together to establish "intercivilizational" human rights.[11]

The Bangkok regional meeting did not simply dismiss human rights as tools of foreign oppression. There is a move from a defensive to an offensive stance: Asian governments intend to assert the legitimacy of Asian norms of social and political order. Some may hear in the 1993 Bangkok Declaration what sounds like the first salvo in the clash of civilizations foretold by Samuel Huntington. According to Huntington, world politics is entering a new phase in which "the great divisions among humankind and the dominating source of conflict will be cultural."[12] He predicts that a central focus of conflict for the immediate future will be between Western states and several Islamic-Confucian states as the Confucian and Islamic civilizations cooperate to challenge Western interests, values, and power.

Huntington's "clash of civilizations" is no less controversial than Fukuyama's "end of history." Critics question the unity of civilizations and their ability to provide motivations for political action; they argue that Huntington overstates the hostility generated by differences and underplays the mutual influence and interdependence between civilizations.[13] Huntington is aware of the opportunities coexisting with the dangers of increased interactions, but he considers conflict the more likely outcome, since he believes that interactions intensify civilization consciousness, the awareness of differences between civilizations and commonalities within each civilization. His pessimistic forecast may be proven right if too many Western governments continue in their aggressive and often sanctimonious efforts to promote their values of democracy and liberalism as universal values while they maintain their military dominance and advance their economic interests at the expense of others.

However, the clash of civilizations can be avoided. Western countries would need to develop a more profound understanding of the basic philosophical and religious assumptions underlying other civilizations and the ways in which people in those civilizations see their interests. We could do better than a cultural détente.[14] For a peaceful and progressive world order, all parties, East and West, must participate in constructing a common framework of communication and exchange, which is neither Western nor Eastern but truly global. Western countries should respect the desire of other countries to become modern without becoming Western. They might even be able to learn something from non-Western countries that would help them solve some of their pressing social problems.[15] Non-Western countries have achieved much through modifying what they learn from Western countries and integrating it with their indigenous cultures. The danger of greater awareness and pride in their own cultures lies in closing their minds to outside influence and in adopting a hostile stance to all things Western out of insecurity or arrogance.[16] If both Western and non-Western countries could maintain an open mind while being clear about their own convictions, if they remain committed to dealing peacefully with one another on terms of mutual respect and constantly strive to understand one another better, then the future could turn out to be one of diverse, flourishing, and mutually enhancing civilizations.

Whose Confucianism?

While the voices of governments have been jarringly loud in the Asian challenge to the existing conception of universal human rights, the claim that there are valuable Asian cultural and political identities distinct from Western ones has a wider resonance. Asians who have no desire to shield governments from criticisms of human rights abuses and economic protectionism would not necessarily side with Western universalist claims in this debate; nor would Westerners critical of specific human rights abuses and other governmental actions in Asian countries be necessarily unsympathetic to exceptionalist arguments. The debate about culture and human rights is part of a larger "soul-searching" on the part of Asians, part of a wider discourse about the future of Asian countries and their peoples. It is erroneous and unproductive to portray the debate as simply having to do with "whether Western-style democracy or Asian-style authoritarianism is likely to prove the better antidote in the long run." Neither is attractive for most Asians; they prefer Asian democracies—of which Confucian democracy is one possibility.[17]

While he allows that Asian societies may meet "the formal requisites of democracy," Huntington considers these political systems "democracy without turnover. It represents an adoption of Western democratic practices to serve not Western values of competition and change, but Asian values of consensus and stability."[18] Democracy may be possible in a Confucian society, but Confucian democracy is a "contradiction in terms." Such conclusions view Confucianism as inherently collectivistic, patriarchal, and authoritarian. Lucian Pye's analyses of China are among those that focus on its authoritarian aspects, which he attributes mostly to its Confucian legacy. For him, Confucianism's lack of a concept of individual autonomy and this value's conflict with Confucian values prove that Confucianism sanctions oppressive governments.[19] Though more balanced in his assessment of the pros and cons of the Confucian legacy, Donald Munro also opposes the individual and the social and sees "selflessness" as "one of the oldest values in China, present in various forms in Taoism and Buddhism, but especially in Confucianism." Such "selflessness," which makes the individual no more than "a cog in an ever more efficient social machine," allows the state to subordinate individual interests to social interests as defined by the state.[20]

Nor is this reading, some would say *mis*reading, of the tradition limited to Western Sinologists. There is no lack of Chinese, Japanese, or Korean scholars who believe that Confucianism is inherently authoritarian and incompatible with democracy. At the very least, embracing a Western idea of democracy would mean abandoning the traditional "rule of virtue" for the "rule of law," and this, in Yu Ying-shih's view, "led inevitably to the end of Confucianism as a dominating political force."[21] During the May Fourth movement, the idea of filiality, seen as central to Confucianism, was attacked for "turning China into a big factory for the production of obedient subjects."[22] Confucianism was vilified for obstructing China's modernization and democratization, and "Down with the Confucian shop" became a May Fourth slogan in its quest for democracy and science.[23] Nor has iconoclasm died out among Chinese intellectuals. The controversial 1988 Chinese television documentary, *River Elegy* (*heshang* 河殤), contrasts the stagnation of Chinese culture with the dynamism of Western civilizations. The message of its authors is unmistakable: to be modern, to be democratic, China must stop being Chinese, which includes being Confucian, and must become Western.

Since its establishment as the orthodoxy of the Chinese empire in the Han dynasty, Confucianism frequently has been misappropriated by those in power for their own selfish interests at the expense of those they ruled, so much so that many have viewed those distortions as constituting Confucianism itself. Even when we leave aside the blatant distortions, Confucianism as a tradition has never been homogeneous and monolithic. It is a complex and continuously changing discourse that has transformed itself and other traditions, and it has in turn been transformed by other traditions. It has had significant impact on several East Asian societies; it also has adapted to social changes that occur independent of it. Bruce Nussbaum, arguing against Huntington that culture is too porous to explain anything, asks "What is 'Confucianism' in 1997? Is it the centralized authoritarian collectivism of China's delegitimized elite, which uses extreme nationalism and anti-Westernism to replace a lost communist ideology? Or is it the market democracy of Taiwan? And what about Korea, with its labor unions, free elections, and recent jailing of one-time military dictators?"[24]

Different societies have practiced Confucianism differently at different times. The Confucian society of Qing China was different from that of Tokugawa Japan. The Confucianism that Max Weber once argued was responsible for the nondevelopment of capitalism in imperial China was not the Confucianism being credited with the success of the East Asian capitalist economies in the second half of the twentieth century.[25] Tu Wei-ming distinguishes political Confucianism from Confucianism as a way of life: the former is a doctrine that mandated a certain form of hierarchical political authority centered around the emperor and a state bureaucracy; the latter has to do with family relations, work ethics, and personal cultivation of the ordinary people.[26] Once we recognize the openness of the Confucian discourse, we could counter current misappropriations of Confucianism by Asian champions of authoritarianism more effectively, not by claiming superiority for Western values but by a broader, deeper study of the Confucian tradition and its relevance to the present and future.[27]

There have been various attempts to democratize Confucianism. Despite ideological and philosophical differences, Carsun Chang 張君勱, Tang Junyi 唐君毅, Xu Fuguan 徐復觀, and Mou Zongsan 牟宗三—signatories to the "Manifesto for a Reappraisal of Sinology and Reconstruction of Chinese Culture" and prominent representatives of twentieth-century Chinese scholarship, join forces in advocating a democratic reconstruction of traditional Chinese culture. Many participants in what Tu Wei-ming has called the "third epoch of Confucian humanism" share these scholars' commitment to a Confucian democracy. While sharing their new Confucian aspirations, Liu Shu-hsien criticizes the specific attempts of various twentieth-century Chinese scholars who attempt to marry democracy and Confucianism; he finds their solutions either impractical or hermeneutically unconvincing, because they underestimate the tension between Confucian and democratic values. Liu advocates surrendering some components of the tradition and radically transforming others to make room for democracy within Confucianism.[28]

Chenyang Li rejects the new Confucian approach completely, convinced that the essential incompatibility of Confucian and democratic values renders any attempt to democratize Confucianism harmful to the "real value and spirit of Confucianism." Instead of Liu's internal pluralist approach, he argues for an external pluralist approach, wherein democracy and Confucianism will remain independent value systems but "good neighbors" in China's future. But neighborliness may not be possible if no agreement is reached about what kind of neighborhood all should live in. Just admitting to the possibility of mutual influence and encouraging dialogue may not be enough when practical choices have to be made about governance, among other questions. Moreover, Li's preference for this minimalist approach is premised on an essentialist view of Confucianism, as evident in his talk of "the *real* values of Confucianism," which are "*essentially* conflicting" with those of democracy, despite admitting that "as a value system Confucianism is not unchangeable."[29]

The survival of Confucianism is not dependent on preserving an *idem* identity, requiring some kind of essence to remain the same; it has to do with an *ipse* identity that lies in meaningful continuity. Even if we grant that Confucianism might not be recognizable without "values such as emphasis on the family, filial morality, loyalty and respecting the old," what these values *mean* and how they are actualized could change over time and space. In any case, not everyone agrees that these values represent what is most valuable to Confucianism; they could be seen as derivative of the primary notions of *ren*, *yi*, and *li* in contingent social contexts. The following chapters recognize the contestedness of the Confucian tradition and lay no claim to *the* correct interpretation. I am concerned with what Confucianism could mean now and in the future, not with what Confucianism is *essentially*. Nor is the reconstruction an attempt to present the picture of an entire tradition, since detailed analysis is limited to the three pre-Qin texts, and other Confucian works are mentioned only in passing. The link with the past that this work is interested in maintaining involves understanding the past, texts and events, in new ways conducive to finding better alternatives for the future. The proposed conception of Confucian democracy is meant to guide an experiment well worth trying in some contexts.

This proposal of a Confucian democracy aiming at a synthesis of two traditions is more radical and difficult than Chenyang Li's solution. Li mentions the two value systems learning from each other, but such learning will remain superficial unless the possibility of syntheses remains open. Li says little about how such mutual learning will occur; I will attempt to illustrate such mutual learning in the following chapters. Li takes the meaning of democracy for granted, hardly going beyond a cursory discussion of the definitional problem of democracy before adopting the liberal framework as the starting point of his comparison. A more nuanced approach that discusses in greater detail and depth the difficult problems of defining democracy is necessary. A Confucian democracy requires a certain understanding of democracy, which will be elaborated through the discussion of Dewey's philosophy that is critical of some liberal theories.

WHICH DEMOCRACY?

Confucian democracy requires not only reconstruction of Confucianism, it also requires reconstruction of democracy. The democracy that crusading Westerners usually preach to Asian societies is a liberal one that emphasizes the rule of law and universal rights, based on the assumptions of individual autonomy and of the government as a necessary evil to be limited as much as possible. Bhikhu Parekh points out that the democratic part of liberal democracy has been far more attractive outside of Western Europe and North America than the liberal components. As Asians understand it, "liberalism breaks up the community, undermines the shared body of ideas and values, places the isolated individual above the community, encourages ethos and ethic of aggressive self-assertions ... weakens the spirit of mutual accommodation and adjustment." For most Westerners, "the power and appeal of democracy come from the idea of autonomy"; for most Asians, the philosophical baggage of liberal autonomy slows down the spread of democracy.[30] A Confucian democracy would not be a liberal democracy à la America.

The conjunction of liberalism and democracy is contingent; there are ambiguities in their relationship. According to David Beetham, "liberalism has provided not only the necessary foundation for, but also a significant constraint upon, democracy in the modern world." While we may have just cause to agree with John Dunn, that "all states today prefer to be democracies because a democracy is what [it] is virtuous for a state to be," it is quite another thing to claim that liberal democracy has gained universal acceptance.[31] Whatever consensus there is on the value of democracy, it tends to be at the expense of specificity of content. Democracy is government by the people, but who constitutes the people? What does it mean for them to govern? What institutions and practices best serve that purpose? Is democracy merely procedural or more substantive? Values commonly associated with democracy, such as liberty, equality, and pluralism, are susceptible to a variety of interpretations.

The concept of democracy is an essentially contested one—consensus on its content is impossible, because different analysts read into it their favored values. As David Held notes, "An uncritical affirmation of liberal democracy essentially leaves unanalyzed the whole meaning of democracy and its possible variants." Fareed Zakaria, arguing that constitutional liberalism and democracy are historically distinct and theoretically different, and that "democracy is flourishing; constitutional liberalism is not," concludes that "Western liberal democracy might prove to be not the final destination on the democratic road, but just one of many possible exits."[32] For him, this is a dangerous possibility; for others, the possibility could be enriching for both East and West.

Actually existing democracies are so dominated and controlled by a bewildering array of external and impersonal forces that some claim that government by the people "can now hardly amount to more than empty verbiage."[33] Many who believe in the ideal of democracy nevertheless find too big a gap between ideal and existing democracies. Sympathetic critics, such as Benjamin Barber, Robert Dahl, Carol Gould, Susan Okin, and Amy Gutmann, have suggested various ways in which existing democracies must be reformed if autonomous individuals are to be able to set their own life plans and participate in the collective life of the community.[34] Their advice ranges from countering the power of bureaucracies, corporations, and the media, reforming processes of collective decisions, and democratizing the workplace to reforming education, gender, and family relations. While they disagree on its causes, an increasing number of commentators detect a spreading discontent in Western democracies. Some argue that this discontent cannot be entirely attributed to the usual problem of reality falling short of the ideal; it cannot be solved by having "more democracy" if by democracy it is meant the current prevalent strain of liberal democracy.

Critics who have been described as "communitarian" reject the overemphasis on individual autonomy dominating liberal democracy, and they argue that democracy, both in theory and in practice, needs to be rejuvenated with communitarian concerns. This internal critique of Western democracies resonates well with the quest for Asian versions of democracy. At the very least, Asian democracy would have to strike a better balance between individual rights and the interests of the wider community than liberal democracy has hitherto managed. Daniel Bell argues that justifications based on individual autonomy would not win Asian support for democracy any more than instrumental justifications; the best chance for democracy in Asia lies in communitarian justifications.[35] The Western communitarian critic of liberal democracy and the Asian communitarian in search of a democratic alternative may benefit from each other's project. Both have something to contribute to a much-needed reconstruction of democracy.

LIBERALS AND COMMUNITARIANS

Most communitarian critiques of liberalism reject the conception of self and the ensuing individualism at the heart of the liberal tradition. They are dissatisfied with liberalism's neglect of community and shared values and concerned with civic virtues that they believe liberalism cannot underwrite. But their views are varied and not always compatible with one another. According to Michael Sandel, at the heart of the American democracy's discontent are "the fear that individually, and collectively, we are losing control of the forces that govern our lives" and "the sense that, from family to neighborhood to nation, the moral fabric of community is unraveling around us."[36] This anxiety about the loss of self-government and the erosion of community is engendered by the politics of "the procedural republic" that has at its core the ideal of a neutral political framework. According to this ideal, freedom consists in our capacity to choose our ends for ourselves. In the procedural republic, politics should not try to form the character or cultivate the virtue of its citizens, for to do so would be to "legislate morality." Government should not affirm through its policies or laws any particular vision of the good life. Instead, it should provide a framework of rights that respects persons as free and independent selves capable of choosing their own values and ends. John Rawls, Ronald Dworkin, Joel Feinberg, Joseph Raz, and Robert Nozick—despite important differences among their theories—are all proponents of such rights-based liberalism.[37] It is this rights-based liberalism that is considered inappropriate to Asian societies by those who argue for the cultural distinctiveness of Asian countries.

Western critics of Asian societies such as the People's Republic of China and Singapore often point to the governments' interference in the people's private lives. However, such criticisms often overlook a genuine and fairly widespread belief in these societies that governments have a responsibility to educate the people through various measures, including legislation as well as public campaigns, in quest of a vision of the good life, the good society. If critics acknowledge the belief at all, they tend to dismiss it as some kind of "false consciousness" and to view the people of these societies as having been brainwashed into "hugging their chains" because of their long history of being oppressed. It is precisely such patronizing attitudes that provoke much Asian resentment (and not just on the part of the governments).

Joseph Chan, who declares his sympathies to be more on the side of critics of Asian governments in the debate on human rights, nevertheless argues that most Asian political moralities that have to be developed to support human rights in Asian terms "would probably endorse the principles of perfection-ism, moralism, and paternalism."[38] A Confucian democracy would differ from Western liberal democracies on the issue of political neutrality to conceptions of the good, on the limits of government. However, one cannot be too san-guine about this difference. History has shown that governments' interference in people's lives often is not benign but intrusive, oppressive, and stultifying to personal development, preventing a person from living a good life—and the same could be said of the pressures of social opinion. The challenge for those supporting Confucian democracy is to articulate an alternative that would be sensitive to cultural requirements while taking seriously the liberal concern about governmental and social tyranny. What is needed is a politics that avoids authoritarianism without neglecting the joint realization of a common good in free discussions.

Linking the discussion of the possibility of Confucian democracy with the Western liberal-communitarian debate serves a number of purposes. It helps bridge cultural differences and bring the debate about the future of Asian soci-eties closer to a public outside of Asia by establishing a connection with a dis-course that is more familiar to the latter. It enables both Western publics and those in Asia to link their concerns with what might prove to be an emerging global communitarian trend, and it allows each to learn from the other in widening communitarian perspectives and refining theories and practices. Such an approach, however, is not without its own risk. The dialectical ten-dencies of Western academic discourse are such that it is easy to overstate the opposition between the communitarian and the liberal stands. Dualistic thinking is inhospitable to Confucianism. The task is to find a more specific reference within the Western liberal-communitarian debate that would avoid dualism and resonate well with Confucian discourse.

In actual fact, few occupy the extreme ends of the range of opinions in the Western liberal-communitarian debate. An increasing number gravitate toward the middle in the continuum between two extremes on most issues that divide communitarians from liberals. The area of overlap between liberalism and communitarianism is increasing. Communitarians differ on whether liberalism should be completely rejected or merely reformed. In contrast to Sandel, MacIntyre, and Taylor, who reject liberalism, Michael Walzer argues that Western communitarian critiques do not lie outside of liberalism but constitute a recurrent and an inconstant feature of liberalism. Roberto Unger characterizes his critique of liberalism as "superliberalism." Amy Gutmann argues that the role of communitarian values may be to supplement rather than supplant liberal values.[39]

Those who insist on the incompatibility of liberalism and communitarianism tend to take a fairly narrow and often rather unreasonable (often described as "strong," though "extreme" might be more accurate) interpretation of the opposing camp's position, when it actually includes a wide variety of theories. The more reasonable recognizes that each side "accords in its view some status to the values on the center stage in the other view." An increasing number seeks some kind of rapprochement, "a fruitful convergence of what is best in liberalism and communitarianism, not a victory of one over the other."[40] What is at issue is not an irreconcilable conflict between the values of individual liberty and community but a matter of ascertaining what the best balance is between the two.

Some communitarians do not even view liberalism as the target of their critiques to begin with. Henry Tam, the chairman of UK Communitarian Forum, claims that the target of communitarian critiques is market individualism, not liberalism—although many would argue that the two are closely linked. He argues that liberalism, as much as conservatism or socialism, could be pursued within the communitarian framework. "Communitarianism is not to be located alongside conservatism, liberalism, and socialism as a rival ideology. Instead it challenges all those attracted to elements of conservative, liberal, or socialist ideas to avoid making the assumption that such ideas can only be pursued within a framework which mixes varying degrees of individualist and authoritarian practices." The Communitarian Movement in the United States, spearheaded by Amitai Etzioni and William Galston, also sees itself as providing a third alternative to "the Authoritarians (such as Moral Majority and Liberty Bell) and the Radical Individualists (libertarians such as the intellectuals at the Cato Institute; civil libertarians, especially the Civil Liberties Union; and laissez-faire conservatives)."[41]

The liberalism that Tam considers compatible with communitarianism includes the liberalism of J. S. Mill, L. T. Hobhouse, and John Dewey.[42] These are liberals who launched communitarian critiques against classical liberalism in an earlier period. They too attempted to reconcile individuality with sociality, and among their revisions of liberalism are a conception of the individual that is decidedly social and an emphasis on the value of community.[43] Though those whom communitarians would consider favoring individual autonomy at the expense of community have often cited J. S. Mill, Gerald Gaus argues persuasively that community is more important in Mill's liberal doctrine than is often acknowledged by contemporary liberalism. In the current liberal-communitarian debate, both sides in aid of their respective positions have cited Dewey. Though Dewey identified himself as a liberal, he is justifiably seen as offering a communitarian program, given his identification of the idea of democracy with the idea of community. David Hall and Roger Ames use Dewey's communitarian view to criticize liberalism in their discussion of the prospects of democracy for China.[44] However, if he were alive today, Dewey would no doubt dismiss the liberal-communitarian dualism as a false dichotomy, as he was wont to do with all dualisms. Drawing on the philosophy of John Dewey, my proposed Confucian democracy aims for a third alternative that would address the concerns of both liberals and communitarians without siding entirely with either.

DEWEY AND CONFUCIUS

Dewey spent more than two years (May 1919 to July 1921) in various parts of China during one of the most interesting periods of Chinese history. Dewey's connection with China began earlier: at Columbia, he had taught a group of Chinese students who were to play important roles in China's history between the two world wars, and whose thinking continued to influence Chinese intellectuals thereafter. It is partly due to the careful preparation and skillful sponsorship of these Chinese students, Hu Shih 胡適 and Jiang Menglin 蔣夢麟 among them, as well as the timeliness of his own message on democracy in the context of China immediately after the First World War, that "Dewey became a fad" while he was in China.[45]

To Benjamin Schwartz, "the encounter between John Dewey and modern China is one of the most fascinating episodes in the intellectual history of twentieth-century China."[46] When Dewey was in China, he often was referred to as the "Second Confucius." The flattering comparison was first made by the then-president of Beijing University, Cai Yuanpei 蔡元培. Though the comparison with Confucius was intended as an accolade, ironically, Dewey's Chinese audience was more interested in Dewey's philosophical differences from Confucianism, which was then associated with the obsolete monarchy and other despised institutions of "Old China." As Cai Yuanpei puts it, "Confucius said respect the emperor, [Dewey] advocates democracy; Confucius said females are a problem to raise, [Dewey] advocates equal rights for men and women; Confucius said transmit not create, [Dewey] advocates creativity."[47] The prevalent interpretation of Confucianism, and the iconoclastic attitude toward it during his visit, probably means that Dewey learned little directly from Confucianism on a philosophical level that could benefit his democratic theory. Still, one could speculate that the close contact with a Confucian society on an everyday basis for over two years might have left some marks on Dewey's subsequent thinking. It is to be hoped that the current encounter between Dewey's pragmatism and Confucianism would be more reciprocal.

In the reconstruction of Confucianism that follows, we shall overturn the contrast with Dewey's pragmatism that Cai Yuanpei drew, not because it was entirely inaccurate, but because circumstances have changed. The Confucianism that would give us Confucian democracy in the new millennium is a different breed from the state orthodoxy believed to have sustained imperial China but also led to its eventual demise. The Chinese intellectuals of an earlier period looked for an alternative to Confucianism as a route to democracy; we shall look for a Confucian route to democracy.

Barry Keenan showed how Dewey's ideas played a role in defining the content of liberal reform movements in the early Republican period in China. The "Dewey experiment" to introduce democracy to China through first transforming its culture has been judged a failure by Keenan and other scholars, but Dewey's encounter with China is, in a sense, still an incomplete story. A new chapter has begun with the simultaneous revival of interest in Confucianism and in Dewey's pragmatism on both sides of the Pacific. What follows will hopefully reinforce Dewey's claim to the title of "second Confucius" and demonstrate the resonance between their philosophies: their conceptions of the individual as a social person; their views of community, its value, and how to bring it about; and the consequent inseparability of the questions "How should one live?" and "How should we live together?" In synthesizing their philosophies, the concerns of ethics and politics merge in a philosophy of democracy as a community of flourishing, unique persons.

While both see the person as social, Confucius' notion of authoritative personhood (ren 仁) emphasizes the role of community more than Dewey, whose aim is to correct rather than completely reject liberalism, and hence it gives a greater role to individual choice (albeit a reconstructed concept of choice) than Confucius. Though both believe that building a community requires working on all aspects of human interaction and not separating feeling from thinking, Confucius emphasizes the aesthetic in "ritual practice (li 禮)," while Dewey emphasizes thinking in "cooperative inquiry." The different contexts of their thought give rise to important philosophical differences. Confucius emphasizes "government for the people" but is silent on "government by the people"; Dewey pays a great deal of attention to the connection between the two. Their similarities often highlight Dewey's departures from other Western philosophies and, combined with their differences, suggest possible means to realize Dewey's ends other than those offered by Western contexts. Their differences are most evident on points (e.g., liberal concerns) that Dewey shares with other Western philosophies and usually brings out the weaknesses of Confucianism in its historical practice. Their similarities and differences combined suggest ways in which the problems of Confucian societies might be solved in future and alternative ways in which Deweyan democracy might be realized.

Introducing Dewey into a discussion of Confucian democracy illuminates Confucianism in new ways that contribute significantly to the reconstruction of Confucianism that we need to undertake to make Confucian democracy possible. At the same time, being introduced into a new context also throws a light on aspects of Dewey's philosophy that might not otherwise be as clearly revealed, and it is suggestive of new possibilities for Dewey's project of reconstructing democracy.

Chapter 2

Social Individuals

Asians challenging what they perceive as cultural hegemony of Western nations in the human rights debate and Western communitarians within liberal democracies criticizing liberalism reject the overemphasis on individual autonomy that is based on a conception of the individual as a ready-made self conceptually and ontologically prior to social relations. The central disagreements between liberals and communitarians stem from different understandings of individuals and societies. To find a balance between liberal and communitarian concerns, we need notions of individuals and societies that do not posit any kind of radical separation and inherent opposition. An adequate understanding of individuals needs to bring in the irreducibly social dimension of being human and show how this is connected with, rather than merely opposed to, individuality. This chapter aims to show how the views of individuals and of societies in early Confucianism and in Dewey's philosophy meet this requirement without succumbing to the problem of subordinating either to the other.

LIBERAL SELF AND AUTONOMY

The conception of the individual as an autonomous self dominates Western modernity. It underlies the individualism central to liberalism and characteristic of contemporary Western capitalist societies.[1] Though there are terms that could be translated as "self" in Greek and Roman philosophy, the philosophical problematic of self concerned with radical inwardness and independence from others emerged only with the consciousness of subjective, self-conscious experience as the principal medium of self-articulation. Charles Taylor traces the sense of "inwardness" to Augustine's "Do not go outward; return within yourself. In the inward man dwells truth."[2] While the ancients sometimes adopt a reflexive stance in their philosophizing, reflexivity does not become radical until we not only experience ourselves as in the world, but more important, we experience the world as *for us*. Without this radical reflexivity, there could be no disengaged subject and its associated ideals of self-responsible freedom and dignity, which are so important to modern individualism; nor would there be an emphasis on the kind of self-exploration or self-knowledge predominant in individualistic, modern cultures.[3]

The belief that no life is truly good unless freely and wholeheartedly chosen by one's own will—thereby placing personal choice and commitment at the center of moral life, contributing significantly to the status of the individual as an autonomous agent—has its roots in Augustine's thinking about the will. His thought combines two ideas about the will, resulting in some tension and difficulty: the will as the power to confer or withhold assent, and the will as our basic disposition. The will in the first sense may be strong or weak; in the second sense, good or bad. The varying strength of the will introduces potential conflicts between knowledge and desire; knowing what is good, contrary to Socrates' teaching, is no longer enough for one to *do* good. As Augustine quoted St. Paul's words to the Romans: "For the good that I would I do not: but the evil which I would not, that I do."[4] *Akrasia*, weakness of the will, for Augustine poses not an intellectual problem but a central crisis of moral and religious experience. His cry, "A question have I become for myself," acknowledges this moral and religious struggle.

Augustine retained the ancients' belief in an ontic *logos*. The turn inward is to open the inward man to God, "As the soul is life of the flesh, so God is the blessed life of the man."[5] The inwardness becomes truly modern and the disengagement of the subject from the world complete, with the fading of that ontic *logos*, so that the only order and certainty to be found must come from within. Self-questioning became first an epistemological struggle before a moral one. The problematic of the self as reflexive meditation on the positing of the subject begins with Descartes's doubts and his answer to the question, "Who, or rather what, am I?" "*Cogito ergo sum . . . sum res cogitans.*" For Descartes, the mind becomes the exclusive locus of thoughts and values; what once existed between the knower/agent and the world, linking them and making them inseparable, becomes located *within* the subject. This defines a new understanding of the subject and object, where the two are independent— the subject is over and against the object.[6]

In moral and political philosophy, the Augustinian-Cartesian legacy gives rise to the modern notion of freedom as autonomy that portrays the subject as radically independent, determining her own purposes without interference from external authority, whether natural or social. This is most evident in seventeenth-century contract theories that take autonomous individuals as their starting point. Political legitimacy in these theories is grounded in the consent of autonomous individuals—normative orders must originate in individual wills. Rousseau enlarges the scope of the inner voice and raises the status of the autonomous individual. The result was the transformation of modern culture toward a deeper inwardnesss and a radical autonomy. His philosophy is the origin of much of the contemporary culture of self-exploration that makes autonomy the key to virtue.

Rousseau propounds the idea of recovery of contact with nature as the key to an individual's self-realization, the realization of the freedom that he or she was born with but had lost to enslaving social arrangements. The idea, which many of the Romantics take up later, represents an escape from calculating other-dependence, from the ambitions it engendered and the force of opinion, through a kind of fusion of reason and nature. It is not a return to a presocial or precultural state but rather an aspiration to an ideal society-culture that does not betray the true voice of nature. Hence, central to Rousseau's philosophy is the idea of conscience, which is the voice of nature as it emerges in a being who has entered society and is endowed with language and, hence, reason (i.e., the voice of true human nature). The idea of the general will is the product of all consciences speaking in one voice. It represents the demands of true human nature, free from all distortion due to other-dependence or opinion, embodied in publicly recognized law. The moral source of both conscience and the general will is the autonomy of the individual.

Rousseau is a key influence on Immanuel Kant, whose philosophy marks the zenith of the rise of the modern notion of freedom as autonomy. As opposed to heteronomy, autonomy is radical independence from all phenomenal attachments; it replaces laws of nature with self-imposed laws of reason. With Kant, the conception of the self as autonomous becomes the very foundation of morality. The moral law emanates from the autonomous will of a rational agent. It is this autonomy that gives a rational agent dignity and worth as an individual. This autonomous individual dominates Western modern culture. In the words of Iris Murdoch, "How recognizable, how familiar to us is the man so beautifully described in the *Grundlegung*, who even confronted with Christ turns away to consider the judgment of his own conscience and to hear the voice of his own reason. Stripped of the exiguous metaphysical background which Kant was prepared to allow him, this man is with us still, free, independent, lonely, powerful, rational, responsible, brave, the hero of so many novels and books of moral philosophy."[7]

It is this Kantian hero so celebrated in Western modernity that Michael Sandel attacks in his critique of John Rawls's *A Theory of Justice*. Sandel argues that a Kantian conception of the moral subject is indispensable to Rawls's deontological liberalism. It is presupposed in Rawls's procedures for deriving the principles of justice, procedures that also justify those principles.[8] To Sandel, the Kantian moral subject fails to account plausibly for some indispensable aspects of moral experience; any moral principles that will meet the needs of moral life would have to be based on an entirely different conception of the moral subject. Moreover, this conception of the moral subject could not even support Rawls's own principles of justice.

Rawls's principles of justice as fairness are equivalent "to an undertaking to regard the distribution of natural abilities as a collective asset."[9] Sandel argues that the only way to make sense of such a common claim on natural abilities is to posit an intersubjective self, tying the notion of collective assets to the possibility of a common subject of possession.[10] Unlike material possessions, I *have* natural abilities and talents in a way that no one else can have them, as far as we refer to those particular traits rather then merely traits of the same kind. Possession in this sense would certainly require an intersubjective being for common possession. However, this admittedly special relationship is not morally significant for Rawls, because he conceives the moral subject as independent of such traits. The collective claim on natural abilities in Rawls's theory is not based on this conception of possession.

The morally justified possession that concerns Rawls has to do with rights of ownership, rights to the benefits (of use and products) arising from those natural traits. Others can enjoy the benefits in question, which can be distributed among separate individuals. Sharing the benefits of natural abilities would not require an intersubjective self. Regarding the natural abilities as "collective asset" amounts to no more than saying that the initial rules for distributing the benefits from natural abilities are to be set collectively, in the original position. The parties in the original position do not have to deserve or collectively own these assets prior to the selection of the principles of justice. The situation they face is selecting first principles that will decide the distribution of benefits from natural abilities, knowing that these abilities are arbitrarily and unequally distributed among free and equal individuals.

Rawls thinks that the parties in the original position would select his principles of justice as fairness instead of other alternatives presented to them (e.g., the libertarian alternative, in which the distribution of benefits corresponds to the distribution of natural abilities, or absolutely equal distribution of benefits). No assumption of an intersubjective being would be required for this exercise to work. The arbitrariness of the distribution of natural talents justifies its being screened out by the veil of ignorance; it then becomes rational for the parties in the original position, ignorant of what their share of natural talents would be, to select the principles of justice as fairness, not because *society as a whole* (some kind of intersubjective being) has a claim on these talents but simply as a matter of maximizing benefits while minimizing risks from individual viewpoints.

Sandel claims that what we have behind the veil of ignorance in Rawls's theory is not a contract among distinct persons (even abstract ones) but the coming to awareness of an intersubjective being.[11] He argues that by removing all differences in interests and preferences and knowledge and power, the veil of ignorance does not bring about fair agreement or bargain in the original position; instead, it makes bargain and agreement impossible, since depriving the parties of all distinguishing characteristics calls into question their plurality and distinctness. It might be argued on Rawls's behalf that at the most basic levels, these persons, admittedly abstract beings that cannot actually exist, can still be individuated by occupying different space. If that appears too trivial, then stronger individuation is possible because of their link to what lies on the other side of the veil of ignorance—the world in which particular characteristics, positions, interests, and aims distinguish persons. They are choosing principles for a society characterized by the circumstances of justice. "They assume that each [of those they represent] has a conception of the good in the light of which he presses claims against the rest. So although they view society as a cooperative venture for mutual advantage, it is typically marked by a conflict as well as an identity of interests."[12] The parties in the original position are choosing the principles for the persons in that latter world, not for themselves *as they are*. Being representatives of real, distinct persons individuates the parties in the original position.

While Sandel's arguments, that Rawls's principles of justice require the conception of the moral subject as an intersubjective being, may not be convincing, one could still sympathize with his view that the Kantian moral subject cannot make sense of moral experience fully, because it is disembodied and presocial when human beings are actually not so. The boundaries of Rawls's moral subject are fixed once and for all in such a way that they are impermeable, invulnerable to transformation by experience. It is disembodied: its identity is given prior to, and independent of, its interests and aims, in contrast to a radically situated self that is not separable from its interests and aims. It connects itself to its interests and aims in an act of the will. "Thus a moral person is a subject with ends he has chosen."[13] The Kantian moral subject also is presocial: it is antecedently individuated with respect to other selves—it is a distinct individual first, and then it enters by choice into relations with others. Sandel argues that Rawls's conception of the moral subject treats social relations as ends to be chosen. It thereby excludes the possibility of social relations constituting self-identity.

To regard ourselves as radically independent of our ends, including our relationships with other people, undermines loyalties and convictions whose moral force lies not in their being objects of choice but in their being constitutive of who we are. For Sandel, a person without such constitutive attachments is not "a free and rational agent" but "a person wholly without character, without moral depth."[14] Furthermore, the possibility of character in the constitutive sense is required for an important ingredient of our moral experience—self-reflection. "Where the self is unencumbered and essentially dispossessed, no person is left for *self*-reflection to reflect upon."[15] If our choices are to be more than exercises in arbitrariness, our deliberations must be conducted against the background of who we are. The conception of an autonomous self also limits others' contributions to one's good. Acts of friendship become parasitic on a good identifiable in advance; "love and benevolence are second order notions: they seek to further the good of beloved individuals that is already given." As Rawls admits: "Even when we take up another's point of view and attempt to estimate what would be to his advantage, we do so as an adviser, so to speak."[16] This fails to recognize that friendship is "a way of knowing as well as liking."[17] It undervalues the contribution of friendship, and relationships in general, to our moral identity and experience.

While communitarians such as Sandel consider the liberal autonomous self an inadequate moral subject, liberals are concerned that the communitarian alternative, the "encumbered self," is so embedded in its social relations, in ends not chosen by itself but dictated by others, that it becomes little more than an automaton. It is not necessary, and it may not even be possible, to question all ends and all relations every time, but if there are some ends and some relationships that one is *never* able to question, then does one not lose control over that aspect of one's life and thereby lose control over how we live, whether we live well or not? Is a life, even if it is flourishing in some sense, still valuable from an ethical perspective if one is not in control of it? The answer does not lie in either of these dichotomous extremes. We will attempt to find in the philosophies of John Dewey and Confucius a way between the autonomy of the disembodied and presocial self, on the one hand, and the automatic behavior of the overly encumbered self, on the other hand.

UNIQUE RATHER THAN AUTONOMOUS INDIVIDUALS

Dewey rejects "the traditional psychology of the original separate soul, mind, or consciousness . . . [which] implies first the severance of man from nature and then of each man from his fellows."[18] He is no believer in the disembodied and presocial self. In his later works, frustrated by the difficulties of weaning people away from the traditional conception, Dewey often prefers to speak of "the biological cultural human being" instead of "the self." But though he objects to "self" (also "subject," "mind," and "knower") as "an original separate entity set over and against objects and the world," it is difficult to do without the *self* as a philosophical term altogether.[19] Even if it is possible, the philosophical price may be too high. The relationships among terms such as *human being*, *self*, and *person* bring out complex issues that we must contend with in our quest for self-understanding and in understanding others.

A human being is an individual not merely because she occupies a unique time and space, for other entities share that form of individuation. And if one is prepared to engage in some science-fiction-like thought experiments, such temporal-spatial individuation is by no means obvious or certain. For practical philosophy, the significance of the notion of the human individual has to do with *valuing* a human being as an individual. This often is justified by the claim that, unlike individual objects, individual humans are selves or persons. Dewey concedes that there is no getting away from the fact that individuals *are* selves (M14.202). The question is, "What kind of self"? By referring to individuals as "selves" philosophically, at least within Anglo-European cultures, we mean more than the fact that people use the reflexive pronouns in their language and engage in self-referential thinking. Charles Taylor argues that one's perspectives on the world, one's moral orientation that guides action, are all part of an identity that, for the modern Western man, is partially constituted by the sense of himself as a being with inner depths, with a special sense of inwardness that underpins the notion that he is a self.[20] The difference between Dewey's conception of self and the prevalent liberal conception is that, for Dewey, the "inner depths" do not exist prior to an individual entering into relations with the rest of the world; they are acquired in association with others, through experience involving interaction with our environment, both social and natural.

To capture the ethical significance of individuality, we need other concepts in addition, if not as alternatives, to "human beings." Other than "self," another alternative is "person." The concept of person is as vague and controversial philosophically as the concept of self. Amélie Rorty argues that there is in fact no single concept of "person"; instead, the concept fulfills various overlapping functions. Each of these functions bears a different relation to the classes of persons and human beings, with different contrast classes. In its widest use, "person" may appear synonymous with "individual human being."[21] However, in contemporary Western philosophy, it seems to be accepted that "the notion of a human being is a notion of a biologically defined entity; the notion of a person is however normatively and ideologically charged."[22] This brings "person" and "self" closer to each other than each is to "human being."

But are "self" and "person" interchangeable? Hume took "self identity" and "personal identity" to be the same thing, and others continue to do so.[23] While "self" and "person" are frequently used interchangeably, there usually is a different emphasis: "self" emphasizes the first-person perspective and "person" the third-person perspective. As John Locke points out, "person" is a forensic term. Questions of personal identity occur in practical matters, such as who actually is the beneficiary of a will, or who actually commits a crime. While personal identity questions are asked more often about others than about ourselves, self-identity questions are asked only in the first person. Self-identity concerns each person's "sense of self," an inner life to which each presumably has privileged access.

In Dewey's philosophy, the first-person perspective does not carry the kind of weight that it has in some Western conceptions of self. Darnell Rucker, working from an unpublished typescript by Dewey, titled "Things and Persons," argues that, in Dewey's philosophy, just as a biological individual human being develops into a self, a self develops into a person. A person is a self that has acquired office, representative functions recognized and defined in social interactions.[24] The differences drawn out by Rucker expose an important aspect of the sociality of individuals. However, I shall use the words "self" and "person" interchangeably, especially since (as Rucker acknowledges) Dewey nowhere distinguishes self and person directly, and in fact he uses the two interchangeably, even in "Things and Persons." What we need to keep in mind is that, except in some of his very early works, when Dewey talks about "self," he does not emphasize the first-person perspective to imply the kind of radical reflexivity underlying the autonomous self, and this brings "self" much closer to "person" in his philosophy.

Other than deemphasizing the first-person perspective, the concept of person reveals a conception of individuality that contrasts with the conception focusing on radical independence. Consider our use of the adjectives "human" and "personal." What is described as "human" characterizes members of the biological species in general. It does not distinguish one human being from another. On the contrary, it implies that all who have that characteristic are similar in being "human." When something is "personal," it characterizes a particular individual distinguished from others. The term *human being* tends to focus attention on species membership, and thereby it emphasizes similarity, or at least resemblance, at the expense of uniqueness. In contrast, "person" emphasizes the uniqueness of individuality which, Dewey claims, always implies contrast with a kind, sort, or *class* and "calls attention to those traits which are unique, non-repeatable, which are differential, and which accordingly require special treatment, particular re-adaptation of general or class methods or standards" (M7.238). Probably there are few characteristics unique to one individual, even when we take into consideration the infinite variety of degrees in which each general characteristic may manifest itself. It is more plausible to say that what is unique is the particular combination of characteristics of each individual, implicating that individual's entire life experience which makes a particular person who she is. "No two of us are the same self.

This is not accidental, but essential. . . . We are not members of a class: each of us is unique" (M7.403).

This conception of individuality that emphasizes uniqueness, in contrast to a conception emphasizing the radical independence of autonomy, is more acceptable in the Chinese context. "The Chinese believed, by and large, in a unique personal existence, no doubt fortified by the concept of a structure of kinship ascendants and descendants, stretching indefinitely forward into the future, in which the individual occupied his unique place."[25] The value of a unique individual lies in its character as a single and an unsubstitutable particular. This uniqueness is defined contextually, in terms of one's contribution to the character of one's natural and social environment as well as the environment's contribution to oneself. Access to and development of uniqueness in an individual is through these relationships.

The contextual uniqueness valued in Confucianism differs from the uniqueness of Romantic "expressive individuation," an idea that developed in the late eighteenth century, that each individual is different and original, and that this originality determines how he or she ought to live.[26] While the value of individuality lies primarily in uniqueness rather than in the radical independence of autonomy in Confucianism and Dewey's philosophy, it is not the source or primary criterion of morality. This contrasts with the value of uniqueness in Romanticism, which often works not as an alternative but as a supplement to autonomy, thereby intensifying the sense of inwardness and the isolation of the individual. Though the Romantic movement strongly resists Kant's separation of autonomy and nature, autonomy is still a central good, understood primarily as freedom of self-expression. The Romantics argue that nature is the source of good, and that the only way we can access it is through an inner voice, through articulation of what we find within us. In contrast, Dewey and Confucianism link unique individuality and morality not through autonomy but sociality.

Dewey's Social Self-in-the-Making

Already present in Dewey's early works is a conception of self as "essentially social, being constituted not by isolated capacity, but by capacity acting in response to the needs of an environment—an environment which, when taken in its fullness, is a community of persons" (E3.335). This social self is not ready-made, prior to experience. Even when he still views the self as "a real unity" that accounts for the connectedness of experience, the unity of the self lies not in any single permanent thing but in the continuity of process—"the self is a connecting, relating activity" (E2.210, 216). Dewey subsequently abandons the idea of the unifying self and seeks unity in a person's "doing and undergoing," that is, within experience itself. He develops a more pragmatist conception of self as self-in-action through a philosophical psychology focusing on action.

Dewey rejects William James's concept of the transcendental ego in the form of the "I" that is the judging Thought, which remembers and so appropriates past constituents of the stream of consciousness of which it is a present unit. For Dewey, thought presupposes habit and involves action. Their subsequent differences notwithstanding, James's *The Principles of Psychology* is the major influence leading Dewey away from a traditional, speculative, armchair approach of introspecting into consciousness to understand the mind. After 1890, Dewey paid more attention to physiology and laboratory experimentation, which view human beings as parts of a natural world. This later approach reveals that "sensations are not the units or elements of knowledge, but are rather the occasions for adaptive adjustments to the environment" (M7.346). Developed in the interaction between the organism and the environment, the mind is "an organ of service for the control of the environment in relation to the ends of the life process" (M2.41).

Dewey's own major contribution to this psychology is found in a highly influential essay, "The Reflex Arc Concept in Psychology," in which he gives an account of the unity of action that illuminates his conception of self. Dewey rejects the "reflex arc" as a new guarantee of the connectedness and coherence of behavior. He objects to the dualism of stimulus and response and psychology's attempt to find lawlike causal relations between the two. He argues that actions are not composed of separate phases of stimulus, internal processing of stimulus and external response, causally connected. Analyzing the action-reaction of a child to a candle flame, he shows that the sensations arising in the retina and elsewhere as well as overt movements and adjustments "lie inside not outside the act" of seeing (E5.98). What are mistakenly seen as separate components of action are in fact functional distinctions within unified action.

James Tiles describes the key to Dewey's view of the reflex arc concept as the pattern of functional differentiation within an organic whole.[27] This is made explicit in an article that Dewey published in 1928. "The beginning is with action in which the entire organism is involved, and the mechanism of reflexes is evolved as a specialized differentiation within an inclusive whole of behavior" (L3.33). The results of the act of seeing-and-grasping the flame refer back to the original impulse and habit associated with the act, thereby modifying the meaning of the impulse and habit. One becomes aware of something as an external stimulus, as requiring some kind of response only when it is indeterminate, as with the child whose habitual response of seeing-and-grasping has been a mixture of enjoyable and painful experiences in the past. Part of the reaction is the interpretation of that stimulus to render it determinate. A reaction is a circuit in which one's sensibilities governing the interpretation of stimulus and one's response adjust to one another, rather than a linear causation.

What is critical in the appearance of a stimulus is that it is problematic, a disruption of the otherwise smooth flow of experience, a "falling out" of an organism with its environment (hence, the contrast between the stimulating and the routine). Reaction is an attempt to reestablish a rapport between the two. The unity of action need not be imparted by something separate from action but is to be found in the interconnectedness and active interactions between the organism and its environment. Such unity could be disrupted, and it is then restored by a process of reconstructing the problematic situation to bring about a successful integration between antecedent conditions and desired consequences. Therefore, there is no need for any unifying entity or separate activity of "unifying" actions and experience.

Those still preoccupied with *identity* often complain that Dewey's view is that of a "self-in-action without a self."[28] They miss the point of Dewey's protest against traditional conceptions of the self. For Dewey, there could be no self outside of experience, outside of human doing and undergoing. The distinction between "self" and action is "after the fact." Unity precedes distinctions in experience; to think otherwise is to commit the "retrospective fallacy"—to mistake a distinction introduced into experience by later reflections as fully present in the original experience. "Looking back, there is the sad event *and* the saddened me; the fearsome bear *and* my fright; the encouraging symptoms *and* my elated hopefulness, but the original situation came with no such duplicity" (M7.37). Selfhood is an eventual function that emerges with complexly organized interactions, organic and social (L1.162).

One's self is constituted partly by one's habits, which are formed and operate in action (M14.21). Habits are social functions that do not exist separately from actions. Habits, for Dewey, are not just conditioned responses or passive routine; they are active, projective means, energetic and dominating ways of acting that could be intelligent and capable of change. In singling out habit, Dewey is not excluding from the self impulse and intelligence—the other components of human nature in his *Human Nature and Conduct*. The three overlap significantly. Habits are impulses organized through social interactions into tendencies for action; habits can be intelligently controlled. Habits are secondary and acquired, "outgrowths of the unlearned activities which are part of man's endowment at birth" (M14.65). A human being is therefore not born with a ready-made self. The process that develops the self is irreducibly social.

George Herbert Mead, with whom Dewey was closely associated, offers if not a more thorough account then certainly a more concise and focused account of this process than is available in any of Dewey's own works. Mead develops the conditions enabling reflection on self, which is necessary to becoming a self, from a theory of the origins of specifically human communication and sociality.[29] The use of signs makes it possible to represent possible actions in the imagination. With key notions such as "generalized other" and "role-taking," Mead develops a theory of social interaction as symbolically mediated, so that one's representation of others' possible reaction to one's imagined action influences one's actual action. One becomes a self when one is able to represent oneself as an agent distinct from, yet related to, other agents in the imagination, and this is only possible with an actual experience of social interactions in which one is treated as an agent who reacts to others and to whom others react.

A baby begins life in instinctive activities, which are "as meaningless as a gust of wind on a mud puddle apart from a direction given it by the presence of other persons, apart from the responses they make to it" (M14.65). It is only in interaction with others that a baby could become a self. As the individuation of a self is not only individuation in the observation and description of another but also individuation of self by oneself, becoming a self is concomitant with acquiring a sense, a consciousness, of self. This sense of self requires distinguishing between self and other, but the distinction does not imply a presocial self or a self that is radically separated from others. A newborn individual has to learn the distinction from those around him. It is only with the responsiveness of nurturing, talking, caring, soothing, and stimulating in others' treatment of him as differentiated from others that a baby learns to organize his experiences into a self.

Not only is the distinction first made through others but it continues to be sustained by interactions with others throughout the baby's life. To sustain such distinction, "a contrast is required. When living beings live together under conditions where they have to consult, in directing their experiences and forming their ends, the welfare of others, each is compelled to distinguish others from himself, and, by a correlative process, his own being and aims from those of others" (M7.340). The self therefore emerges and is sustained in social interactions, so that "without the consciousness of the *alter*, there can be no consciousness of the *ego*; and the more distinct the consciousness of others, the more definite the thought of one's ego" (M7.340). The distinction between self and others implies not radical separateness but the connectedness of individuals. We learn to be the people we are, to a large extent because of what others approve, disapprove, protest, encourage, share, and resist.

We are social selves, because the recognition that our actions affect others, whose reactions in turn affect us, is central to our conduct. We act in a social environment, even when others may not be immediately present. As this age of environmental concerns requiring global solutions has shown us, the very fact that we share a world with others means that immediate proximity is not necessary for our actions to have an effect on others. "Every act brings the agent who performs it into association with others" (M5.404). James Campbell points out that Dewey is making a point not primarily about evaluation of action but about the interpretation of action (though the former follows from the latter), when claiming that "conduct is always shared. . . . It *is* social, whether bad or good."[30] A human action is distinguished from a mere physical event only because the former has meaning that comes from participation in the larger activity of a social group with shared tools, goals, and traditions. Through the meaning it contributes to our actions, our social environment shapes our desires, interests, and motives (M9.21). Even as we act to shape our environments, our environments shape our selves.

Dewey, like communitarians, rejects the conception of self as disembodied and presocial; like liberals, he does not see the self as "encumbered" or "embedded" in a static or passive manner. The self is the product of experience, which involves interaction between a person and her environment. Therefore, it is partially the product of environment. But Dewey is not guilty of reducing the self to an automaton, as some liberals have accused communitarians of doing. The self, in Dewey's conception, acts on the environment, even as the latter acts on it. In the interaction between a person and her environment, she modifies her environment by interpreting past and present and acting to change the future environment. The self is neither completely independent of nor completely determined by the environment. We do not have the autonomy of the disembodied and presocial self; neither are we condemned to the automatic behavior of the encumbered self. The interaction between a person and her environment allows mutual modification to different degrees in different situations, so that individuality and sociality could mutually enhance each other.

CONSTRUCTING A CONFUCIAN CONCEPTION OF SELF

Having examined how Dewey's conception of self combines individuality and sociality, we now turn to how Confucianism deals with the problem of individuality versus sociality. What is the Confucian alternative to the liberal conception of the individual as an autonomous self that many consider incompatible with Confucianism?

Unlike in the history of Western philosophy, there is actually no *problematic* of the self in the early Confucian tradition. Of course, there are a number of terms involving self-reference in the ancient Chinese language. They distinguish between self and others contextually: what is "other" in one context would be "self" in another. *Wo* (我), still commonly used today, and *wu* (吾) can be either "I" or "we," depending on the context. The characters *zi* (自) and *ji* (己), both reflexive, are the terms most frequently rendered into "self" in

English. Another term, *shen* (身), with the basic reference of "body," is sometimes also translated as "self." As Herbert Fingarette suggests, it is important
not to reify these grammatical equivalents of "self" into some kind of inner
ego by giving them the independent noun form in English; they are more accu-
rately translated as "oneself" rather than "one's self."[31] Had the question arisen,
Confucius, like Dewey, would not have believed in any "self" that is an original separate entity set over and against objects and the world.

   The central question for Confucianism is "What is to be done?" rather
than "Who am I?"[32] The latter could of course be part of the former, and vice
versa, but the unfolding of the philosophical quest becomes very different,
depending on which is considered the primary issue. Even though what has
been translated as "self-cultivation" is a key philosophical issue in Confucianism, it is about development of a way of living by engaging in certain
practices. The radical reflexivity, so central to the relatively late Western
problematic of the self, is not an issue in early Confucianism. Fingarette argues
that there is a relative lack of "inward" orientation in the *Analects*.[33] We should
not exaggerate what may seem, at first glance, a startling claim. Fingarette certainly does not mean to suggest that the Chinese people lack an "inner life"
in the sense of feelings and thoughts that others are not privy to. A Chinese,
like anyone else, feels, reflects (*si* 思), and "examines herself within (*neizixing*
内自省)" (*Analects* 4.17). She may even acknowledge the complex and frequently obscure character of that inner life. That "the human heart-and-mind
is difficult to fathom (*renxin bece* 人心叵測)" is a Chinese idiom, traceable to
the early Han dynasty.[34]

   Nevertheless, a persuasive case can be made that the "inner life" is not a
serious philosophical problem, and if there are any questions about this "inner
life," they arise in experience that is not primarily viewed as "inner." In fact,
the "inner life" is never completely separable from the outer.[35] Notions involved
in describing the "inner life" have the radical *xin* (心), the heart-mind in which
the psychological and the physical are united. This is the same character used
to refer to "the core," "the center." What begins in the *xin*, as the "inner" center
of personal experience, is almost invariably connected to "outer" expressions
and actions accessible to others; what begins as an "outer" experience, must
reach the "inner" center to have any significance. Furthermore, answers to
questions about the inner life cannot be found by merely looking "inward." As
Confucius testifies, "Once, lost in my thoughts, I went a whole day without
eating and a whole night without sleeping. I got nothing out of it and would
have been better off devoting the time to learning" (*Analects* 15.31).

   While Confucius and his followers did not discuss the origin or the
concept of the self, one could still construct a Confucian conception of self
that is compatible with, and even enhances, our understanding of the key concerns of Confucianism. Such a conception would be that of a social self con-

stantly reshaped by its environment, even as it shapes the environment through action. It is a conception bearing remarkable similarities to that of pragmatists such as John Dewey and George Herbert Mead. David Hall and Roger Ames, drawing inspiration from Mead, offer a focus-field conception of the Confucian social self. The relationship between the focus and the field may be illustrated by a holograph in which a three-dimensional image appears suspended behind a photographic plate, while at the same time each small chip that makes up the plate gives the whole image from certain angles. The field constitutes each focus, even while the foci simultaneously constitute the field. In this model, "the variety of specific contexts defined by particular family relations, or sociopolitical orders, constitutes the fields focused by individuals who are in turn shaped by the field of influences they focus." The self is always particular, as each field can only be entertained from particular perspectives. It is always an open-ended process, as there is an infinite reservoir of fields offered by familial, social, cultural, and natural environs. One *makes* oneself in a process of contextualization that "allows the focal individual to ally herself with those contexts that she will constitute and that in turn will constitute her."[36]

The continuous "making" of a Confucian focus-field self is evident in the idea of *xiushen* (修身), translated as "self-cultivation" or "personal cultivation." The basic reference of the character translated as "self" in this case, *shen* (身), is "one's body," but as various scholars point out, Chinese philosophy in the pre-Qin period did not share the Western mind-body dualism, so that by "body" is meant a combination of configurational energy (*qi* 氣) and raw stuff (*zhi* 質)—a psychophysical process rather than a purely physical entity.[37] A notion such as *shen* indicates the importance of physical spatiotemporal existence, inseparable from any psychological life, in a Confucian conception of self. *Shen* is the human being seen from within and, hence, it has a connotation of "self." Fingarette sees it as "a reference to the self more as objective phenomena than as subject." From a Confucian perspective, "body" is always the "lived body," or embodied existence—the emphasis is on what Dewey calls the "fullness of experience." One's *shen* is one's "life"—*zhongshen* (終身) means "for one's whole life," and *shenshi* (身世) means one's "life story," "the times of one's embodied existence."

Understanding *shen* as "lived body" brings us close to Dewey's conception of self as a product of experience, of one's doing and undergoing. Like Dewey's conception, a Confucian conception of self as *shen* is not a ready-made self; it is always in the making, being cultivated. A similar mutual modification of person and environment is evident in Confucianism. Personal cultivation is the first step in bringing about an ideal world order. As the famous passage in the "Great Learning" chapter of the *Book of Rites* elaborates: "Those in ancient times who wanted their pure and excellent character to shine in the world would first bring proper government to the empire; desiring to bring proper government to the empire, they would first bring proper order to their families; desiring to bring proper order to their families, they would first cultivate their persons."[38]

In cultivating ourselves, we change our environment, but the process is not linear; there is a feedback effect. Our environment also affects us, contributing to or hindering our efforts at self-cultivation. Therefore, to cultivate ourselves often also requires changing our environment. We find in this process of personal cultivation a parallel to the way interaction between a person and her environment allows a mutual modification of self and environment in Dewey's philosophy, a mutual modification that enables individuality and sociality to enhance, rather than to restrict, each other. A Confucian self, like a Deweyan self, is neither autonomous in the sense of being disembodied and presocial, nor capable only of the automatic behavior of a radically encumbered self.

TENSION BETWEEN DISTINCTNESS AND CONNECTEDNESS

Individuals as social selves, as persons interacting with their environment, neither completely determined by their social relations nor completely determining those relations, are crucial to Deweyan and Confucian ethical life. The development of a social self is a critical part of becoming moral, which Dewey sees as a form of growth (L7.14). Both moral judgment and moral responsibility are social products. He describes the formation of conscience, for example, as basically a socialization process in which "the community without becomes a forum and tribunal within" (M14.216; M11.124). Attributing moral responsibility is, for him, prospective rather than retrospective, influencing the formation of habits and aims, and influencing future acts (M14.216; L7.303). The "community" that forms our moral outlook is not necessarily the immediate social group around us, except in the very early stages of childhood; it also could include ideal communities that exist only in our imagination.

If "community" is defined too narrowly, then Dewey's ethical theory would have no way of explaining how, in some cases, an individual could have very different moral beliefs from the immediate social group in which she is situated. Such cases are important in Dewey's philosophy. He distinguishes three levels of conduct: the first comprises behavior motivated by various biological, economic, and other nonmoral impulses or needs that yet had important results for morals; in the second level, an individual accepts with relatively little critical reflection the standards and ways of her group as these are embodied in customs or *mores*; and in the third, an individual thinks and judges for herself, considers whether a purpose is good or right, decides and chooses, and does not accept the standards of her group without reflection (L7.12). The last stage of reflective morality requires an ability to think in relation to some community better than one's immediate social group. It does not, however, need to posit the kind of radical independence from all social groups traditionally associated with the concept of autonomy, because pragmatist epistemology precludes absolute separation of subject and object of knowledge.[39]

Morality is social, for the same reason that self is social: because others do take account of what we do and respond to our acts accordingly. The resistance and cooperation of others are the central facts in the furtherance or failure of our schemes and activities constituting our selves, but the social saturation of our activities alone does not guarantee that they are right or good (M14.218). The social self and the moral self are not identical; the latter is a subcategory of the former. Even with a social self, we can still act immorally. What this means is that the difference between moral and immoral conduct is not a difference between the social and the individualistic, contrary to mistaken assumptions underlying disputes in moral theory about egoism and altruism. Dewey distinguishes between spontaneous selfishness and reflective selfishness (M7.340). The spontaneously selfish, like a child grabbing all of the food from the table because she is hungry, is unself-consciously engrossed in certain objects and pursues a course of conduct without thinking of their relation to herself and others. As impulse-based, direct responses to situations that are without reflective quality, deliberation, or conscious end, such acts are, strictly speaking, nonmoral. It is nevertheless an appropriate subject of moral approbation only because, if unremarked, it would form a habit toward socially objectionable acts (L7.294).

Reflective selfishness involves a conscious, deliberate privileging of oneself and one's own welfare above others. Conscious reference to one's own welfare and others' welfare as part of the *aim* of conduct becomes possible only after a child has become aware of herself and others as distinct beings who are differently affected, positively or negatively, by her acts. This comes about in the process of adults approving or reproving the results of her behavior (L7.294). Both egoism and altruism, as habits and therefore constituents of character, are acquired. Genuine moral conduct requires regard for both self and others, rather than a disregard for self. "The distinction between a selfishness with which we find fault and an unselfishness which we esteem is found in the quality of the activities which proceed from and enter into the self" (M14.202). The key moral question in our conduct is not about the priority of self or others, it is "what *kind* of a self is being furthered and formed. And this question arises with respect to both one's own self and the selves of others" (L7.295).

Dewey points out that building up a social self by making conduct more intelligent and social is not yet moral progress in the fullest sense. What is needed is that such conduct should itself be valued as good, and so should be chosen and sought (L7.14). People vary in the degree to which they acknowledge and value their sociality. There is consequently an existential ambiguity in the nature of the self (L1.186). In the opacity of one's bias and preferences, one tends to isolation and discreteness—the private and incommunicable aspect of experience is emphasized, and one is doomed to a blind solitariness. Focusing solely on this aspect of experience, one will undermine one's capacity to relate to others, and sociality becomes dysfunctional. But this narrow-mindedness is unnecessary. The problem is a practical and moral one: to widen the horizon, to recognize the plasticity and permeability of one's needs and desires. One needs to acknowledge that a self "belongs in a continuous system of connected events which reinforce its activities which form a world in which it is at home, consistently at one with its preferences, satisfying its requirements" (L1.188). A self is not simply a social product; it could change the environment that has produced it. The irreducible uniqueness, that could "add a bitter loneliness to experience" if one allows it to isolate oneself, could be the source of a creative transformation of self and the world. Instead of denying our sociality, we could make it work for us.

In Dewey's conception of self, there is a tension between distinguishing self from others and the connectedness of self and others. We need to constantly struggle against sliding from distinguishing ourselves from others to assuming some kind of radical separateness, necessitating opposition and conflict. Ethical life is achieving a precarious balance between distinctness and connectedness. Most of the time we fall short of this balance, but instead of merely bemoaning it, Dewey sees in this an opportunity for growth. It is important to recognize that conflicts do occur in social interactions, but they need not be irresolvable, and resolutions need not eliminate the distinction between self and others. Instead of always viewing the social environment as invasive, we should instead recognize social arrangements, laws, and institutions as possible "means of *creating* individuals" (M12.191). The ethical self, from the perspective of unique individuality, is an achievement—the difficulty or ease of the achievement depends partially on the environment.

As an achievement of initiative, inventiveness, varied resourcefulness, and assuming responsibility in choice of belief and conduct, individuality cannot be taken for granted; it is always at risk. This is something that, in Dewey's view, often has been ignored in a philosophy that deals in general categories such as "the individual" and "the state." By neglecting concrete situations, theories that claim organic relations between the individual and the state end up justifying the social status quo. The difference between such theories and Dewey's philosophy is brought out clearly in his critiques of the concrete situation of the United States of his time, especially in *Individualism Old and New*. He analyzed the way in which the "corporate civilization," produced by new forms of production and consumption, suppressed individuality, despite a professed belief in a "rugged individualism." In the acute maladjustment between individuals and the social conditions under which they lived, there was "a disintegration of individuality due to failure to reconstruct the self so as to meet the realities of . . . social life" (L5.73). The "deepest problem" of reconstructing the self to recover social individuality, a functional sociality that is the basis of ethical life, is not only a problem of his time, but a problem that must be faced by every culture and generation living in rapidly changing times (L5.56).

A kind of tension between distinctness and connectedness between self and others also may be detected in Confucianism when we examine the use of zi 自 and ji 己. Both are translated as "self," and Herbert Fingarette finds nothing significantly different between them.[40] Using psychologist Arthur Deikman's distinction between "the observed self" and the "observing self," Livia Kohn differentiates ji from zi as "selfhood" and "spontaneity," respectively. In her view, both Confucianism and Daoism "strive for cultivating and subduing selfhood in favor of spontaneity."[41] We shall explore another philosophically significant difference between zi and ji. Ji occurs in one of the most important passages in the *Analects*—*keji fuli wei ren* (克己復禮為仁)—which D. C. Lau translates: "To return to the observance of the rites through overcoming the self constitutes benevolence."[42] Rendering *keji* (克己) as "overcoming the self" leaves something to be desired insofar as it implies some kind of definable ego self that is to be overcome or sacrificed in a person's ethical progress. Ames and Rosemont translate that passage: "Through self-discipline (*keji* 克己) and observing ritual propriety one becomes authoritative in one's conduct." Usually, "self- . . ." is used to translate terms involving zi (自)—for example, self-examination (*zixing* 自省), "self-so-ing" (*ziran* 自然). So why not *zike* (自克) instead of *keji* (克己)?

Zi is used in contexts of reflexivity when the act in some other contexts may involve more than one person. The main import is indicating the speaker as both the source—a related meaning of zi is "from"—and the object of the act.[43] When it comes to ji, there is not only reflexivity, although that is certainly involved, but a contrast with others—I/me *rather than* others. This is not necessarily reprehensible, as Confucius himself says that learning should be for oneself (ji) rather than for others (*Analects* 14.24). Distinctions, as Dewey points out, are more than legitimate *in their place*. "Petrifaction of distinctions of this kind, that are pertinent and recurrent in specific conditions of action, into inherent (and, hence, absolute) separations is the 'vicious' affair" (L16.248). In contrasting oneself (ji) with another, one is drawing a boundary, however transitory.[44] Disciplining oneself (*keji* 克己) is to give others as much emphasis as is required rather than emphasizing one's own concern at the expense of others. It deemphasizes the contrast, the boundaries between self and others, and it gives one's own as well as others' concerns as much weight as is appropriate to the situation.

How is disciplining oneself a means to authoritative humanity (*ren* 仁)? *Ren* also is translated as "benevolence" or "humanity". Peter Boodberg translates it as "co-humanity" to register its inherent sociality. Tu Wei-ming calls it "man in society."[45] Authoritative humanity involves extending and improving the network of relationships that constitutes a person. It is about preventing boundaries from being petrified, and about breaching petrified boundaries between persons. The same point could not have been made as well with *zi*. One could reinforce this with a passage from the *Xunzi*, where Confucius is said to grade "self-love (*ziai* 自愛)" above "causing others to love oneself (*shiren aiji* 使人愛己)" and "loving others (*airen* 愛人)" as the answer to the question, "What is authoritative humanity (*ren* 仁)?"[46] Using *zi* instead of *ji* avoids emphasizing the contrast between self and others, whereas the other two answers, despite having some merit, emphasize that contrast by their use of *ji* and *ren* (人).

The possibility of varying the boundaries between self and others, of giving the distinction between persons different emphasis and value, indicates the presence of a tension resembling that between distinction and connectedness in Dewey's conception of self. Confucians recognize the possibility of self-imposed isolation that neglects one's sociality. The emphasis on boundaries between oneself and another, captured in the use of *ji*, also enables Confucianism to acknowledge that a person can be and often is selfish, self-centered, while maintaining the claim that humans are intrinsically related. While people still constantly refer to themselves as *ziji* (自己), as emphatically bounded and differentiated from others, it is little wonder that they so often fail to think of themselves as intrinsically related, despite a 2,500-year-old tradition urging them to the contrary.

Isolation is not always self-imposed. Sociality becomes dysfunctional when any one party undervalues or exploits it. Social conditions could be dysfunctional through others' behavior, so that maintaining one's ethical integrity becomes concomitant with isolation. This sense of isolation is common in Chinese literature throughout the ages, and it is especially bitter for "unsuccessful" officials of Confucian persuasion, because the tradition places such high value on public office as actualization of ethical life. There is a long list of frustrated scholar-officials who had to choose between their integrity and success, or even just survival, in the imperial bureaucracy, including Du Fu 杜甫 (712–770 A.D.), whose poetry is quoted at the beginning of Mark Elvin's "Between the earth and heaven: conceptions of the self in China." Elvin argues that the Chinese everyday view of the self is neither strange nor inaccessible to the modern Western imagination, and he analyzes poet Qu Yuan's 屈原 (ca. 343–ca. 277 B.C.) most famous work, "On Encountering Trouble (*Lisao* 離騷)"

as a "psychological self-portrait" evoking "the isolation felt by the egoistic type of suicidal personality."[47]

While the sense of isolation does show that despite the high value set on sociality the Chinese do not ignore the distinction between individuals and solitariness as a possible mode of existence either chosen or forced upon us, Elvin misreads the significance of such literature, at least for the Chinese, if he sees Qu Yuan as being primarily individualistic and egoistic in the Western sense. From a Confucian perspective, it is because of the corruptness of those around him that Qu Yuan was "not in accord with the men of [his] day," and not because he was an "egoistic type." The boundaries between self and others in his case are not just self-imposed. He did not undervalue sociality, but sociality has become dysfunctional through the behavior of his corrupt colleagues and superiors at court. The very fact that he did not simply retire from the corrupt world and "cultivate himself" is evidence for the importance of connectedness with others. So important is this connectedness that his extreme isolation in the end drove the poet to suicide. For the Chinese people, he gains a different form of life in his death: not immortality of an eternal soul but a connectedness with other distinguished personalities through the ages, with others for whom he is an inspiration of ethical living and with whom he therefore shares a continuity of experience.

Confucian conceptions of self may be social, but there is no guarantee that sociality will be acknowledged and valued, hence, there is always a possibility of sociality becoming dysfunctional. It is therefore important for Confucianism to recognize, as Dewey does explicitly, a difference between the social self and the moral self (contrasted with the immoral rather than the amoral) or the ethical self.[48] We can construct a Confucian conception of self as a focus of fields of social networks in which each of us is enmeshed, whether we like it or not. But not all social relations are to be valued, since they could be dysfunctional, in that they could retard individual growth and obstruct ethical living. It is this kind of dysfunctional bonds and relationships that later Chinese intellectuals such as Tan Sitong 譚嗣同 and Kang Youwei 康有為 protested against. This distinction between the social and the ethical is important if we are to reconstruct Confucianism so that it would not endorse all of those social evils that May Fourth intellectuals such as Lu Xun 魯迅, Hu Shih 胡適, and others fought to abolish. Confucians are social reformers as well as self-cultivators. To be an ethical self, one must contribute to relationships that enhance the quality of experience of both oneself and others and consciously value one's intrinsic relationality. One should not perpetuate a dysfunctional social relation but should attempt to change both oneself and others so that the relation can become functional again.

There is a difference between the "background sociality" embodied in oneself as *ji* (己) and the ethically valued sociality embodied in oneself as an

authoritative person (*ren* 仁). The focus-field conception is much more useful
if it avoids collapsing the two. One becomes *ji* as soon as one is capable of
self-reference, but one has to work much harder to achieve *ren*. As *ji*, one is
distinct from others, even as one is irrevocably related to them. The difference
between an ethically backward and an ethically advanced individual lies in
the value that she places on relationality and whether she recognizes that
boundaries between herself and others are always contextual and transitory
and should never be reified. When one achieves *ren*, the intrinsic relations
between self and others become mutual incorporation, so that one is engaged
in a situation constituted by an entire field of self-other concerns, where
each concern, in being given its due, is not distinguished by ownership. The
tension between distinction and connectedness becomes creative rather
destructive.

This is why, in the passage from the *Xunzi* mentioned earlier, Confucius
says that one who is truly enlightened would see *ren* as "self love" (*ziai* 自爱)—
the truly enlightened goes beyond the transitory boundaries between self and
others and focuses on every aspect of a situation, as appropriate to the situation, without overprivileging any party (*Xunzi* 29/143/11). The message is
similar to that of Dewey, who argues that in morality, "the kind of objects the
self wants and chooses is the important thing; the *locus* of residence of these
ends, whether in you or me, cannot of itself make a difference in their moral
quality" (L7.295).

In order to bring about an ethical outcome, the resolution of the tension
between distinction and connectedness must not be at the expense of either
party's individuality. The method for achieving this in early Confucianism is
found in the concept of *shu* 恕, the one thread that unifies Confucius' teachings (*Analects* 4.15). It has been translated as "altruism," "consideration," "reciprocity," and "deference." Confucius himself elaborates it as "Do not do to
others what you yourself do not want" (*Analects* 15.24). *Shu* is the method of
ren that is described as "correlating one's conduct with those close at hand"
(*Analects* 6.30). Creatively extrapolating from the composition of the ideogram
(the cognate *ru* 如 meaning "like, as if, to resemble," and *xin* 心 meaning "heart-
and-mind"), one might suggest that *shu* involves making the hearts-and-minds
of oneself and of others alike. This does not mean presuming that others are
the same as oneself and imposing one's likes, dislikes, and beliefs on them; nor
does it mean uncritically taking over others' likes, dislikes, and beliefs and suppressing one's own. Instead, one strives to appreciate the situation, including
others' and one's own desires and beliefs, from the other's unique perspective
as well as from one's own perspective. In switching between perspectives, some
integration is achieved, so that one tries to appreciate every desire and belief
in relation to the whole situation without favoring any. Every perspective can
end up modified in the process. This task resembles the process that Mead

calls "role-taking," which contributes to the emergence of the self in social interactions.

The nature of the tension between distinctness and connectedness is critical to the kinds of selves being created. In Confucianism, as in Dewey's philosophy, the quality of a created self is linked to the quality of its social relations. What kind of selves (one's own and others') one makes defines one's ethical accomplishment. The key ethical question for both Dewey and Confucianism is not the priority of self or of other but the kind of selves (oneself and others) being created in a relation and sustained in any situation.

CHOICE IN THE LIBERAL-COMMUNITARIAN DEBATE

The view of ethical life focusing on the quality of the tension between distinctness and connectedness without completely sacrificing either is different from the liberal view that finds answers to the question "How should one live?" in individual acts of choice. Choice is central to liberal morality and the Western problematic of the self. Charles Taylor identifies an "individualism of personal commitment" as an important aspect of modern Western culture. It is rooted in the ability to choose and the concomitant responsibility attributed to an individual as a "self" that wills. The individual thereby gains an important status that sets her apart from others.

Choice is a central issue in the debate between John Rawls and Michael Sandel. Sandel distinguishes between two models of agency by which the self might come by its ends—an account he calls "voluntarist," which relates the self to ends as willing subject to objects of choice, and an account he calls "cognitive," which relates the self to ends as knowing subject to objects of understanding. He argues that the central role of choice in "deontological ethics" such as Rawls's requires the voluntarist model of agency, which is based on the priority of the self over its ends.[49] According to Sandel, the cognitive account of agency captures important aspects of our moral experience that the voluntarist account misses. Will Kymlicka criticizes Sandel's contrast of choice with self-discovery for excluding from self-discovery the questioning of given ends. Kymlicka argues that "no matter how deeply implicated we find ourselves in a social practice or tradition, we feel capable of questioning whether the practice is a valuable one."[50]

One should not underestimate the difficulties of questioning social traditions and practices in which our selves are embedded. Moreover, when it happens, it is not clear that the event is adequately described as a choice and not as a discovery. Questioning social traditions and practices in which our selves are embedded indicates that the "embeddedness" is being loosened by new experience. This is a process in which one's previous self-identity is partially dissolving, setting off a process to reconstitute self-identity to make sense of the new experience. It may take the form of reinterpreting previous constituents (or roles, as liberals would call it), or, in more serious cases of displacement, some constituents may be completely rejected, and in some cases replaced by new ones.

I agree with Kymlicka that "interpreting the meaning of our constitutive attachments" may not be enough, and the real question is whether we can reject them entirely, should we come to view them as trivial or degrading. But the possibility of an end or attachment being rejected means that it may not be constitutive of the self in the future; it does not imply that it has not been constitutive before rejection. Constitutive ends and attachments would have to be absolutely unquestionable and indispensable only if we assume erroneously that the self must be some kind of unchanging essence. If we recognize that the unity of self lies in the continuity of changing experience rather than in the persistence of some unchanging entity, then whether some specific ends and social relations are constitutive of self would not depend on whether it is questionable or dispensable.

When we examine the phenomenon of what Kymlicka calls "rebellion against one's identity as a possible mode of expressing it," it becomes evident that choice, as some liberals understand it, may not be an appropriate description, or at least it misplaces the emphasis, of the questioning process. While the process of deliberation over alternatives may take time, a choice is made in a moment. Constituents of self-identity are seldom rejected in a momentary grand gesture of rebellion. After that crucial mental or verbal moment, the rejection, if it is to be effective, requires continued practice—which may be a matter of thinking differently henceforth—that removes those constituents over time while it adds new constituents. We do not experience a "identity crisis" as a matter of choice but more as if we are lost and trying to find our way again. In choice, we cannot choose effectively without first being clear about the alternatives. The crucial moment comes after achieving that clarity. In discovery, finding our way, achieving that clarity is the crucial experience—after that clarity is achieved, it already shows the way one should take; no further choice, in the significant liberal sense, is required. Reconstitution of self or person is not about choice as an autonomous exercise of the will; it is about discoveries, stimulated by new experiences, in a process of interaction with others over which we have only partial control.

Communitarians are concerned that the liberal conception of choice underestimates the role of social confirmation in individual ethical judgments and of social practice in sustaining individual ethical life. "The concern is that this [liberal] vaunting of 'free individuality' will result not in the confident affirmation and pursuit of worthy courses of action but rather in existential uncertainty and anomie, in doubt about the very value of one's life and its purposes."[51] This does not leave us, as Kymlicka assumes, with only the alternative of advocating unacceptable practices (by the government, for example) of providing "external causes," as opposed to reasons, for people's beliefs—and thereby reducing them from agents to automatons, pawns in the palms of those controlling the causes. There is another alternative: the search for the good life is carried out in social practice, in one's interaction with others, in which one both teaches and learns.

There is a tendency in some liberal theories to understand the reasoning process as being ultimately solitary, a view that may be traced to Kant: "we cannot possibly conceive of a reason as being consciously directed from outside in regard to its judgments; for in that case the subject would attribute the determination of his power of judgment, not to his reason, but to an impulsion. Reason must look upon itself as the author of its own principles independently of alien influences."[52] Just as we live life "from the inside," we think "from the inside." But is reasoning really so individualistic? Thinking with others, and for others, does not necessarily exclude thinking for oneself. Communitarians could argue along with Dewey that inquiry into "How should I live?" or even "Who am I?" achieves better results as a social practice.

DEWEY ON WILLING AND CHOOSING

Dewey's sympathies lie closer to the communitarians on the question of choice. In Dewey's philosophy, ethics begins with a problematic situation, an uncertainty when faced with conflicting goods. Dewey's account of how an ethical question is answered by making the indeterminate situation determinate seems more a matter of discovery than a matter of autonomous exercise of the will. He views ethical reasoning as a cooperative inquiry employing social intelligence rather than a solitary exercise of individual reason. But Dewey would reject the false dichotomy of autonomous choice that attributes total control to the individual versus self-discovery that denies the ability of individuals to think for themselves. A more plausible conception of choice lies between the two. This conception, wherein control is neither total nor nil, has a central role in Dewey's philosophy. Dewey considers choice "the most characteristic activity of a self," and "only deliberate action, conduct into which reflective choice enters, is distinctively moral, for only then does there enter the question of better and worse" (L7.286; M14.193).

Dewey distinguishes between preferences and choice. Preferences include appetites and impulse, however blind, anything that selects one thing and rejects others. It is choice only unwittingly, in that to prefer something is to declare in act, though not necessarily in thought, that it is better than something else (L1.320). "We prefer spontaneously, we choose deliberately, knowingly" (L7.286). Occasions for choice in the sense of deliberate decision occur when preferences conflict so that action is obstructed. There is confusion and uncertainty, thinking becomes necessary, one explores competing ends and how one feels about them, one assesses the various means available and their likely consequences, one rehearses in one's imagination the various courses of action, and eventually one arrives at some conclusion about which course of action is better and which is worse (M14.132).

In the conclusion about what is better and what is worse, a choice is already made. One *could*, even recognizing a course of action to be worse, still embark on it, but then one would be rejecting one's own deliberation—and insofar as choice is *deliberate*, one would then be acting not from choice but out of some preference in the form of blind impulse or appetite. Choice as deliberate decision is therefore not arbitrary, even though in its more general sense of picking one of several alternatives, choice may be arbitrary in any particular case (L1.67). Choice is not an exercise of some mysterious independent faculty of will; it results from, and is inseparable from, a process of deliberation beginning from the moment efficient, overt action is blocked, and progressing as "a work of *discovery*," uncovering the conflict of preferences in their full scope so that "an adequate stimulus to the recovery of overt action" may be revealed (M14.150, emphasis added). Choice is made as soon as a "unified preference" emerges out of conflicting preferences in the deliberation (M14.134).

Choice could be reasonable or unreasonable, where reason, instead of being opposed to desires, is "the attainment of a working harmony among diverse desires" (M14.136). Deliberation is conducted well when there is sensitivity to the integrity of a situation in its full complexity, when every constituent is given consideration appropriate to the entire situation. The resulting choice would be a unified preference that incorporates as many as is practical of the initially conflicting preferences—it would be a reasonable choice. In contrast, an unreasonable choice would result if some particular constituents overwhelm the others. This may be compared to the principle of "inclusiveness" that Rawls includes among his "principles of rational choice."[53] However, Dewey gives more weight to feeling, as inseparable from thinking in the mutual adjustment of constituents to achieve harmony in a situation.

Rawls recognizes the complexity of the process of deliberation, especially about life plans and conceptions of the good. It is doubtful if he would insist on any strict reduction to rules of rationality. In *Political Liberalism*, Rawls differentiates between rationality and reasonableness: the rational involves "a single unified agent with the powers of judgment and deliberation in seeking ends and interests peculiarly its own"; the reasonable involves a "particular form of moral sensitivity that underlies the desire to engage in fair cooperation as such."[54] Dewey does not separate the two. The "reasonable" for Dewey applies to both preferences belonging to one individual and those belonging to more than one individual. Though his account of reasonable choice was in terms of a single individual's preferences, it applies to situations involving more than one individual as we see from his discussion of egoism and altruism (L7.295).

Though Dewey emphasizes an element of "discovery" in choice, this does not mean that he considers any end beyond revision. He differs from liberals in that he does not consider an autonomous self, independent of social attachments, customs, and traditions, a precondition for that revision process. We begin as embedded selves, and our thinking is dependent on cultural institutions, what Hegel calls the "objective mind" and Dewey describes as the "mind in individuals."[55] Mind becomes individual rather than merely informing individuals (i.e., one thinks for oneself) only when the mind in individuals proves inadequate in experience, when an individual deviates from customs and traditions in order to reconstitute a problematic situation. Individual minds are eventual functions emerging in "the novel reconstruction of a pre-existing order" (L1.164). Independence (and only *relative* independence) from social attachments, customs, and traditions is the result, not the precondition, of revising what one's self was once embedded in.

The stability of ends that are "constitutive" of oneself may often be good, but if the ends are not revisable under *any* circumstances, Dewey would see that as evidence of arrested growth that is detrimental for both self and society. Arrested growth, in Dewey's view, results from choosing a static self over a dynamic self that "goes forth to meet new demands and occasions, and readapts and remakes itself in the process." To treat ends as not revisable is to make the perpetuation of the static self the standard of our valuations and the end of our conduct at the expense of the dynamic self—it is to contract and harden the self (L1.307). Contrary to Gordon Allport's criticism, Dewey does not exaggerate change within any given individual.[56] While Dewey has faith in the possibility of change and dynamism, he is emphatic about the "self-assertiveness" of habits, the oppressiveness of customs, and the difficulties of achieving individuality, and about how little of human history has been the work of intelligence. What he believes in is that, regardless of how difficult it is, we must try to bring about communities that enable individuals to guide their conduct with intelligence— for it is the only choice that would not betray our humanity.

Choice is, in Dewey's view, especially characteristic of our selves because "in choosing this object rather than that, one is in reality choosing what kind of person or self one is going to be" (L7.287). A self is constituted by habits; habits are formed over a continuous course of action; and action, insofar as it is not unthinking, begins with choice. Self-reflection is indispensable to the making of an ethical self in Dewey's philosophy. Without it, a self would still be formed, accumulated from impulsive and unthinking routine actions—such a self would still be social, but not ethical. Living ethically requires thinking;

it requires the use of intelligence in one's conduct. Just as inchoate and scattered impulses coordinate into serviceable powers and habits in social interactions from which a social self emerges, intelligence emerges and operates in actions in a social environment.

According to Dewey, "thought is born as the twin of impulse in every moment of impeded habit" (M14.118). In *Human Nature and Conduct*, Dewey sometimes alternates between intelligence and thought without explicitly specifying their relationship. Elsewhere, he characterizes intelligence as "active and planning thought" (M12.134). Intelligence is "the power of using past experience to shape and transform future experience" (M11.346). It is not synonymous with thought, which applies also to contexts where the shaping of future experience may not be involved, or where it is involved but no learning from the past is employed. When habit is impeded, from the agent's standpoint, there is shock, confusion, perturbation, and uncertainty, and, consequently, "a new impulse is stirred which becomes the starting point of an investigation, a looking into things, a trying to see them, to find out what is going on" (M14.127).

The new impulse born of impeded habit gives rise to thinking. Impulse provides the forward, prospective tendency in thinking so that it moves toward restoring the unity of interrupted actions. But the contents of thinking, if it is to be effective rather than mere "daydreaming," are retrospective, taken from past experiences, past interactions between the thinker and the environment, both physical and social. Not just any kind of thinking but intelligence is required to remove the obstruction to habit and overt action. Intelligence draws on the resources of the past produced by actions of many rather than one. It is social rather than the possession of an individual (L2.366; L11.48). In attempting to shape future experience, which takes place in a social environment, the effect of intelligence is more than individual; it is social.

Consistent with his conception of choice, Dewey rejects the view of the will as some mysterious faculty with transcendental status, or "a power of choosing, having no ground or reason outside the arbitrary choice itself which isolates the moral agent from all social relations" (L7.341). Instead, he identifies the will with habits, as "dispositions," tendencies to act, potential energies needing only opportunity to become kinetic and overt (M14.21, 34). As with habits—even though the use of nouns may suggest otherwise—no entity separate from action is being referred to. The will is a functional aspect of action. When one wills something, there is present "an active tendency to foresee consequences, to form resolute purposes, and to use all efforts at command to produce the intended consequences in fact" (L7.175). Dewey argues that whatever unconvincing psychology traditional moral theories may subscribe to, "common sense" understands willing as practical and moving, "a *cause* of consequences; it is causation in its personal aspect, the aspect immediately preceding action" (M14.33, emphasis in original). The will is defea-sible—external conditions could frustrate the action so that it does not reach the intended consequences—but the will is active whenever some action is initiated deliberately.

Willing is closely linked to desiring. Desire occurs only when activity is obstructed and its satisfaction or fulfillment is the resumption of the obstructed activity (M14.172). Desire is therefore determined by reference to the habit that shapes the pattern of that activity. Hence, habits "form our effective desires," and "in any intelligible sense of will, they *are* will" (M14.21). Action may occur in which there is only a vital impulse or a settled habit reacting directly to some immediate sensory stimulation, but action also may occur with "ends-in-view" (L13.222). In the latter, desires are present in which the ends-in-view are foreseen consequences, the anticipation of which provides the pro-pelling force in the action toward the actualization of those consequences. Desires therefore involve effort, unlike wishes, which occur in an absence of effort (L13.204). Desires, in their propulsive character, involve impulses, but they also involve sensations and ideas, which are affected by habits, manifested in the acts that give rise to them (M14.25). When desires first present them-selves, they are the products of "a mechanism consisting of native organic ten-dencies and acquired habits" (L13.217). Maturity in conduct consists in not immediately giving way to such tendencies but in remaking them through con-sideration of the consequences *if* they are acted upon—the will consists of such desires "remade" by thought (L7.190).

It is the absence of intelligence, of critical scrutiny of aims and foresight of results, that distinguishes obstinacy from will; what the two share are per-sistence and energy in striving to execute aims (M9135). Desires, and will, by extension, are behavioral attitudes with a biological basis; they arise when there is an obstruction in a creature's life-activity. Desire "is activity surging forward to break through what dams it up. The object which then presents itself in thought as the goal of desire is the object of the environment *which, if it were present*, would secure a re-unification of activity and the restoration of its on-going unity" (M14.172, emphasis in original). From this account, desiring and willing are clearly involved in the same situations that call forth deliberation and choice. Choice is the beginning of action, because what is chosen also is what is willed (L17.338).

Confucian Choice: Learning and Thinking

While Dewey reconstructs the concepts of the will and of choice, one might ask if such concepts are even found in Confucian vocabulary. Choice appears to have little importance in a philosophy that Herbert Fingarette character-

izes as a "way without a crossroads." He points out that the image of the crossroads, so perfectly suited as a metaphor of choice in view of the prevalence of
roads and travel metaphors in the *Analects*, is *never* used by Confucius. One
could suggest that choice between alternatives as an inseparable part of action
is captured in the ideogram *xing* 行—usually translated as "action," "practice,"
"to walk," or "to travel"—which develops from a pictograph of a crossroads.[57]
Fingarette is not denying that Confucius recognizes people as making choices
in their daily lives and considers them responsible for their actions to varying
degrees. His specific claim is about the philosophical significance of such acts.
The choice that he argues is absent in the *Analects* is a specific conception of
choice as an autonomous exercise of the will, "intimately intertwined with the
idea of the ontologically ultimate power of the individual to select from
genuine alternatives to create his spiritual destiny."[58]

There is an unfortunate equivocation about what "genuine alternatives"
are in Fingarette's view. He equates them with "real options" when he says that
Confucius does not allow for choice, "if we mean by choice a selection, by
virtue of the agent's powers, of one out of several equally real options."[59] This
implies that choice is somehow illusory, unreal—when in fact his account of
the alternatives to "treading the true Path (*dao* 道)" as walking crookedly,
getting lost, or abandoning the path makes a more modest point: in any one
specific situation, there are no equally *good* options. The alternatives of walking
crookedly, getting lost, or abandoning the path are as real as treading the path;
they are just not as good. Once this equivocation is cleared up, the contrast
between early Confucianism and Western philosophies on the matter of choice
has to be qualified.

Even Augustine would not consider choice being between options that
are equally good, but there is still a difference. Fingarette makes a persuasive
case that, for Confucius, unlike Augustine, ethical failure is more a matter of
ignorance than weakness of the will. While the Augustinian understanding of
moral choice is dominant in the Western problematic of the self, there also is
a far from negligible strand of thinking, going back to the ancient Greeks, that
links ethical action with knowledge, as in the alternative offered in Sandel's
"cognitive" model of agency. Instead of simply concluding that early Confucianism is compatible with only the cognitive model of agency and is therefore not primarily concerned with individual choice, I would contend that
there is room in Confucianism for a Deweyan conception of willing and choosing that balances individual control over situations with the discovery of components of the situation, including oneself, in a social practice of cooperative
inquiry.

A case in point, which Fingarette rejects as concerning choice, is Confucius saying that he could do nothing with one who does not constantly ask
himself, "What is to be done? What is to be done?" (*Analects* 15.16). On

Dewey's terms, it involves choice—it is a problematic situation in which a selection from alternatives is necessary, requiring a thinking process. The question "What is to be done?," symptomatic of a problem, can only be answered with a combination of learning (*xue* 學) and thinking (*si* 思), a combination that comes close to Dewey's concept of intelligence as "the power of using past experience to shape and transform future experience."

Though it is reduced to "studying" in later ages, the early meaning of *xue* is much wider. It means to "become aware," and it covers practically all kinds of learning from experience—not just learning from one's own past experience but also from the past experience of others, from one's cultural legacy. Confucius describes himself as "being eager to learn," and he praises his favorite student, Yan Hui, for the same.[60] Learning is the first step in self-cultivation, the first move in ethical progress, and it must continue without ceasing to sustain ethical living, for without learning, even the love of authoritative humanity (*ren* 仁) would lead to foolish action (*Analects* 17.8). Though Confucius refers to "those born with knowledge," he does not actually identify anyone as having such knowledge. His chief concern is with knowledge gained from learning, which he describes as being found in using one's ears widely and following what is good in what one has heard, and using one's eyes widely and retaining what one has seen in one's mind (*Analects* 7.28). In drawing on such experiential knowledge to answer the question "What is to be done?," Confucianism approaches Dewey's account of choice as intelligent deliberation employing resources of the past to shape the future through reconstituting a present situation.

Confucius sometimes speaks of *si* (思), translated as "thinking" or "reflecting," in contrast to learning, "Once, lost in my thoughts, I went a whole day without eating and a whole night without sleeping, I got nothing out of it, and would have been better off devoting the time to learning" (*Analects* 15.31). This is not to say that *si* is completely useless; rather, it must complement learning: "learning without due reflection leads to perplexity; reflection without learning leads to perilous circumstances" (*Analects* 2.15). *Si* is used as a generic term for various modes of thinking, each with a different relationship to knowledge gained from past experience. Thinking is fruitless when it is "ungrounded" and empty, speculative, and mere "daydreaming." When based on experiential knowledge, it is critical and evaluative and enables the thinker to extend knowledge to new circumstances and to resolve problematic situations.[61] Unless past experience is made relevant to present circumstances through intelligent thinking, one is no clearer as to how to proceed (and, hence, the perplexity); if one attempts to think without learning from past experience, and worse yet, to proceed according to such "ungrounded" thinking, then action would be unintelligent, and the results are often unproductive and even dangerous.

One should not overemphasize the contrast between *xue* and *si*; they form a polarity so that each is always in the process of becoming the other. Thinking *in vacuo* is not the norm, and there is already an element of critical and evaluative thinking in learning. Confucius says, "if you listen broadly, set aside what you are unsure of, and speak cautiously of the rest, you will make few mistakes. If you look broadly, set aside what is perilous, and act cautiously on the rest, you will have few regrets" (*Analects* 2.18). Even as you hear or see something, you are already evaluating how far you should rely and act on it. When faced with a problematic situation, one draws on past experience, with its inseparable observation-evaluation, and learning from that experience one reflects further to extend its relevance to the present and future, in the mode of intelligent thinking. In this way, one deliberates to find a good answer to the question, "What is to be done?"

While there are enough similarities in the concern about and approach to problem solving to justify our drawing a parallel between Dewey's and Confucius' views of the thinking-acting process required for ethical life, we must be careful not to exaggerate their similarities. Dewey has a well-developed theory of inquiry that draws on his understanding of the scientific method; no such theory is available in early Confucianism. Deliberation in Dewey's philosophy tends to be thinking about ends and means, both instrumental and constitutive, while there is no philosophical theory of means and ends in the early Confucian texts. Although both recognize the importance of customs and traditions, and their positive aspects, Dewey emphasizes deviation from customs and traditions in the emergence of individual minds, while Confucius emphasizes continuity with the past. When past resources prove inadequate, Confucians usually prefer to reinterpret rather than reject the past. Keeping those differences in mind, one could nevertheless argue that Confucian use of the term *thinking* (*si* 思) is vague and elastic enough to accommodate Dewey's more developed theory of deliberative thinking, even though it includes other less structured forms.

Are we overemphasizing questioning and deliberation in ethical action as understood in early Confucianism? Although Irene Bloom recognizes that "choice is not necessarily to be viewed as part of the complex of ideas which involves moral responsibility, guilt, retributive punishment, and repentance, as it is at the point where we encounter the Augustinian notion of *liberum arbitrium*, or free will," she nevertheless sees the "obvious point" of Mencius' discussion of the "four beginnings (*siduan* 四端)" as rejecting the role of conscious deliberation or choice in moral action that is not the subject of alternative interpretations or judgments.[62] Based on Deweyan psychology, the man who moves to save the child about to fall into the well is not simply following his instincts. He responds thus only because his past experience, both observing and evaluating, and extending actual experience by imagination, allows him to know, to foresee, the consequences of the child falling, and thereby he reacts to that knowledge.

Another child as inexperienced as the one at the rim of the well would not react to the scene in the same way the adult would. Insofar as learning from past experience brings about an attempt to shape future experience, however "spontaneous" the reaction, there is an exercise of intelligence similar to that in more conscious deliberation and choice. The continuity and open-endedness of experience is such that it would be misleading to focus on only a limited period of time in considering the role of choice and deliberation in ethical action. Still, such examples do show that despite considerable weight given to reflecting, early Confucianism emphasizes the acquisition, through ritual performance, of dispositions that would ensure that actions are spontaneously appropriate, rather than a less spontaneous practice of inquiry. In contrast, even while Dewey recognizes the importance of feeling and dispositions, he emphasizes verbalistic thinking found in cooperative inquiry.

Bloom also believes that "in classical China, where persons were characteristically defined in terms of biological inheritance, identities and roles were not chosen but received along with the gift of life itself."[63] In that case, some "constitutive ends" are beyond questioning and revision, as Sandel has argued. However, Confucianism could be reconstructed so that constitutive ends are revisable. It is true that one does not choose one's parents or siblings, or even the community in which one is born. Although with regard to the last, one at least has the choice, within limits, of which community one continues to live in. Confucius left his native state of Lu to attempt to find a ruler who would put his political program into practice, and at one time he considered going to live among the eastern tribes whom the people from the central states considered "crude" (*Analects* 9.14). While modern modes of transportation appear to have expanded such choice, political boundaries today, being more formalized, actually impose greater constraints.

Bloom overemphasizes the stability imparted by biological ties in human relationships that define our roles and identities in Confucianism. The cultural significance of the family is not due entirely to "biological inheritance." Adoption is accepted practice in Chinese society, and an adopted parent does not have fewer claims than a biological parent. The *Analects* recognizes, as a matter of ethical significance, that a biological parent does not necessarily act appropriately in terms of the ethical requirements of parenthood (*Analects* 12.11). Family and other social relations are significant in one's ethical life not because of "biological inheritance" but because they are *ethical* relations. Ethical relationships require conscious effort to bring about and sustain. Relationships based on biological ties, in extreme circumstances, could be rejected and further contact with the relative terminated. A student of Confucius, Sima Niu, disowned his brother because of the latter's unethical behavior, and when he lamented that he had no brother, Zixia consoled him by saying that if one relates to others with respect and propriety, "all within the four seas are brothers" (*Analects* 12.5). Mencius defended Kuang Zhang as a filial son, despite the fact that the latter had been estranged from his father over an ethical matter.[64] The ethical significance of a relationship lies in its developing and being sustained by ethical conduct, and in this aspect, relationships—and the roles and identities they define—are deliberately cultivated.

CONFUCIAN PERSONAL COMMITMENT

The comparison of Dewey and Confucius has focused on the thinking process involved in choice, and on defending Confucianism against the charge of denying our ability to question, revise, and even reject our ends and social attachments. With Dewey, I have noted that intelligence is social rather than individual. I shall explore further the sociality of choice in Confucianism by examining the Confucian view of personal commitment in ethical life. It is important to see that this sociality does not negate individuality in choice.

In Dewey's psychology, deliberation and choice are associated with desiring and willing. In the *Analects*, there appears to be no classical Chinese term equivalent to "choice." Situations that we could interpret as calling forth deliberation and choice are sometimes discussed in terms of *yu* 欲—the generic term variously translated as "wish," "want," or "desire"—and *zhi* 志, often translated as "will." Fingarette characterizes *yu* and *zhi* as imparting a "directed dynamism" to the self, and *zhi* can "motor and direct action."[65] Like the will in Dewey's philosophy, *yu* and *zhi* do not refer to any faculty or entity separate from the willing act. As Dewey discovers, it is so difficult to "reclaim" Western philosophical concepts such as "the will" from its traditional influence that some translators, anxious to avoid misunderstanding, prefer to abandon the term *will* and, based on the character's composition, render *zhi* as "to set one's heart-and-mind on" something.[66]

As with Dewey's distinction between desiring and willing, there is a greater degree of thought, even deliberation, in *zhi*, which reveals effort and persistence in striving to execute aims. Unlike Dewey, who distinguishes obstinacy from the will, *zhi* also is used in the *Analects*, on one occasion, for obstinacy (*Analects* 4.18). However, the most prominent use of it is in relation to ethical purposes, and among its objects are learning, authoritative humanity (*ren* 仁), and the way (*dao* 道). We shall see how these instances of personal commitment to ethical living reveal that, in contrast to most Western views of willing, setting one's heart-and-mind on something is part of a social practice rather than a purely individual endeavor. Confucius says, "From fifteen, my heart-and-mind was set upon learning." This is the first of several stages of a process that extended to the time when Confucius, from seventy, "could give his heart-and-mind free rein without overstepping the boundaries" (*Analects* 2.4). By any standard, Confucius' life is a remarkable exemplar of personal commitment. Personal commitment is an ongoing process, traveling a long road even when the burden is heavy and the going gets tough (*Analects* 8.7). It begins in the heart-and-mind, the center of one's becoming, and it extends throughout one's life. A personal commitment, in Confucius' teaching, is not a solitary undertaking. Not only are there always fellow travelers along the way, but we are led into it by exemplars preceding us, and in achieving consummation in the process, we lead those who come after.

In what Charles Taylor calls the "individualism of personal commitment," the act of willing carries justificatory weight—the choice makes a chosen way of life good (though it may not be right). This is a liberal view of the role of choice in morality.[67] In contrast, "setting one's heart-and-mind" on something does not in itself justify it in Confucianism. If anything, the results achieved justify the initial act of embarking on a particular path. Ethical tasks may be evaluated according to *dao* 道, usually translated as "the way" (although the Chinese language does not use the definite article).[68] However, the results are not evaluated by some standard independent of individuals and their communities. I disagree with Fingarette, who describes *Dao* as a standard with "an inherent generality, an absence of essential reference to a unique individual," and Munro, who argues that "in Confucianism the common traits of the sage-like types stand out as the ideal features for people to copy," and people differ only "in the means to achieve universal goals."[69] If we reduce ethical action to a matter of meeting transcendental standards, then all individuality is lost.

One could not deny that Confucian ethics has to be understood through a group of key terms fairly general in their application—among them, excellence (*de* 德) authoritative humanity (*ren* 仁), appropriateness or propriety (*yi* 義), ritual practice (*li* 禮), wisdom (*zhi* 智), keeping one's words (*xin* 信), and courage (*yong* 勇). But these are not absolute principles that individuals follow, each ethical act an instantiation of some fixed universal, and the sage does not distinguish himself only by providing prominent examples of such instantiations. As Tu Wei-ming points out, "since the Way is not shown as a norm that establishes a fixed pattern of behavior; a person cannot measure the success or failure of his conduct in terms of the degree of approximation to an external ideal."[70] For an understanding of Confucianism more conducive to Confucian democracy, one needs an approach that combines intersubjectivity with a focus on particularity, thereby allowing articulate evaluations and judgments that combine social affirmation with individual creativity.

We could do worse than follow Fingarette's lead in turning to the arts for an approach to understanding Confucianism, but in his use of the analogy of music, individuality is arguably still subordinated, since "the true artist's style serves the work."[71] Dewey would say that he has confused the art product (the tangible music score) for the work of art, which is constituted by each particular interaction of the music concept with the performers and audiences, and therefore constantly changes (M10.218). There is no static "work" independent of those who interact with a product of artistic activity; there is no one way independent of individual treading of particular paths. The unique quality of each artistic performance cannot be ignored in its evaluation, but the value attributed cannot be determined entirely by this uniqueness. Evaluation must have intersubjective validity. Therefore, there are two aspects to evaluation—one pertains to the unique feelings in that particular encounter with an art product, and the other pertains to thinking about why that experience is excellent. The latter is an attempt at articulation in a shared vocabulary of the experience—not according to some a priori rules (though there may be some "summary rules") but in relation to previous experiences (not just one's own) relevant to the present experience. Even as the articulation of each individual experience is guided by the shared vocabulary developed in past experience, it could modify that vocabulary at the same time.

This is one aspect in which "exemplifying" differs from instantiating or following a law, principle, or rule. In the latter, there is unilateral determination—the law determines whether something is an instantiation of it; in the former, there is mutual modification between what is being exemplified and what is exemplifying. Evaluation of a work of art is an attempt at persuading others in a community who are sharing experiences that are subject to such an evaluation, which refers back to the unique feelings involved in the experience of the particular work—there must be a fit between the excellence articulated and the feelings experienced. Furthermore, not everybody's articulation of the excellence of a work of art counts equally in such a community, thus there must be an acceptance of one's qualification as a judge, a complex process that again involves persuading others in the community.

This analogy reveals how sociality contributes to the value of one's choice, especially one's personal commitment to ethical living, without denying individuality altogether. When one is able, by traveling one's particular *dao*, to extend the *dao* visible to and valued by one's community, then one's commitment gains value. One carries out one's commitment like an artist creating a work of art. One's individuality creates something new, a "novel reconstruction of a pre-existing order," which contributes to one's community. One's work is "justified," given enduring value, when it brings into focus, with intensity, the richness of human experience in an embodied form that could be shared with others and further enriches the life of the community. Ethical value involves both the individual and the communal.

While individuality has a significant role in one's ethical progress in early Confucianism, the unique qualities of individuals are not valued for their uniqueness in disregard of everything else—something Munro sees as an important ingredient of Western individualism inherited from the Romantics.[72] Confucians value only those unique qualities that contribute to a particular individual's ethical growth. If a person has a unique capacity that inhibits ethical growth of self or others, or causes suffering, then should it still be valued? According to Confucianism, and Dewey's pragmatism as well, it should not. Few people, and certainly no reasonable liberals, would be fanatical enough to subscribe to an individualism that answers in the positive.

INDIVIDUALITY AND ORGANIC SOCIALITY

Liberalism is not usually so individualistic that it denies the importance of society completely. John Rawls recognizes "the comprehensive good of social union . . . to which everyone can contribute and in which each can participate" as one of the political goods that complement the principles of the right.[73] What troubles communitarians is that liberal acknowledgment of the importance of society often is inadequate due to its understanding of sociality. Historically, conception of the autonomous self as moral agent is concomitant with an atomistic understanding of society as a collection of preformed individuals. This mechanical conception of society underlies social contract theories, which are still closely associated with liberalism today. Hegel criticizes this conception of society as "a heap, an aggregate of atomic units," for confusing society with an association of private persons. Such a conception can make no sense of the fact that it is not up to us whether or not we are born into or belong to society.[74]

In response to Hegel, Rawls concedes that "we have no prior identity before being in society," but he insists that this does not pose a problem for maintaining the distinctness and plurality of persons. While taking seriously communitarian critiques inspired by Hegel, he continues to resist any supposition that "society is an organic whole."[75] Although organic conceptions of society are more common among communitarians, Gerald Gaus argues that "new liberals," including John Dewey, J. S. Mill, and even John Rawls, also conceptualize society as an organism of some sort.[76] A move from a mechanical to an organic conception of society is required to reconcile individuality and sociality. In an organic conception, society is viewed as an organism, wherein individuals are related to one another, and to the social whole, as cells are organized into organs, which are organized to form the organism.[77]

Organic relations are internal, in contrast to mechanical relations, which are external. In an external relation, the participants can be conceived or thought of, if not actually exist, in isolation; an internal relation affects or contributes to the identity of its participants, the very way we are able to think of them. "The limbs and organs . . . of an organic body are not merely parts of it: it is only in their unity that they are what they are, and they are unquestionably affected by that unity, as they also in turn affect it." Logical atomists consider all relations external; Hegel views all relations as internal.[78] Dewey does not consider all relations internal, but he does consider social relations internal, and to that extent, he may be said to subscribe to an organic view of society.

Dewey subscribes to an organic view of society as late as 1928, although he had some reservations about the organic conception of society even while defending it.[79] Despite his view of social relations as internal and his use of the language of organicism even in his later works, Dewey's conception of society varies from organic conceptions such as Hegel's, of which liberals are most critical. In the view of its critics, Karl Popper and Isaiah Berlin among them, Hegelian organic conceptions of society justify political and social tyranny, because they are holistic and teleological. On the other hand, scholars such as Shlomo Avineri and Taylor argue that those who accuse Hegel of totalitarianism or authoritarianism misunderstand him.[80]

The social whole in organic conceptions of society could appear as some kind of super-individual subject with aims and interests of its own—it has a *telos*, a final end, the realization of which is the realization of its true nature. For Hegel, the *telos* of the social whole is the actualization of *Geist*, the full realization of reason and freedom. Such teleology often has an element of historical determinism that denies individual autonomy and responsibility.[81] Taylor describes the implications of Hegel's notion of the "cunning of reason" in history in these words: "We are caught up in a drama we do not really understand. Only when we have played it out do we understand what has been afoot all the time. . . . That reason realizes itself means that the outcome arises out of human action which is not really conscious of what it is doing, acts while seeing through a glass darkly, but which is guided by the cunning of reason." We are not in control of our own destiny, let alone of the destiny of the world. Agency is not merely individual. *Geist*, as individuals' "soul," "an unconscious inner sense," "exercises a force on them which they surrender to even against their conscious will."[82]

Liberals would reject any conception of the "social individual" that implies such organic conceptions of society. From their perspective, these conceptions end up sacrificing individuality. We need to defend Dewey's philosophy and Confucianism against such a charge in order to maintain the claim that they offer an alternative that balances individuality and sociality rather than sacrificing either. Dewey started his philosophical career as a Hegelian. Though he abandoned his early Hegelianism, "acquaintance with Hegel has left a permanent deposit in [his] thinking" (L5.154). This "permanent deposit" refers to "Hegel's idea of cultural institutions as 'objective mind' upon which individuals were dependent in the formation of their mental life." But Dewey is not among "the upholders of the collective *mystiques*" of which Berlin is so critical. Dewey does not posit society, or any social entity, as a super-individual subject. In his philosophy, "the metaphysical idea that an absolute mind is manifested in social institutions dropped out; the idea, upon an empirical basis, of the power exercised by cultural environment in shaping the ideas, beliefs, and intellectual attitudes of individuals remained." This removes him from the holistic, teleological collectivism characteristic of organic conceptions of society that, according to Berlin, is "metaphysical and normative" rather than "sociological and psychological."[83]

It is undeniable that Dewey often adopts a holistic perspective. His accounts of the mind and the self, for example, are genetic ones that reveal progressive functional differentiation within an organically structured whole. He does not, however, propose that we need to know the nature of the whole before we could know the parts; he examines the empirical functional differentiation itself for knowledge of both the parts and the whole. Moreover, "an organic whole" is only relatively whole. A situation is an organic whole vis-à-vis its components, which must be differentiated and reconstituted to solve a problem, but it is a part of the ongoing process of experience. Though he philosophizes about "the generic traits of existence," Dewey does not speculate about the nature of some kind of final, absolute whole.

Dewey is even wary of speaking in terms of "society as a whole." In his view, such "pure abstractions" lead to the frequent mistake of opposing *the* individual and *the* social. "There is no single thing denominated 'society'; there are many societies, many forms of association" (L7.324). And when each form of association is taken to be *a* society, it does not exist apart from individuals. Associations are significant not because of the presence of any super-individual subject but because of the existence of interaction and operative relations among individuals. Any social purpose, common good, would not be the given possession of a super-individual subject; it would have to be constructed by individuals interacting with one another.

While he abandons the mystifying, totalizing teleology of Hegelianism, it would be a mistake to conclude that teleology has no place at all in Dewey's philosophy. According to Dewey, the sense of "the organic . . . shades into teleological and is opposed to mechanical" (M2.177). Human beings are more preoccupied with enhancing life than with bare living, more interested in consummations than in preparations. Human action goes beyond mere maintenance of the life process; it is concerned with the consummatory phase of experience, with direct enjoyment, which is concerned with "final objects" (L1.69). As directly experienced, "things are poignant, tragic, beautiful, humorous, settled, disturbed, comfortable, annoying . . . immediately and in their own right and behalf" (L1.82). Because "*any* quality as such is final; it is at once initial and terminal; just what it is as it exists, . . . nature in having qualities within itself has what in the literal sense must be called ends, terminals, enclosures" (L1.82). "Since common sense is concerned, directly and indirectly, with problems of use and enjoyment, it is inherently teleological" (L12.81).

All natural events are natural ends, in the sense of objects and qualities being immediately experienced. Contrary to traditional teleologies, natural ends are not necessarily good. Dewey admits that, linguistically, "ends" do seem to have connotations of something valued and sought after. Such ends, he argues, are not natural ends but ends-in-view. A natural end becomes an end-in-view only when, because of its experienced quality, it is actively sought for and reached as a conclusion (L1.93). Unlike natural ends, which may relate to their so-called means externally, in mere sequential order, an end-in-view is internally related to its means. Things become means "only as the end-in-view is actually incarnate in them, in forming them. Literally, they *are* the end in its present stage of realization" (L1.280). An end-in-view "is in constant and cumulative reenactment at each stage of forward movement. It is no longer a terminal point" (L1.280). It is "end" in no exclusive sense; it belongs integrally to the means that produce it. Ends-in-view and their means are not merely causally related; they share connections of meaning that develop continuously in a flexible, freely moving process, so that without a fixed prior design determining everything, events could still move in a particular direction, a direction that may be furthered or frustrated but that is internal to the process.

Ends-in-view play a crucial role in providing direction to human action in a world in which events are "on-going and as such unfinished, incomplete, indeterminate," and consequently "possess a possibility of being so managed and steered that ends may become fulfillments, not just termini, conclusions not just closings" (L1.127–28). In an indeterminate, unfinished, open universe, progress is not inevitable; it is up to us to bring it about (L14.113). While direct worth is found only in the immediate experience of certain qualities and meanings of things, that is, in natural ends, as things not immediately present, the intrinsic qualities of which are not directly experienced, then ends-in-view are primary from the standpoint of control (L1.96). Ends-in-view are central to the intelligent control of activities and therefore to Dewey's melioristic social philosophy. We may safely assume that teleology has an important role in Dewey's thinking. But this teleology is ad hoc, context-specific; it differs from the kind of totalizing, absolute teleology that subordinates the individual to the social.

Dewey's teleology is very different from Hegelian teleologies in which the organic whole, even if it "may be wholly or partially manifested in and as a temporal process, . . . is not itself temporal, but transcends all temporal series."[84] Hegelian teleologies privilege a transcendent/immanent order, a whole that is complete and self-enclosed—they value stasis over dynamism, so that change has value only as a means to permanence. In contrast, the stability of an organic whole is always relative in Dewey's philosophy. Every existence is an event, that is, each is always *becoming*—having come into being, each will pass away. In such processes of becoming, what are designated "structures," providing the stability of "systems," are only "the slower and the regular rhythmic events."[85]

The finality of ends in Dewey's philosophy is not absolute; it is relative to particular parts of experience. From a wider perspective, "nothing in nature is exclusively final" (L1.99). "Any event is at once both beginning of one course and close of another; is both transitive and static" (L1.85, 90). Dewey rejects any teleology that posits "rows of inferior ends which prepare for and culminate in something which is *the* end" (L1.89). Just as "there is no one single and all-at-once beginning of everything," there is no one single final end for everything (L1.83). Ours is "a world which is not finished and which has not consistently made up its mind where it is going and what it is going to do" (L1.67). Though teleological in one sense, Dewey's philosophy neither posits a final end to subordinate individual ends nor implies historical inevitability that denies individuals any control over their destinies.

The influence of Hegel on organic conceptions of society also is felt in accounts of Chinese society and Chinese thought. Chinese society often has been portrayed as the epitome of an "organic society" in which the individual is completely subordinated to the social. Western writers often have projected their own understanding of the organic view of society onto Chinese thought. Munro noted that "anyone who scans the histories of China written by foreigners during the past two decades will find the assertion that the Chinese favored the analogy of the organism in explaining nature" and society. Ann Kent considers "the view of society as an organic whole whose collective rights prevailed over the individual, the idea that man exists for the state rather than vice versa" a significant obstacle to the struggle for civil and political rights of individuals in China. Randle Edwards describes the typical Chinese view of society as "an organic whole or a seamless web," and in a rather unfortunate mix of metaphors, he goes on to say that the Chinese consider each individual "a cog in an ever more efficient social machine."[86]

The Confucian conception of the focus-field self constructed in this chapter, wherein individuals are situated in a social network as the holographic focus of a field, supports Munro's view that "most of the Confucian and Taoist writings suggest the coimplication of self and other, and coimplication implies organic relation." However, that Chinese thought implicitly treats social relations as internal does not, as we see from the discussion of Dewey's conception of society, imply that the Chinese view subordinates the individual to the social. Recognition that social relations are internal cannot alone justify the claim that the holism prevalent in Chinese thinking assigns purposes or goals to wholes such as clans, families, society, or nature, and that for the Chinese, "the destiny of individuals is a function of their relation to the whole and its purposes."[87]

The "social whole" in most Western organic conceptions requires structure and a self-closure that precludes endless progression. According to Giovani Sartori, "What is known about a system, the level of integration of the components, and its boundaries, is the logical equivalent of the closure of that system."[88] In contrast, the use of terms such as *organism* and *whole* in a contemporary English discussion of Chinese philosophy does not always imply structure and closure. Taking up Frederick Mote's theme of the Chinese view of "cosmos" as an organismic process, Tu Wei-ming considers "wholeness" a basic motif of this process—the other two being "continuity" and "dynamism"—but he emphasizes that the organismic process is an open, not a closed, system. "As there is no temporal beginning to specify, no closure is ever contemplated. The cosmos is forever expanding; the great transformation is unceasing."[89] This differs from the Western understanding of the organism that implies a complete whole with clear boundaries (at least conceptually).

As Chinese scholar Fei Xiaotong points out, while we could not avoid the use of terms with Western philosophical baggage as long as we discuss Confucianism in a Western language, "western innovations [including concepts] are never precisely appropriate; we need to sinicize them."[90] Unless the modifications, different connotations, or even different meanings are made explicit, borrowing Western philosophical terms could distort our understanding of Chinese thought. This is what happens with the language of organicism. We do not find the metaphor of organism or imagery of a body applied to any social group in the *Analects*. The one use of body-related imagery in the *Mencius* compares the *relationship* between the ruler and his ministers to that of the heart-mind to the four limbs (*Mencius* 8.3/41/1). The *Xunzi* at one point refers to "all under heaven" following a true king "as though it were of a single body with him, just as the four limbs follow the heart-and-mind" (*Xunzi* 12/60/17). According to Munro, the Song philosophers go farther and "refer to the organic whole composed of heaven, earth, and all things, with its mind and its pervasive life force."[91] But is the Chinese *yiti* 一體, translated as "single body," the same as the organism as a whole in Western theories?

There is strong evidence in Chinese thinking, as in Dewey's philosophy, that something is "whole" only relatively. In Western thought, an organism is a combination of physical discreteness and functional interdependence of parts forming a whole. In Chinese thought, the human body is a dynamic network of patterns of energies wherein boundaries, if present at all, are at best fuzzy.[92] The lack of emphasis on physical boundaries within an organism is repeated in the relation between organisms and the environment. Bodily energy patterns do not form a self-contained whole; energies are exchanged with the environment viewed as different, interdependent patterns of energies.[93]

Studies of Chinese societies encounter conceptual difficulties with defining "social wholes." Examining Confucian society from three levels—individual (*ji* 己), family (*jia* 家), and nonfamilistic social group (*qun* 群)—Ambrose King argues that the "group" outside of the family, certainly "society," is only vaguely defined in Confucianism.[94] There is no formal treatment of *qun* as a social group in early Confucianism. The term refers to any group of more than three, but it appears more frequently as a verb in the classical language. In the *Conversations of the States* (*Guoyu* 國語), it is used to refer to animal groups of three or more, in contrast to human groups, which are referred to as *zhong* 衆, usually translated as "multitude."[95] Since *zhong* has no connotation of cohesion beyond simultaneous presence in a particular location, it is difficult to think of *zhong* "as a whole."

Qun appears in the *Analects* as a distinctly human association. Confucius laments that he could not withdraw from human affairs, because he must associate (*qun*) with fellow human beings rather than with birds and beasts (*Analects* 18.6). He further contrasts *qun* with *dang* (黨): "The exemplary person is self-possessed but not contentious; he gathers together with others (*qun*) without forming cliques (*dang*)," thereby giving *qun* an ethical connotation (*Analects* 15.22). This is strengthened in the *Xunzi*, wherein *qun* is an activity that elevates human beings above all other existents; a good ruler is one who is good at this activity.[96] The use of *qun* in these early Confucian texts focuses on how people associate with one another rather than on drawing group boundaries.

Even the "family (*jia* 家)," the most important group in Chinese society, has no definite boundaries. This involves more than empirical difficulties determining the boundaries. The definition itself is vague about boundaries, because what is distinctive about each group is not really where its boundaries are drawn but how the individuals are related. According to Chie Nakane, "The Japanese family system differs from that of the Chinese system, where family ethics are always based on relationships between particular individuals, such as father and son, brothers and sisters, parents and children, husband and wife, while in Japan they are always based on the collective group, i.e., members of a household, not on the relationships between individuals."[97] The Chinese *jia* sometimes refers to a nuclear family, an extended family living in the same household, but it also can include all members of a lineage or a clan, even servants and other dependents who are not related by blood or marriage.

The common expression, "people of our family" (*zijiaren* 自家人), can refer to any person one wishes to include—"family" can be expanded or contracted, depending upon the circumstances. At one extreme, its classical usage refers to a single person of high rank, a noble, a high official, or the "son of heaven";

at the other extreme, it can be extended to an unlimited number of people, so that "all under heaven belongs to one family" (*tianxia yijia* 天下一家).[98] It is tempting to argue that the use of *jia* to apply to people who are not immediate relatives is simply a figure of speech. As such, it does not really pose any conceptual problems. But this already assumes that the concept should, in its primary meaning, apply only to the biological nuclear family, which is precisely what is questionable in the Chinese context.

Jia in the early texts often appears with *guo* 國, usually translated as "state." In modern mandarin, both *guo* and *guojia* designate a sovereign nation-state. This notion may seem to promise clearer boundaries, as it is distinctly territorial in connotation. One of its meanings is "that which is ruled/administered by the son of heaven, or by a feudal lord." This already introduces indistinctness, as the feudal lords were (at least initially) under the rule of the "son of heaven." The vagueness increases when we compare it to the *Rites of Zhou*, which uses *jia* to refer to territories under high officials and nobles who are below the feudal lords in rank.[99] *Guo* at times does not refer to the entire territory under a ruler but the "capital city" wherein he resides (*Mencius* 10.7/54/28). Fung Yu-Lan claims that, in the past, what is meant by *guo* is in fact *jia*.[100] Without going that far, we need only note that, despite a tentative distinction in terms of relative size (or military might)—*Analects* 5.8 mentions "a family of a hundred chariots" and "a state of a thousand chariots"—the distinction between *jia* and *guo* is unclear in the early texts.[101]

The binomial used to translate "society" in modern usage, *shehui* 社會, was used previously to refer to a gathering around the communal altar to the Divinity of the Soil on festival days. The altar to the Soil (*she* 社) symbolizes social unity and interdependence. The imagery in the term points to an understanding of society as a network around a symbolic center rather than an entity defined by boundaries. Liang Shuming 梁漱溟 observes that Chinese society is based on relationships rather than on individuals or the group.[102] The relationships so important in Confucianism are among particular individuals, not between individuals and a social whole. Central to Confucian social thought is not a conception of the social whole but a set of five fundamental relational norms (*wu-lun* 五倫): affection (*qin* 親) between father and son, appropriateness (*yi* 義) between ruler and subject, differentiation (*bie* 別) between husband and wife, order of precedence (*xu* 序) between the elder and the younger, and trust (*xin* 信) between friends. So conspicuous is the absence of the social whole as a key ethical or social concept that in 1981 there was an outcry in Taiwanese society to establish a sixth relational norm between individual and group (*qun-ji lun* 群己倫) in response to the increasing "individualism" or, rather, one should say, the rampant selfishness in modern capitalism.

With all of the difficulties in applying the concept of a social whole to Confucian thought, it is reasonable not to think of ideal Confucian society as a super-individual subject with its own interests and aims that could subordinate individuals' ends. It might be argued that even without positing any super-individual subject, the individual could still be subordinated if there is a "final end" that need not belong to any specific social whole, or a totalizing ordering principle independent of any social whole. A prime candidate for such a teleological ordering principle would be "the way (*dao* 道)." As David Nivison describes it, "the *dao* allows and enables everything to be what it is; it claims no credit, does no pushing, and all is ordered." Among scholars of Confucianism, Fingarette defines *dao* as "a single definite order," and the only alternative to it is chaos. In Song-Ming neo-Confucianism, *li* 理, often translated as "principle," "reason," has been interpreted as a single, nonempirical, ordering unity that penetrates all things.[103] These accounts are influenced by a dominant Western conception of order that underlies the claim of any totalizing teleology. Some kind of organic whole, a closed and self-sufficient system, is always implicit in totalizing teleology.

Joseph Needham and Frederick Mote reject the claim that Chinese thought manifests any kind of totalizing teleology. As Mote puts it, instead of a cosmos, the Chinese have an "organismic process" without beginning or end, without boundaries. Mote probably exaggerates that the Chinese "are apparently unique in having no creation myth." Derk Bodde considered the Pan Ku legend, which he traced to no earlier than third century A.D., the only myth that could qualify as a creation story. Anne Birrell's study of ancient Chinese myths traces the earliest extant recorded version of cosmogonic myth in China to the fourth century B.C., but she notes that "compared with other cosmogonic myths in the ancient world, Chinese accounts appear relatively late," even though the earliest written records in China date from circa 1300 B.C.[104] Birrell also shows that Chinese creation myths tell of the cosmos being created from some primal element, but not of *creatio ex nihilo* involving a creator, divine will, or benevolent intelligence, supporting Mote's claim that the traditional Chinese worldview is wholly different from Western "conceptions of creation *ex-nihilo* by the hand of God, or through the will of God, and all other such mechanistic, *teleological*, and theistic cosmologies."[105]

According to Needham, in Western philosophies, "the animal organism may be projected onto the universe, but belief in a personal god or gods meant that it always had to have a 'guiding principle.' This was a path the Chinese definitely did *not* take. To them . . . cooperation of the component parts was spontaneous, even involuntary, and this alone was sufficient." Hall and Ames argue that ancient Chinese thinking is *acosmotic*, in that most of their speculations do not depend on the notion that the totality of things constitutes a single-ordered world with a radical beginning.[106] In Chinese cosmology, instead of a cosmos created *ex nihilo* and guided toward a final end by a unitary principle, a process without beginning or end organizes itself. The cosmic process is self-sustaining and ever changing without conforming to any given or fixed pattern; it is not directed by any final end, but it is so of itself (*ziran* 自然).

To make a case for Confucian democracy, it suffices to note that whatever mythic elements there might be in pre-Qin Confucian texts, they do not pertain to cosmogony. Moreover, according to the prominent Chinese scholar of ancient Chinese mythology, Yuan Ke, one of the obstacles preventing the full development of Chinese myths was "the negative attitude of scholars of the early Chinese empire and throughout the centuries, especially scholars of the Confucian persuasion."[107] It seems quite safe to assume that rather than final ends and social or cosmic wholes, it is the interaction between individuals that is at the center of the Confucian conception of society. Drawing inspiration from Dewey's philosophy, one could reconstruct Confucianism to avoid the kind of holism and teleology that subordinates the individual to the social. Both will then be able to balance individuality and sociality without sacrificing either in their conceptions of individuals as social and of society as comprising networks of internal relations among individuals.

Chapter 3

Harmonious Communities

John Dewey's philosophy, which does not radically separate an individual from others nor reduce one to a pawn under others' control, offers an alternative view of individuals that is compatible with early Confucianism. Such a view does not imply a conception of society as some mystical, super-individual subject. In rejecting conceptions of individuals as atomistic selves, one does not have to deny the value of individuality. Such rejection usually emphasizes the value of community. A community is not simply any kind of society or smaller social group. The discussion of sociality in chapter 2 is only preliminary in articulating a viable alternative Confucian democracy that values community.

We need a clearer conception of community and some idea of how to bring it about and sustain it. In constructing such a conception with resources from Dewey's philosophy and early Confucianism, this chapter will argue that a Confucian community need not stifle individual creativity in favor of social conformity, that its unity is not based on exclusion entrenching an unhealthy "us-them" mentality, and that the differentiation within a Confucian community that many consider hierarchical could be justifiable and democratic.

SOCIETY AND COMMUNITY

Society did not emerge as the key concept for understanding the relations between individuals and groups until rather late. John Locke first contrasted it with the state. Ferdinand Tönnies contrasted it with community in *Gemein-*

63

schaft und Gesellschaft (*Community and Society*).[1] The distinction captures an important element that many consider essential to community but not present in society: a sense of belonging. Gerald Gaus points out: "Social life is not the same as community; whereas the former is premised on interaction and asso-ciation, community involves a sense of belongingness and devotion to the group."[2] Mere recognition of belonging is insufficient; there also must be a feeling of belonging to a community. If the feeling of belonging required is premised on "commonality and similarity," understood in a strong sense as "sameness," then we would conclude with Gaus that a sense of community is in tension with individuality, which implies diversity and differences.

Jack Crittenden pushes the implications of this required commonality and similarity farther. He calls the *Gemeinschaft* idea "the total community," which he attributes to communitarians—MacIntyre, Taylor, Walzer, and Sandel—and which, in his view, leaves no room for individual autonomy.[3] Crittenden's paradigmatic community involves sharing a total way of life and not just sharing specific and limited interests or associating as a means to one's own end. It consists of face-to-face relationships that foster concern for the well-being of all members and ensure the centrality of the community to one's iden-tity. If this conception of community precludes self-reflection completely, as Crittenden argues, then it would also be incompatible with the growth of indi-viduality by which Dewey judges all human forms of life. Crittenden pushes the criteria he lists to unnecessary extreme in his critique of communitarians—"*centrality* of community to one's identity" becomes community *determining* one's identity. But the centrality of community to individual identity need not prevent the questioning of customs, traditions, and so on, nor does it neces-sarily determine an individual's behavior.

The belief that community requires "fundamental similarity," a common-ality understood as homogeneity in beliefs, outlooks, and attitudes governing behavior, underlies two related criticisms against community. Internally, it stifles individuality, since there is no room for diversity or individual creativ-ity. There is only one right way of thinking, of doing things; any deviation is considered a betrayal, an attack on the community. Whoever is not for us is against us. Externally it is, at best, indifferent and, at worst, hostile to out-siders. The sense of belonging, central to the life of a community, depends on an "insider-outsider, us-them" mentality. Such communities are sustained by what Richard Sennett calls the "ethos of the ghetto."[4] It emphasizes a way of life to the exclusion of all others and builds an invisible wall against the world. Outsiders are treated as aliens and are reduced to subhuman or even non-human. Unknowns are avoided. Intolerance of differences is the very essence of community, or so its critics argue.

I shall argue that we find a very different conception of community as an ideal in Dewey's philosophy, which is compatible with Confucianism. A

Deweyan and Confucian ideal community is neither intolerant of differences within nor hostile to strangers without. It deemphasizes group boundaries without sacrificing intragroup bonds; it accommodates diversity without surrendering integrity.

NONEXCLUSIONARY COMMUNITY

Both Deweyan and Confucian views of society focus on the characteristics of interactive processes in which individuals participate, rather than on the maintenance of the boundaries of social entities. "Society *is* individuals-in-their-relations. . . . Individuals develop not in a remote entity called 'society' at large but in connection *with one another*" (L8.80). Though Dewey considers the question of how society is possible the most artificial of questions, he provides an account of how human beings form society as "association, coming together in joint intercourse and action for the better realization of any form of experience which is augmented and confirmed by being shared" (M12.197).

Social processes are basically communicative processes involving signs. Human beings act with reference not only to the immediate present but also to a situation that includes what is absent, the remote in both time and space (L1.213). This is made possible by the use of signs to represent entities absent in the immediate environment. Signs arise in joint action in which their use enables human beings to influence one another's behavior to bring about a desired result. Animals engage in behavior that influences other animals' behavior, for example, the peacock unfolding its tail or an animal making a sound that warns its herd of an approaching predator. But such "signaling" behavior, at least in the lower animals, functions as a direct stimulus. The response is determined by some biological mechanism, and it is not a response to a sign. The behavior is purely instinctive, in which "existing organic structures practically enforce correct participation" (L1.261).

Response to a sign is, in contrast, response to its meaning, involving a selective focus of many conditions and wide-ranging consequences. Processes of interpretation in which some indeterminacy always remains replace causal mechanisms. Dewey illustrates this by comparing a hen's alarmed response to a farmer throwing grain to it and an infant's learned response to preparatory events leading to the satisfaction of his hunger (L1.140). The causal determination connecting stimulus and response cannot be overridden; the connection between a sign and its response can be overridden by other connections within a situation. The attribution of meaning, connecting sign and response, requires an undetermined, flexible reconstruction of the situation by the agent. Repeated encounters and a history of shared experience may establish a general working consensus of meaning of a network of signs, but the risk of misunderstanding always remains in any particular situation. Signaling for humans is a joint act in which a successful outcome depends on each person putting herself in the position of the other as sharing the situation.

Human association in itself is not unique or significant. "Interactions, transactions, occur *de facto* and the results of interdependence follow" (L2.330). Interdependence is not limited to the human world. We find various other forms of life existing in association, and Dewey believes that "everything that exists in as far as it is known and knowable is in interaction with other things" (L1.138). The consequences that flow from the distinctive patterns of human association are significant. When these consequences, being known, are esteemed and sought after, societies develop. The pursuit of consequences of association requires a conscious, deliberate sharing of ends-in-view, following a common plan of action, and the coordination of the actions of participants; all involve interpretive processes going beyond instinctive, stimulus-response behavior.[5]

Human association distinguishes itself from other forms of association when it becomes communicative, when it establishes "cooperation in an activity in which there are partners, and in which the activity of each is modified and regulated by partnership" (L1.141). Communication is the prerequisite of sociality; it makes the difference between brute and man (L1.134). To learn to be human is "to develop through the give and take of communication an effective sense of being an individually distinctive member of a community" (L2.332). Without communication, there can be no community. "Natural associations are the conditions for the existence of a community, but a community adds the function of communication in which emotions and ideas are shared as well as joint undertakings engaged" (L13.176). It is the quality of communication, rather than exclusionary boundaries, that will create and sustain communal bonds.

Dewey is not always clear about what distinguishes society from community. At times he seems to equate society with community, in contrast to mere association (L2.330), but then he also distinguishes "society, in the sense of an association," from a community (L13.176). One way out of the confusion lies in remembering Dewey's distinction between de facto and de jure meanings of ambiguous words such as "society" and "community," even though he does not always make it clear in his writings which meaning is involved. Separating the two meanings is more difficult than one may think, as experience does not come in neat packages. Take, for example, the proposition that social processes are basically communicative: are the social processes in question de facto or de jure, or both? If communication is involved in both, it too has two kinds of connotation—how are they differentiated?

If a woman orders me to clean her boots and I understand her but do nothing about it, is there communication? There is transmission of meaning, which is shared, so that I understand her words, and there is enough shared cultural background so that I know what boots are and what cleaning them involves—this qualifies it as communication in the everyday usage of the word. But Dewey understands communication as a process of sharing experience to the extent that it modifies the position of the parties who cooperate in a joint activity to attain a common goal. By this standard, the above boot-cleaning example is not yet communication. The sharing achieved in any human inter-action is a matter of degree; Dewey's conception sets up a de jure standard that de facto cases approach to different extents.

Is the account of society as communicative processes a de jure account? Not entirely. As Dewey explains: "any existing society is marked by both pos-itive and negative value" (L8.83). Dewey's account is about de facto societies; it recognizes as social processes interactions with different degrees of sharing, however, it also is a de jure account in that it enables, apart from identifica-tion of a group as a society, a critique of it in terms of how much (or little) sharing is achieved by everyday interactions. This is why Dewey declares de jure meanings "almost always uppermost" in social philosophy (M9.88).

Society and community converge in their de jure meanings: a way of living together that fosters personal-social growth. De facto societies and communi-ties each approach it in different ways. As a matter of general usage, "com-munity" and "society" are sometimes used interchangeably, but "community" also is used with a narrower application to refer to a specific kind of associa-tion, in contrast to "society," which is used to refer to all forms of human asso-ciation. When used in contrast, "community" has more shared experience than "society," and insofar as shared experience is necessary to personal-communal growth, "community" comes closer to de jure association. In lamenting that "the machine age in developing the Great Society has invaded and partially disintegrated the small communities of former times without generating a Great Community," Dewey emphasizes the difference between a de facto society and a de jure community, and the need to bridge that gap (L2.314).

The move from the Great Society to the Great Community is a move toward de jure association, an increase in the positive value in human relations, and an improvement in the quality of communication. It is easy to think of the Great Community as a more perfect replica of past communities under-stood as *Gemeinschaften*, especially when Dewey speaks of "the traditions, out-looks, and interests which characterize a community" (L2.331). Speaking of the need to achieve the Great Community in the same breath as the destruc-tion of "small communities of former times" makes critics suspect Dewey of a kind of nostalgic conservatism. Despite his sometimes misleading language, Dewey's conception of ideal community is not simply the perfect *Gemeinschaft*, characterized by complete stability and cohesion imparted by a common

Sittlichkeit with a given common good within rigid group boundaries. Dewey's ideal community is nonexclusionary.

A successful gang of thieves communicates effectively in terms of achieving its common end and sharing its ill-gotten gains among its members. The same gang, with no better organization and communication, would more closely approach an ideal community if it were a charity. There would be no difference between the two if boundaries separating the common values, interests, and goals of a group from others were definitive of community. Dewey's philosophy distinguishes them partly by the consequences that each group has on others: "How full and free is the interplay with other forms of association?" (M9.89). A group is not a community in the ideal sense unless it contributes to the growth of other groups, of individuals outside it but affected by its actions. A community is a group that interacts flexibly and fully in connection with other groups to form a greater community (L2.328). When it fails to do so, it limits the possibilities for growth of its own members and therefore of itself. A community's boundaries should remain porous. Its value as a community (or perhaps subcommunity may be a better description) depends partly on relations that cross those boundaries.

A Deweyan community does not have rigid boundaries, because it is held together not by homogeneity but by the process of communication. "There is more than a verbal tie between the words common, community, and communication. Men live in a community in virtue of the things which they have in common; and communication is the way in which they come to possess things in common" (M9.7). Communication requires interaction and continuity, not identity or homogeneity. If "putting oneself in the place of another," the basis of communication, is only possible between people who are identical in some way, then we end up with Gaus's view that the "sense of community, i.e., fraternal bonds based upon sympathy, seems to require that those so bonded perceive themselves as fundamentally similar."[6]

If we can only feel sympathy for those whom we perceive as *fundamentally similar* to us, then we are on the road to an "us-them" bigotry that has no place in a Deweyan community. Both similarity (in the sense of resemblance rather than identity) and difference are required in communication; neither is more fundamental than the other. Any attempt to bridge the gap between unique individuals that starts from an assumption of "fundamental similarity" runs the risk of what Richard Rorty calls the "worst form of cruelty," humiliating another through redescription. By defining another on one's own terms, one denies her "otherness," her self-definition on *her* terms. Such cruelty is characteristic of a narcissistic culture that turns social relations into a "mirroring of the self," which undermines the possibility of community.[7]

Is communication possible between completely different parties? If we assign completely different meanings to words, then we will not be able to make ourselves understood with those words. Nevertheless, what is required is not identity but "family resemblance," creating an overlapping continuity of meaning. Even in language, let alone nonverbal communication, there is always a certain degree of flexibility in meaning, so that the "overlap" required for understanding varies, and in some cases it can be quite slim. One might still argue that even if one does not start with identity, the point of the exercise is to end up with it. Only when it is achieved can there be community—the end of communication is the increase of meaning "overlap," to the point where there is complete fusion of all horizons into one single horizon shared by all. This kind of homogeneity is not acceptable to Dewey. "The concept of uniformity and unanimity in culture is rather repellent. . . . Variety *is* the spice of life, and the richness and the attractiveness of social institutions depend upon cultural diversity among separate units" (M10.288). Dewey's community is not about creating a single, overarching horizon, which amounts to everyone developing "God's view." It is about creating and deepening an infinite number of overlaps among countless changing horizons. Such nonexclusionary community is not intolerant of differences; it needs differences to flourish.

We can make the same point about differences with the Confucian focus-field conception of self. The field is the dimension of sociality, of overlapping meanings; the foci are distinct centers of unique individuality. The field is infinite, unbounded. The boundaries of what is focused in any one instance are contingent and specific. The only limit to the possibility of extending the focused area is what is practical at any moment. The field itself is constantly growing with more and more foci emerging (individuals being born into or joining the society), each with its unique horizons. The fixation with a "fundamental similarity" in community is erroneously premised upon a one-dimensional understanding of the relationship between individuality and sociality. Regardless of how wide or deep an overlap in meaning within a field is (even in the fantastic case of the field being one single overlap), each focus sharing it with other foci remains distinct and unique. The meaning *as focused* by each of these foci is unique, because each focus retains a unique perspective.

On a less abstract level, imagine a pair of colleagues assigned to a job that must be completed before they can leave for the day. To complete the task on schedule, they must have a common goal and a common understanding of how to reach it. But each, considered on her own, would be performing a task different from the other's, since the job is a cooperative task that requires a different contribution from each (otherwise, we would say that they have been given similar jobs rather than one job). Within the context of the distinctive task that each has to perform, the "common understanding" of the cooperative task is different for each of them. Furthermore, the shared goal could have different meanings from each person's perspective—it may be simply a matter of leaving in time for a date for one of them, or a possible contribution to job promotion prospects to another. Meanings in every area of overlap between horizons are connected to different things in different ways in each participant's unique horizon of meanings.

As long as one cannot *actually* become another person, the centers of horizons will never merge completely. All each can achieve is approximations to another's view, never exactly the *same* view. The recognition that our attempts to "put ourselves in the place of another" can only ever meet with partial success—success relative to specific purposes—contributes to the probability of such attempts achieving satisfactory consequences without harmful side effects, for it introduces a certain tentativeness, an acknowledgment of fallibility, which keeps us alert to any further developments in a situation that may require a revision of earlier conclusions. This acknowledged fallibility that respects another's unique individuality is critical in preventing the pursuit of community from becoming exclusionary and oppressive.

If "putting oneself in another's place" is characteristic of the communicative process, then communication is central to Confucianism. The one thread that runs through Confucius' teaching is *shu* 恕, "Do not do to others what you yourself do not want" (*Analects* 15.24). This involves bridging different horizons by putting one's own perspective in question and attempting to adopt another's with the awareness that success would be partial at best. What is important is to avoid privileging any one perspective, to strive to appreciate each in its own terms in relation to the situation. *Shu*, translated as reciprocity or deference, may be viewed as a cooperative process as well as a matter of how we should treat others. As the method of authoritative conduct (*ren*), it is "correlating one's conduct with those close at hand" (*Analects* 6.30). This may be understood as communication, as "the establishment of cooperation in an activity in which there are partners, and in which the activity of each is modified and regulated by partnership" (L1.141).

We have seen how, in Dewey's account of communication, a person reconstructs situations flexibly by attributing meaning, connecting sign and response. Communication guides one's actions. For Confucius, as it is for Dewey, the quality of communication is critical to community. In his teachings, Confucius often mentions the *Songs* (*shi* 詩) and the *Rites* (*li* 禮), treasuries of shared meanings of the Chinese civilization.[8] He recommends studying the *Songs* so that one may communicate well. "If you do not study the *Songs*, you have no means of speaking properly" (*Analects* 16.13). Good communication is the basis of social efficacy. "Close at hand [mastery of the *Songs*] enables one to serve one's father, and away at court it enables one to serve one's lord" (*Analects* 17.9). Rites, or ritual practice, which we shall discuss in greater detail when we consider how to bring about and sustain community, may be viewed as involving signs, verbal and nonverbal, whose shared meanings facilitate the coordination of participants' actions and achieve harmony and stability in social interaction.

In the *Analects*, Confucius says that the first thing he would do, if given the reins of government, would be "the proper establishment of names (*zheng-ming* 正名)," because otherwise "speech [i.e., communication] will not flow properly . . . affairs will not culminate in success . . . rites and music will not flourish . . . punishments will not fit the crime . . . the common people will not know where to put hands and feet" (*Analects* 13.3). *Ming* attributes meaning, as in positive significance, approbation. It is in this sense that "the exemplary person despises the thought of leaving this world without having made a name for himself."[9] We could employ Deweyan vocabulary to unpack this: we act in response to the meanings that we attribute to each particular situation that we are in. When the meanings attributed ("naming") are inappropriate vis-à-vis the situation as socially constituted, our response will not be ethically efficacious. *Zhengming* is the establishment of proper meanings of important constituents of social situations, so that everyone, sharing them, would act appropriately and efficaciously. Meanings must be communicable; what is communicated must indicate the appropriate means for participants in a situation to attain some common end-in-view jointly (*Analects* 13.3). Unless we communicate properly, attribute appropriate meanings, and connect appropriate responses to signs, community will fail.

This implicit focus on communication is not surprising, since Confucianism is a relation-based rather than a group-based or an individual-based philosophy. In emphasizing relations, it emphasizes not the boundaries of social entities but the processes of human association which, as Dewey points out, are basically communicative. Boundaries of social groups in Confucianism are conceptually vague and temporary, even when they exist. Where the boundaries are drawn between two social groups is not really a matter of great import, since Confucianism is more concerned with the nature of specific relationships and how they interconnect with one another in a continuous social network than with determining the exact location of boundaries. The margins of a social network fade into obscurity, with less and less attention paid to them; little effort is spent attempting to determine exactly where the network stops. A network grows more in terms of hitherto unimportant and unnoticed connections becoming important and prominent, usually through cooperative efforts, rather than connections coming into existence *ex nihilo*, since initial contacts among people often occur unremarked.

In practice, social groups flourish only when their boundaries are porous and constantly shifting. However, there is always the risk of boundaries rigidifying, and as a result, a social group may develop an "ethos of the ghetto." In Chinese society, this criticism is most often leveled against families. Concern for the family has been seen as exclusionary in what has been called "Chinese familism," which prompted Bertrand Russell to wonder what concern is left over for society and strangers in the face of such an inordinate investment in immediate human relations. Chinese scholars such as Liang Shuming and Lin Yutang also consider limiting one's concern to one's family as undermining China's unity and strength as a nation.[10]

An exclusionary community, whether a family or some other social group, distorts rather than actualizes the Confucian ideal of community. Social groups, insofar as they are distinguished from one another, are related in a continuous, interactive process. Mencius says, "There is a common expression, 'The empire, the state, the family (*tianxia guojia* 天下國家).' The empire has its basis in the state, the state in the family, and the family in one's own self" (*Mencius* 7.5/36/23). We first learn to relate to others in our most immediate relations (i.e., within the family). But "you extend to other aged persons the manner you treat the aged in your family, as befitting their age; you extend to other young people the manner in which you treat the young in your family, as befitting their youth."[11] Instead of excluding others from one's horizon of concern, the family enables one to extend that horizon. "Family fidelity (*xiaoti* 孝悌) is the root of authoritative conduct."[12] One's ethical achievement is measured by how far one's concern for others, one's authoritative conduct, extends. The whole world turns to one who is an authoritative person; the sage is greater than an authoritative person, because he has "extended beneficence broadly to the masses and is able to assist the multitude."[13]

While there are no pregiven limits to the extension of one's ethical consideration, of one's authoritative conduct, and therefore of one's relational network, Confucianism does not advocate equal love for everyone. That is the doctrine for which Mencius vehemently attacked the Mohists: by loving everyone equally, one fails to acknowledge the ethical significance of family relationships (*wufu* 無父: "doing away with fathers") and thereby sinks to the level of beasts (*Mencius* 6.9/35/1). However, no rigid boundaries exist between "insiders" and "outsiders" in an authoritative person's practice of "graduated love." Her network of relations is like a ripple—no matter how far it extends, the energy is always greatest at the center, decreasing proportionally to the distance from the center. How far a ripple could extend depends on the amount of energy at the center.[14] According to this model of ethical relations, investment in central relations, instead of precluding concern for more remote relations, enables us to include them in our ethical consideration and influence. Confucianism, properly understood, would condemn a lack of concern for those outside of our central relations as inhibited ethical development.

No membership in a social group, no matter how central to our identities, can claim absolute precedence over all other relations. We can see this by considering the status of family relations in Confucianism.[15] Confucius' disagreement with the governor of She about what "uprightness" requires of a son whose father "takes a sheep on the sly"—whether or not to report the latter to the authorities—often has been cited as an indication of the priority of family relations in Confucianism.[16] But we find a student rejoicing that Confucius, in his teaching, did not show any partiality toward his own son (*Analects* 16.13). When his favorite student, Yan Hui, died, Confucius' grief exceeded his grief at his own son's death (*Analects* 11.10). Commenting on sages Yu and Ji "passing their doors three times without entering" while serving the community, Mencius attributed their actions to the closeness of their relations with the people.[17] Yu and Ji did not allow their concern for their families to distract them while serving the people; family relations did not take precedence in this case.

Confucian persons are not simply locked from birth into hierarchical and closed family networks; the *construction* of relations through interactive practices has always played an important role in Confucian societies.[18] The ethical significance in human relations is not pregiven or absolute. It is invested, and it also can be eroded, by actions of the interacting parties. Which relations are central can change over one's lifetime. A relation on the margins of one's social network may move into the center, and vice versa. In a more complex, modern society, when life no longer revolves around a family or any single social group, flexibility in weighing the relative importance of relations becomes even more important. It is the ethical significance of relations rather than group membership that decides the priority, that guides our action when the situational demands of different relations conflict. The answers to such dilemmas are neither simple nor absolute.

When demands of relations conflict, one tries to find a way to preserve both relations by reexamining the situation from new perspectives. When that is impossible, as so often happens, priority should depend on which alternative course of action would preserve more of one's entire relational network and also provide opportunities for future growth of the network. There are times when "breaking away" from a family relation is necessary for one's relational network to grow. In becoming involved in other relations, one does not simply replace the damaged family relation with others that one attempts to make more central. The new resources that one gains in the resulting personal growth also could enable one to repair the damaged family relation in a way that would be impossible without that earlier break. In today's society, a family cannot flourish in isolation. Even the best parents will have difficulties bringing up their children properly if the wider social environment works against their efforts. Concern for one's family therefore entails concern for a wider community. Even when family relations are all that they should be, there could still be situations wherein it would make sense to give priority to less central relations. As Confucius says: "Those who give no thought to what is distant will find worries much closer at hand."[19]

A cohesive social group is a center in a larger social network. Its cohesiveness depends on the strength of relations among its members, which are stronger than relations between its members and those outside of the group. Given the elasticity of the Chinese view of "family (*jia* 家)," social groups in Chinese society are not necessarily defined by a clear, unitary criterion (or set of criteria). This means that becoming identical with the existing group members is not the only way that "outsiders" could become "insiders." All an "outsider" needs to do is establish a strong relation (or strengthen an existing relation) with an "insider" that is meaningful to other members of the group—the new relation could be completely different from other relations within the group. The shifting of boundaries that results from such new relations could modify without destroying a group's identity. The stronger the relations within a group, the greater its capacity for such growth. Strength depends not on homogeneity of thought or behavior but on effectiveness of communication.

The ideal Confucian community is described in the "Great Learning" chapter of the *Book of Rites* as "peace under heaven (*pingtianxia* 平天下)" (*Book of Rites* 43.1/164/28). This is possible only if states are well governed, and states are well governed only if families are ordered. As a relational center in a social network, a family or any other cohesive group could be both a focus of energy from which vectors radiate into the environment, and the place where vectors act concentrically. Each group may constitute a center, but not the only center. Other groups are centers, foci of energy in their own right. Each center acknowledges the existence of other centers by acting upon them and being acted upon by them. Smaller social groups are nested within larger social groups. For the larger group to flourish, it is not enough that each constitutive smaller group is doing well by itself. Their being part of a larger group implies an organic relation, so that their interaction will affect the well-being of the larger group. A small group flourishes only if it interacts well with, and thereby contributes to the well-being of, other groups with which it forms a larger group. A group approaches the ideal of community only if it interacts flexibly and fully with other groups to constitute a larger community; a community is not yet ideal as long as some members of the human species are excluded. This understanding of the Confucian ideal of community is nonexclusionary. Intergroup interaction is as important in this ideal community as in Dewey's community.

My argument that the ideal community in Dewey's philosophy and early Confucianism is nonexclusionary has focused on denying that a community is necessarily indifferent or hostile to strangers. The basis of the argument, that ideal community requires not a fundamental similarity but interactive differences, also implies that such a community would not stifle members' individuality. We will have a clearer picture of how the diversity of individuality contributes to the flourishing of a community rather than threatens its unity in the following exploration of how to bring about and sustain an ideal community.

THE ART OF COMMUNITY: ACHIEVING HARMONY

For Dewey, "all communication is like art" (M9.9). The communicative process of constructing and sustaining a community is an art. The connection of Dewey's aesthetics and his social philosophy has been rather neglected. Even though judicious scholars always point out Dewey's assertion of the inseparability of art and science, studies of Dewey's views on community generally have focused on the role of the scientific method and social inquiry.[20] When properly conducted, science is an art (L1.284). One is liable to misunderstand Dewey's enthusiasm for science in the task of community building unless one places it within the wider context of his view of experience as art. Without becoming art—a process of making the world a better place to live in—science remains a passive tool with as much potential for evil as it has for good (L1.272).

Communication that achieves community is "uniquely instrumental and uniquely final." It is instrumental "as liberating us from the otherwise overwhelming pressure of events and enabling us to live in a world of things that have meaning" (L1.159). It is final as a sharing of experience precious to a community, "a sharing whereby the meanings are enhanced, deepened, and solidified in the sense of communion" (L1.159). Communication is art and science. Art celebrates consummation in experience; science prepares the way for it (L1.269). Consummation is life from the perspective of immediate enjoyment; preparation is life from the perspective of problem solving. As preparation, community exists to the extent that the problems a group faces together are solved by the method of cooperative inquiry. As consummation, community is achieved when there is a quality of harmony in human relationships.[21] There is social harmony when individuals participate with others in an ordered relation that "bears within itself the germs of a consummation akin to the aesthetic" (L10.20).

In Confucianism, one embarks on the way of the exemplary person by achieving harmony (*he* 和) in family relationships.[22] From the family, social harmony is extended until it embraces all human relationships in the ideal of "bringing peace to all under heaven."[23] I shall try to show that, though harmony in Western thought and *he* in Chinese thought may mean different things, there is enough resonance in the way Dewey understands harmony and some Confucian understandings of *he* in the context of community for us to bring the two together.

For Dewey, harmony is not uniformity, or homogeneity, or instantiation of universals in particulars; it is a "unity in variety," wrought by actual interactions and exchanges of energies, including both material and symbolic exchanges (L10.166). Complexity and minuteness of differentiation widen and enrich aesthetic patterns and "fulfillment is more massive and more subtly shaded" (L10.29). "In so far as people are all alike, there is no give and take among them. And it is better to give and take" (M10.288). Socially, harmony is not uniformity or unanimity. In the early Confucian tradition, there also is a preference for diversity rather than uniformity. As Confucius says: "The exemplary person seeks harmony (*he* 和), not sameness (*tong* 同); the petty person does the opposite" (*Analects* 13.23). The *zhongyong* 中庸 describes the exemplary person as one who "seeks harmony but does not follow the undiscriminating crowd (*he er bu liu* 和而不流)."[24] *Zuo's Commentary on the Spring and Autumn Annals* 左傳 also records an important discourse in which *he*, as harmony in the sense of a minister's views *complementing* the views of his ruler, is distinguished from *tong*, the minister and ruler having identical views. It is harmony, not unanimity, that leads to good government.[25]

However, *tong* is not always used in contrast to *he* in Chinese texts. In the Confucian tradition, there is a social ideal of "the great unity (*datong* 大同)," which makes its first appearance in the "Evolution of Rites (*liyun* 禮運)" chapter of the *Book of Rites*, and which occupies an important place in the thinking of later Confucians. While some might argue that there is a change in the Confucian social ideal from harmony to consensus, others argue that *datong* refers not to "identity" or consensus precluding dissent but to "harmony."[26] I find the later view persuasive, insofar as the ideal is Confucian. The "state of lesser prosperity (*xiaokang* 小康)"—which is contrasted with *datong* in the *Book of Rites*—is contrasted with harmony (*he*) in an assessment of government attributed to Confucius in *Zuo's Commentary*.[27]

In general, early Chinese thought shares Dewey's view that harmony requires a rich variety of constituents. "There is no music with one note, no culture with one object, no satisfactory results with one flavor" (*Conversations of the States* 11679–82). As a passage from *Lü's Spring and Autumn Annals* 呂氏春秋 says of gustatory harmony, "the business of mixing and blending must use the sour, the sweet, the bitter, the spicy, and the salty. Bringing the ingredients together is a very subtle art; each has its own expression."[28] The unique particulars in harmony must continue to be different, even as they mutually transform one another. "There is no sacrifice of the self-identity of the parts. . . . As one part leads into another and as one part carries on what went on before, each gains distinctness in itself"(L10.43). No constituent should stand out at the expense of any other.

Harmony is dynamic instead of static; it is ordered change. Energies are channeled so that there is a cumulative carrying forward, with each successive stage emerging from and temporarily completing the preceding stages. In a harmonious process, each participating element anticipates the one that follows, and the latter is born in response to the former. "The interaction of energies . . . institutes opposition in company with accumulation, conserva- tion, suspense, and interval, and cooperative movement toward fulfillment in an ordered, or rhythmical, experience" (L10.165). Opposition of energies is critical in achieving "dynamic continuity," which "resolves an otherwise uniform mass and expanse into individual forms"—forms in harmony rather than disordered heterogeneity (L10.161). In its rhythmic character, harmony requires not only diversity and contrast but also tension and resistance.[29]

The notion of social harmony consistent with the thinking of Dewey would not reject all conflicts, but it is not indiscriminate with regard to them. Replying to Stephen Pepper's accusation that he denies the importance of con- flict that a pragmatist aesthetics must recognize, Dewey replies that, on the contrary, he emphasizes its indispensable function in his discussion of "resis- tance," but he distinguishes "between the cases of conflict that lead to dis- persion and disruption, and those cases in which conflict and tension are converted into means of intensifying a consummatory appreciation of mater- ial of an individual qualitative experience."[30] While some conflicts may be constructive, there are too many examples of destructive conflicts in the world for us to be sanguine about the desirability of social conflicts. In most cases, social conflicts represent the problems that a society has to solve.

In harmony, diverse constituents are ordered in a focus achieved through previously developed organized responses, so that a situation stands out from the inchoate flow of experience as *an experience*. "An experience has a unity that gives it its name, *that* meal, that storm, that rupture of friendship. The existence of this unity is constituted by a single *quality* that pervades the entire experience in spite of the variation of its constituent parts" (L10.44). Critics who question the consistency of Dewey's aesthetics with his pragmatism, and accuse him of reverting to Hegelianism, of being guilty of an organic ideal- ism, overlook what I have attempted to show in distinguishing Dewey's con- ception of society from Hegelian organic conceptions: that his use of words such as "whole," "integration," "coherence," and so on is relative; these words must be interpreted against the background of his view that experience is process, and that all boundaries are contextual rather than final.[31] Aesthetic focus is a bounded whole, only in the context of a situation as immediate occurrence.

In the wider context of experience as process, the principle of continuity holds. *An experience* stands out in our consciousness, but it is not completely divorced from the stream of experience. "Any experience, the most ordinary, has an indefinite total setting. Things, objects, are only focal points of a here and now in a whole that stretches out indefinitely" (L10.197). The infinite whole of experience is an inexhaustible reservoir of meanings that contextualizes meaning in any particular situation. It is also, in the words of Thomas Alexander, a "horizon of feeling," the source of "the undefined pervasive quality of an experience . . . which binds together all the defined elements, the objects of which we are focally aware, making them a whole. The best evidence that such is the case is our constant sense of things as belonging or not belonging, a sense which is immediate" (L10.198). This pervasive, qualitative whole is only tacitly felt in most experiences, but it becomes intensified and focused in *an experience* distinguished from the stream of inchoate experience by an ordered channeling of energies. In an aesthetic experience, we move from a precognitive, inchoate feeling of a situation to a cognitive, communicative process of understanding its meaning and value in the wider, continuous context of shared experience, and we return to an *appreciation* of the whole, a sense—which is a fusion of feeling and thinking—of the meaning and value as immediately embodied in the situation.

Social harmony is the quality that pervades a social situation when shared meanings and values achieved through communication and participation focus the associative experience with sufficient intensity. In social harmony, each participant contributes to the preparatory phase and enjoys the consumma-tory phase to the best of her abilities. The sense of community, the immedi-ate enjoyment and shared meaning embodied in a socially harmonious situation, is not merely inchoate feeling, nor is it purely intellectual. One has not fully recognized one's membership unless one also feels part of a commu-nity; one's feeling of belonging does not amount to a sense of community unless one also understands what being a member means.

Social harmony in Dewey's philosophy must contribute to personal-com-munal growth if community is to be a regulative ideal. This resonates with the message of the *Zhongyong*: where there is harmony, not only would everybody occupy a position suited to him or her in a community, but everyone also would be "nourished" and therefore would grow.[32] Where there is growth, there is freedom, in Dewey's view. Members of an ideal community would be free, because social harmony increases their ability to "use foresight and insight to shape spontaneous action into enduring fulfillments and to shape both natural and social environment into means for those fulfillments."[33] The aesthetic focus, which gives meaning and value to an experience through closure, paradoxically opens up the world. Experience grows and develops by being controlled and constrained. In this process, each participant, in achieving social harmony cooperatively with others, refines and expands her abilities.

In ordering the fragmentary and discordant elements of a situation, social harmony forges bonds that expand sociality. The experience of social harmony leaves behind a deposit in the character of its participants that disposes them to create harmony in future situations. It creates a sense of mutual trust that mitigates future conflicts. The meanings and values embodied in each experience of social harmony add to the reservoir of shared experience vital to a community's cooperative exploration of the meaning of community life. "The time of consummation is also one of beginning anew" (L10.23). The eternal quality that "Great Art" is supposed to possess is nothing more than "its renewed instrumentality for further consummatory experiences" (L1.274). The art of community is a cooperative human project of expanding and exploring the horizons of meaning, of opening up experience to those ideals that give significance, direction, and fulfillment to human action—it is a project of growing together.

The art of community—achieving harmony through communicative processes—incorporates diversity, resistance, tension and focus without ultimate closure, and it promotes growth with its accompanying freedom. This process of bringing about and sustaining community does not oppress individuals. We will extend this argument specifically in the context of Confucian ritual practice (*li* 禮), which has been seen as the main instrument of social tyranny in traditional Confucian societies. We shall see that when practiced properly, ritual practice fuses the artistic/aesthetic and the social in such a way that it embodies rather than stifles individual creativity. The following exploration of its function in building and sustaining community suggests new possibilities for Dewey's search for the Great Community. It elaborates on the association between art and community that is implicit in Dewey's philosophy.

Achieving Harmony through Confucian Ritual Practice

Dewey considers art an extension of the "power of rites and ceremonies to unite men, through a shared celebration, to all incidents and scenes of life" (L10.275). Such rites and ceremonies are part of *li* 禮, which has been translated as "rites," "rituals," "ritual action," "ceremony," "propriety," "decorum," "manners" "courtesy," and "civility." I shall adopt the translation of "ritual practice(s)" to retain its religious roots while acknowledging its social, habitual aspects. Confucian ritual practice covers a much wider area than Dewey is referring to. Ritual practice is one of the six arts of Confucian education—the others are music (*yue* 樂), archery (*she* 射), charioteering (*yu* 御), calligraphy (*shu* 書), and numbers (*shu* 數)—activities that create value, immediate enjoyment combined with meaning, and make the world a better place to live in. Scholars have worried at times over the "conceptual unity" of *li*, but A. S. Cua thinks that this concern resting on an over-narrow conception of morality/ethics is misplaced.[34] More important, its wide scope, embracing ethical, aesthetic, and religious values, makes Confucian ritual practice an eminent candidate for approaching Dewey's idea of "experience as art." Confucian ritual practice is the Chinese art of human association.

According to Master You (*youzi* 有子), who was said to resemble Confucius, "achieving harmony is the most valuable function of ritual practice."[35] Ritual practice brings about harmony within the family (*Analects* 12.5; *Book of Rites* 9.1/59/29). For Dewey, the art of achieving social harmony requires directing blind impulses and reforming routine habits with intelligence. Impulses are among the interacting energies that must be properly channeled; habits provide both means and meanings from the past that shape the present. Intelligence must direct both to achieve a consummatory outcome. One could view ritual practice as aiming to cultivate what Dewey calls "social habits," set ways of conduct, "patterns of behavior that mark out the activities of any group, family, clan, people, sect, faction, class" (L13.75).

The typical explications of *li* are traditional or conventional "rules of conduct." David Nivison points out that ritual practices "are rules that are flexible and humane." Such rules of conduct should be treated as "intellectual instruments to be tested and confirmed—and altered—through consequences affected by acting upon them" (L4.221). As Cua, another who characterizes ritual practices as rules of conduct, paraphrases Wittgenstein, "ritual rules, like all rules, stand there like signposts for the guidance of our will and action"; it is one's sense of what is appropriate for a particular stage of one's journey that provides guidance as to whether, and how, to follow a particular ritual signpost.[36] Practitioners of ritual practice who act as though they are following universal and immutable rules overlook Confucius' own example of refusing to be inflexible or to insist on certainty (*Analects* 9.4).

As rules of conduct, ritual practice aims to inculcate social habits, ensuring their successful performance. From a performative perspective, a ritual practice itself may be seen as a social habit. When properly performed, it combines habit, impulse, and intelligence. I shall focus more on habit and intelligence, since Dewey emphasizes that art is "intelligent habit" (M14.55). As social habit, ritual practice provides "a principle of organization, continuity, and efficiency" in social life (M6.413). As habits are "the tools which put at our immediate disposal the results of our former experience, thus economizing force," so ritual practices are active means that put at the immediate disposal of participants the experience of previous generations in dealing with the precariousness of life (E4.241). Some ancient Chinese ritual practices are symbolic reenactments of cooperative tasks of great import (e.g., those related to the cultivation of crops, or the waging of battles).[37] These ritual practices began as attempts to communicate with nature, with cosmic forces, with ancestors, to bring satisfactory outcomes to joint human enterprises.

Participants in ritual practice communicate with one another—acknowledging their interdependence and reaffirming their mutual trust and commitment to their shared goal. As the "magical" element loses its importance, or credibility, its communicative aspect becomes more important and ensures the persistence of ritual practice. According to the *Zhongyong*, ancestral worship clarifies and reinforces the order within the clan/family—it rehearses symbolically the attitudes that various individuals should adopt toward one another according to the way that they are related. Tu Wei-ming points out: "The dead are honored, because a loving memory of the forefathers brings forth communal identity and social solidarity."[38] The ritual practices honoring dead ancestors play an important role in building what Tu Wei-ming calls a "fiduciary community." "He who understands the ceremonial sacrifices to heaven and earth, and the several sacrifices to the ancestors, would find governing a kingdom as easy as looking into his palm."[39] Governing is easy when ritual practices achieve social harmony.

Ritual practices celebrating birth, coming of age, marriage, death, and so on are rites of passage marking significant moments in human life, moments of closure and beginning anew. The funereal rites embody the significance of the dead for the living. A funeral celebrates and honors the work and achievement of the departed; it expresses the grief of the living and represents their commitment to the continuity of the words and deeds of the dead.[40] To Xunzi, the greatest disgrace is to have no one but spouse and children attend one's funeral, for it indicates ethical failure in life (*Xunzi* 19/93/17). Ritual practices are never solitary events. Just as others play a part in every phase of one's life, their participation is indispensable to those rites of passage in which every participant acknowledges a key development in a person's relationship to others, her position in the community—which implies changes in expectations and demands on her future conduct, and in what she in turn may expect and demand from others. Other ritual practices (e.g., those regarding dress, greetings, and behavior at feasts) facilitate everyday social interactions. Later Confucians' concern with one's behavior in solitude, traceable to the idea of "being watchful when alone (*shendu* 慎獨)" in the *Zhongyong*, is based on a belief that how one behaves when alone will invariably affect one's behavior when in company; one's habitual behavior with regard to small and apparently trivial details of daily life will affect major events in one's life.[41]

In its broadest sense, ritual practice, as a generic kind of social action, is neither archaic nor exclusively Chinese. As Fingarette has shown, even though external forms vary from culture to culture and generation to generation, there remains a vast area of human experience wherein interaction is ritual: promises, commitments, excuses, pleas, compliments, and pacts.[42] As embodiments of shared meanings, ritual practices function as guides to action so that better coordination can be achieved with less effort than would be possible if one had to search anew for appropriate ways of interacting in every situation. If ritual practices are social habits, they should be intelligent habits, for "the striving to make stability of meaning prevail over the instability of events is the main task of intelligent effort" (L1.49).

From the Chinese character 禮—depicting a sacrificial vessel 豊—it appears that *li* first signifies religious sacrifices, then extends to the modes of conducting religious ceremonies, and farther to all modes of conduct that are deemed proper and should be observed. As Herlee Creel points out, *li* had been used in this broader sense even before Confucius' time; Confucius' achievement lies in linking it with other notions such as *ren* 仁 (authoritative conduct) and *yi* 義 (appropriateness) to form a unique, ethical vision. Li Zehou claims that Confucius' main mission is to restore the ritual practices instituted by the Duke of Zhou, and thereby to restore the clan-based social organization and government.[43] Despite Confucius' characterization of himself as a transmitter rather than a creator (*shu er bu zuo* 述而不作), some scholars argue that Confucius is not as conservative as others such as Li Zehou portray him.[44] Confucius' apparent denial of his own creativity may attest more to his modesty than to a neglect of creativity. The sage is closely associated with creativity (*zuo* 作) in the Confucian tradition. According to the *Book of Rites*, "One who creates is called sagely; one who transmits is called perspicacious. A perspicacious sage means one who transmits and creates."[45] Given that Confucius repeatedly denied being a sage, it is not surprising that he should also consider himself falling short of creativity.

To understand the progressive nature of Confucius' teachings, one must recognize that it is *continuity*, not *identity*, that is critical to his notion of transmission. Given a cosmology in which change is primary, historical and cultural continuity must be a dynamic process. Hence, in transmitting the ritual practices of the Duke of Zhou, Confucius is not handing future generations a mummified past. A legacy is successfully transmitted only when the past is revitalized, so that it is embodied in the different experience of the present. Confucius considers one who "revitalizes the old to realize the new (*wengu er zhixin* 溫古而知新)" worthy of being a teacher (*Analects* 2.11). The continuity with the past is not merely retrospective. As the Chinese like to say, one continues past efforts to open up (new opportunities in) the future (*jiwang kailai* 繼往開來). In tune with the Deweyan view of harmony, Confucian ritual practices, as the core of cultural transmission, should be dynamic rather than static and creative rather than oppressive. Without creativity, historically appropriate changes would not occur, and ritual practices would degenerate into mere customs and conventional rules, thus compliance becomes nothing but routine.

Personal investment of meaning in individual performances brings creativity to Confucian ritual practice. Social change must be initiated by individuals (M9.305; L14.113). To understand the intertwining of the personal and the communal in Confucius' teachings, we need to examine the relationship among three key ethical ideas of authoritative conduct (*ren* 仁), appropriateness (*yi* 義), and ritual practice (*li* 禮). Hall and Ames argue persuasively against translating *yi* as "righteousness" and understanding it as providing some kind of absolute standard. In their view, *yi* has to do with the personal investment of meaning in action, based on the interaction between a person's individuality and her environment in specific situations.[46] From a personal perspective, authoritative conduct is the extension and improvement of one's relational network. As a process extending and improving interpersonal interactions, authoritative conduct builds and sustains community. Chapter 2 discussed how authoritative conduct is achieved through ritual practices. We shall next examine how ritual practices bring into play appropriateness with every observance.

Appropriateness is as indispensable as ritual practice in achieving authoritative conduct. According to Mencius, appropriateness is "the human path" that realizes authoritative conduct.[47] Authoritative conduct brings together person making and community making through mutual enhancement between ritual practice and appropriateness. Ritual practice represents the cultural legacy that transmits meanings created by earlier generations to future generations; appropriateness is each individual's personal appropriation of this legacy and her contribution of novel meaning to it, based on her interaction with her particular environment in each specific situation. The *Book of Rites* describes ritual practice as "the actualization of appropriateness. If an observance stands the test of being judged by what is appropriate, although the ancient true kings may not have done it, it should be adopted for its appropriateness" (*Book of Rites* 9.35/63/26). Confucius describes an exemplary person as one who "has a sense of appropriateness as his basic disposition, and develops it in ritual practice" (*Analects* 15.18).

Ritual practice and appropriateness often occur together in the *Xunzi*. Because human beings can distinguish what is appropriate or significant from what is not, they are considered above animals. They achieve harmony by such distinctions and significations (*Xunzi* 9/39/9). These distinctions or significations are embodied and transmitted in the form of ritual practice. "The ancient true kings, abhorring disorder, established ritual practice and what is appropriate, in order to distinguish between what was acceptable and what was not in nourishing the people's desires and meeting their demands."[48] Cua argues that in Xunzi's philosophy, ritual practice must be explicated in relation to authoritative conduct and appropriateness for an adequate understanding of Xunzi's ethical vision. For Xunzi, it is only "when all three [*ren*, *yi*, and *li*] are attained, then the exemplary person has reached the way."[49] However, instead of being "functionally equivalent in ethical contexts," I believe that ritual practice and appropriateness complement and enhance each other in the process of personal-communal growth.

In exceptional circumstances, usually in times of great social turmoil or political upheaval, one might fall back upon appropriateness alone to achieve authoritative conduct. This is one way of reconciling Confucius' otherwise cryptic assessments of Guanzhong as an authoritative person, even though the latter did not understand ritual practice. There is less reason to think that one could dispense with appropriateness in conducting ritual practice.[50] It is the interaction between ritual practice and appropriateness that results in a growth in meaning that is widely shared and transmitted across generations, a growth in the organizing, articulating, and practicing continuity linking physically separate individuals constituting community.[51] This intertwining of the personal and the communal in the ritual practices-appropriateness conjunction is central to achieving a social harmony that would preclude the oppression of individuals and the stagnation of societies.

Confucian ritual practices are cooperative activities in which all understand what each should do, and each does his or her part so that all act together harmoniously. The shared meaning as well as frequent practice could result in seamless cooperation that embodies harmony, both aesthetic and social. In acquiring shared meanings embodied in ritual practices through a process of education and socialization, participants acquire certain ways of feeling and thinking. They also acquire self-discipline and a disposition for harmony, which comes from an appreciation of the value of harmony that they have experienced. To achieve harmony, self-discipline is required as participants must respond appropriately, instead of simply doing whatever they feel like doing at the moment, or being satisfied with whatever they could manage, which would likely be quite inadequate when they first participate in a ritual practice (*Analects* 12.1). In Deweyan language, self-discipline ensures an appropriate performance that eschews both caprice and routine.[52]

The sensitivity and understanding toward other participants engendered in achieving harmony in ritual practices would favor other tasks in which cooperation is required. Ritual practices, which are designed to achieve harmony in recurrent occasions of daily living, create the nurturing environment for achieving harmony in other more problematic arenas of life. In conflict situations, the predisposition toward a harmonious resolution and the avoidance of an adversarial stance can have a significant impact on the outcome. Polite and nonconfrontational postures, facilitated by ritual acts understood by all, even in situations of a serious conflict of interests, are not always simply hypocrisy; they are, in fact, powerful means of increasing the chances of an outcome acceptable to all. A harmonious outcome is of course never easy to achieve, since it requires that the participants be genuinely disposed toward a harmonious outcome, as well as equipped with the necessary self-discipline, sensitivity, and understanding of the situation and those involved.

Traditionally there has been an emphasis on the "externality" of rites, as with the way Li Zehou understands the textual reference that "*Li* works from the outside (*liziwaizuo* 禮自外作)."[53] But other scholars have challenged this interpretation. Tu Wei-ming argues that there is historical and textual evidence to emphasize the dynamic process rather than the static structure of rites.[54] I shall attempt to show that ritual practice works only if the external form and internal content are balanced. The form of a ritual practice—the visible, tangible details to be observed in every performance—embodies a general meaning, which individuals learn to interpret through processes of education and socialization. As the *Book of Rites* (11.24/72/3) acknowledges, while it is possible to display all of the external modes of a ritual practice, even though its meaning is lost, it is the meaning that is valuable. "Surely the frequent mentions of ritual practice refer to more than gifts of jade and silk?" (*Analects* 17.11). Simply observing the ritual form, following rules that others lay down, is merely going through the motions. Not only is it an inadequate performance by Confucian standards, it is a deplorable form of deception that Confucius condemns as the "ruin of ethical excellence (*de zhi zei* 德之賊)" (*Analects* 17.13). One's ritual performances are successful only if they are enhanced by appropriateness, by the personal appropriation of and contribution to the shared meanings of the community. Only then will there be personal-communal growth.

Each ritual performance, in addition to the ritual form, is constituted by a particular content comprising its unique circumstances. For a successful ritual performance, one must make sense of the situation as a whole by combining the formal meaning embodied in the external modes of the ritual practice with all other specific elements in the situation to achieve a unique, performed meaning. The performed meaning draws on the interactions of the participant's individuality with the unique circumstances of the situation and adds to the reservoir of the shared experiences contextualizing the ritual practice. The interaction of ritual forms, participants, and the environments of performances is required for changes in both the ritual form and meaning. Consider the case of wearing ceremonial caps of linen (*Analects* 9.3). New circumstances arose in which black silk became cheaper than linen, and some individual, interacting with this new circumstance in his own particular situation (perhaps he is relatively poor), felt that it was appropriate to wear a black silk ceremonial cap instead of the usual linen one. This experiment might have failed, that is, it might have been judged simply as a breach of ritual practice. But, as it happened, others responding to their own circumstances, and interpreting the performed meaning when black silk is used, also found it appropriate to wear black silk caps. The experiment eventually brought about a change in the ritual form—the meaning once embodied in black ceremonial linen caps becomes embodied in black ceremonial silk caps.

For an example of the change of ritual meaning, one could turn to ancestor worship. It might once have (and for some, still does) embodied superstitious beliefs about life after death and the ability of ghosts and spirits to interfere with worldly affairs. When circumstances change so that such superstition loses its credibility, then the same ritual forms, if they are to remain meaningful, must embody new meanings—such as those regarding continuity, mentioned earlier—that are not dependent on superstitious beliefs. Where ritual practices have not been reified to the extent that particular individuals or groups dictate what is appropriate or not, changes depend on the judgments of the majority of participants. This does not mean that everyone's judgment would count equally, since some, because of their recognized excellence (or for other reasons), could influence others' judgment. Whether or not a particular change is for the better depends on the quality of the judgments that brought about the change. The ability to change both ritual forms and ritual meanings often becomes critical to the survival of ritual practices. When ritual practices have survived despite their inappropriateness to changed circumstances, it is at the expense of the participants—their growth is stultified, because they are obstructed from interacting freely and meaningfully with their environment.

Unfortunately, the actual practice in Chinese society has not always fulfilled the promise of Confucian ritual practice as a way of achieving a rich and creative harmony. How did ritual practices result in the kind of social oppression of individuals that has sometimes been witnessed in China's history? A comparison of de jure ritual practice with de facto ritual practice shows that when cultural patterns that sustain community become inflexible, when individual creativity is viewed with hostility and prevented from revitalizing cultural patterns, then the pursuit of community and social stability becomes perverted and self-defeating. Social interaction fails the test of personal-communal growth when ritual forms reify at the expense of creative content in performance. Insisting on every minute formal detail, regardless of changing circumstances, and enforcing conformity through coercion (including some really barbaric punishments) sometimes perverted Confucian ritual practices into what Lu Xun condemns as "cannibalistic ritual doctrines."[55]

It is the flexibility of signifying and interpreting the content of each particular performance that ensures the contribution of creative individuality; it is through each participant feeling and thinking freely and creatively that ritual practices could remain vital and responsive to an ever-changing environment. Neglecting flexibility and creativity in favor of the form alone and coercing conformity empty a ritual practice of its creative content and the meaning particular to each performance. There will be no renewal of shared meaning, nor the creation of novel meaning if feeling and thinking are not responsive to the circumstances of each specific performance. Rigidity, in turn, erodes feeling and thinking with regard to the transmitted formal meaning, for one could simply "go through the motions," fulfill the formal requirements of a ritual practice, without the appropriate feeling or thinking about its significance as integrated into one's life. Ritual performances then become meaningless, routine, or, worse, oppressive burdens.

We may illustrate this with an example of a simple ritual practice: bringing a gift when one visits somebody. The gift is a token of appreciation for the invitation and hospitality expected from one's hostess. A ritual practice may be formalized to different degrees, depending on the insistence on specific details. One such detail is the value of a visitor's gift. If it is not rigidly specified, a relatively rich visitor, let us call her "Vanessa," may bring a thoughtful gift (with regard to the particular hostess) that is expensive, though well within her means. The hostess, Harriet, would have to interpret that detail of the gesture as the thoughtful act that it is, or as an attempt to "show off," to stress their different financial circumstances. She then responds based on that interpretation and on her own feelings and attitudes. When the roles are reversed, Harriet might either return a gift of equal value that she could not afford, or a less expensive gift that she could afford but is still a thoughtful gift for Vanessa, who must in turn interpret Harriet's gesture specifically and perhaps modify her own behavior the next time she visits. Thinking and feeling by each participant enter into each specific encounter, which would not occur if the value of ritual gift were rigidly prescribed. Hence, the stricter and the more detailed the formal requirements of a ritual practice, the less flexibility, and therefore the less personal investment of meaning, is possible for the participants. The proliferation of detailed formal ritual requirements in every area of life could render it unnecessary for people to think and feel for themselves at all.

Let us consider breaches of ritual practice. If one is only concerned with form, then when a visitor fails to bring a gift, she is condemned regardless of the circumstances—the meaning of her behavior is entirely determined. Sensitivity and understanding are required on the part of the hostess only if she looks further into the specific circumstances for meaning beyond the general formal meaning of rudeness (or worse) attached to such an event. Individualized feeling and thinking become even more restricted if the hostess's response to such an event is also strictly prescribed, regardless of how she may feel or think (some may be more generous and inclined to overlook such breaches than others). In practice, the rigidity in not understanding and accommodating nonconformity to ritual forms according to specific circumstances and cruel punishments for failure to conform lead to coerced performance.

Over the centuries, Confucian ritual practices have shown a tendency to lose their flexibility, not only among the vulgar but also among some prominent Confucians. Mencius recommended that the ritual practice of not touching a member of the other gender (except for husband-wife, parent-child) in giving and receiving need not apply if grabbing one's sister-in-law's hand is the only way to save her from drowning (*Mencius*, 7.17/38/20). In contrast, Cheng Yi 程頤 (1033–1107 A.D.) admonished widows who remarried out of economic necessity, in that "starvation is a small matter compared with the loss of chastity." This is more inflexible than the *Book of Rites* describing widows not remarrying as the highest expression of "living up to her words (xin 信)," the greatest virtue of a wife, without actually forbidding or totally condemning remarriage.[56] Historically, ritual practices, which should have been a flexible, symbolic network enhancing harmonious feeling and thinking, sometimes ended up as social shackles that oppressed the heart and paralyzed the mind.

The Science of Community: Cooperative Inquiry

Historical failures of Confucian ritual practices show that a *Sittlichkeit* that clings to reified beliefs and values and subjects its members to the tyranny of a tired tradition will not achieve genuine community. In a world of change, even the best habits need modifying sooner or later (M14.41). Continuity must be balanced with development; the old must be remade through union with the new. The Confucian art of creating and sustaining community achieves this when appropriateness and ritual practice mutually enhance each other. From a Deweyan perspective, there also is an element of science in this process. The task involves a certain form of social self-criticism employing intelligence (L11.37). As Michael Eldridge says, intelligence is experience, or culture, criticizing itself.[57] An ideal community constantly transforms itself so that its members would remain "in touch" with a constantly changing environment. What its members hold in common is not predetermined by others or fixed for all time. A community is not simply something that one inherits; every generation must engage personally in a search for its own community. An ideal community avoids being oppressive because it remains in question; like a Deweyan person, it is "ever not quite."

Community, from the perspective of achieving harmony in human relationship—immediate enjoyment of the meaning and value of social life—is art; community, from the perspective of the intentional direction of events required to transform a problematic situation into a unified whole, is science. In Dewey's philosophy, intelligence links art and science. Art is intelligent habit, while science is intelligent inquiry. The method of intelligence is best exemplified in modern science (L13.279). The science of community is a method of solving problems through cooperative inquiry. The method is employed in solving specific problems, but unless the solutions to these problems contribute to the achievement of harmony, they will not be satisfactory as social actions—and thus we fail to solve the problems as *social* problems. Social harmony is not an ultimate, single, final, common good; both Dewey's philosophy and Confucianism resist the idea of a totalistic final end. Social harmony incorporates various common goods, in the plural. Where the realization of these common goods is obstructed, each common good becomes an end-in-view adopted in a specific situation after free and thorough cooperative inquiry. Social harmony has a part in every social end-in-view as it is the quality of the unified whole in relationships, but its specific manifestation is different in every situation.

Richard Rorty, who has done much in reviving interest in Dewey's pragmatism, says that although "Dewey never stopped talking about 'scientific method,' . . . he never had anything very useful to say about it." Other scholars believe that Dewey's understanding (whatever its weaknesses and problems) of the scientific method is central to his philosophy.[58] In advocating a scientific method of social inquiry, Dewey is not laying down fixed rules or procedures for thinking. His notion of "experimental intelligence, conceived after the pattern of science" is a general one: "Concrete suggestions arising from past experiences, developed and matured in the light of the needs and deficiencies of the present, employed as aims and methods of specific reconstruction, and tested by success or failure in accomplishing this task of readjustment, suffice" (M12.134). He certainly does not recommend what Wu Kuang-ming calls the "coercive logic" of the West in the latter's argument that Chinese pragmatic humanism differs from American pragmatic humanism because of their different styles of reasoning. According to Wu, "Chinese argumentation shifts our paradigm of reality to change our pattern of behavior. The argumentation is a movement *of* the situation itself, to move us into a new discernment, to create a new situation."[59] This would actually fit into the Deweyan pattern of inquiry laid out in *Logic: The Theory of Inquiry*. In any event, Dewey would concede that the pattern of inquiry he has laid out is not beyond revision by a study of how people in different cultures solve problems.

Wu Kuang-ming's point is not without merit. Dewey himself would agree that "our logic is molded on the structure of language, which reflects experience," and that it is not something independent of the way we inquire and reflect on problems. Given the linguistic as well as the experiential differences, there would be some differences in the way people in different cultures think and reason. However, we should be careful not to exaggerate the differences between the styles of reasoning in American pragmatism and Chinese pragmatism; nor should we "freeze" the styles of reasoning. Every style of reasoning is capable of change and improvement through, among other ways, learning from other styles.[60] Moreover, within each culture, there is always more than one style of reasoning overlapping with another, just as there could be some overlap in the styles of reasoning of different cultures. Otherwise, attempting to reconstruct a conception of community constituted through cooperative inquiry that Confucianism could share with Deweyan pragmatism would be a nonstarter.

Dewey acknowledges that there are important differences between the physical sciences and social sciences. He does not recommend that we simply apply the procedures and findings of the physical sciences in dealing with social problems; he believes that social inquiry can "develop its own regulative ideas and standards," so that we may acquire powers of directing the social environment, of reconstructing our society, as science has acquired over our physical environment (L4.86; L6.55). He explicitly objects to an "absolutist logic" that attempts to assimilate human sciences to physical sciences (L2.358–60). He maintains, as late as 1949, that "what is needed is not the carrying over of procedures that have approved themselves in physical science, but *new* methods as adapted to *human* issues and problems" (L16.379).

Dewey argues that, despite their differences, it is possible for the social sciences to learn from the physical sciences, to become more scientific, that is, more intelligent, because there is an overlapping pattern underlying inquiries in both areas. Inquiry is "the controlled or directed transformation of an indeterminate situation into one that is so determinate in its constituent distinctions and relations as to convert the elements of the original situation into a unified whole" (L12.108). All inquiries arise in an existential matrix that is both biological and cultural, since human beings are natural organisms interacting with a physical environment and cultural beings interacting with one another through semiotic networks. Inquiries are situation based and problem oriented, they integrate theory and practice, and they are evaluative (L12). We may view inquiry also as a process with different overlapping stages (the movement is not necessarily linear). When a social situation is indeterminate, it is obscure, doubtful, disturbing, perplexing, and full of conflicting tendencies—things do not hang together, and those involved become aware that "This won't do." When the trouble is recognized, and those involved directly and indirectly get together to solve the problem, then social inquiry begins.

An intelligent group whose aim is to solve a problem does not rush into action. Instead, it examines the situation and attempts to formulate the problem. This involves not only a careful observation of what is going on but also requires selecting among the numerous rules of the existing conceptual structure to interpret the factual material. Constituents of the situation observable by sound organs and techniques are "facts," but they only become "facts of the case" through a selection based on their assessed relevance to *resolving* the problem. "Statement of a problematic situation in terms of a problem has no meaning save as the problem instituted has, in the very terms of its statement, reference to a possible solution" (L12.112). Very frequently, conceptual reconstruction—especially of ends, values, and social doctrines that guide social action—is necessary to formulate the problem. This follows from

Dewey's conception of means and ends being internally related. His "instru-mentalism," "experimentalism," or "instrumental experimentalism" is not only a matter of finding means to given ends; inquiry is as much about what the ends should be as it is about what the means should be, and the two are closely related.

An experimental social method manifests itself first by surrendering the notion of preconceived, immutable goals (L2.360). Unless inquirers recognize that these are revisable, however pertinent former interpretations may have been for past occasions, they would be hampered in formulating the problem. Which ends-in-view are appropriate is critical to problem formulation, for "solution comes only by getting away from the meaning of terms [including ends] that is already fixed upon and coming to see the conditions from another point of view, and hence in a fresh light" (M2.273). Only when ends-in-view and other ideas used in the inquiry interact freely with the observable "facts of the case," mutually modifying one another and thereby moving toward greater coherence, will the problem be formulated so that it suggests possible solutions.

Solutions are "working hypotheses" to be tested intellectually before actual experimenting. Intellectual testing, or "reasoning," is "developing the meaning-contents of ideas in their relations to one another" (L12.115). The compo-nents of a proposed solution must be tested for their "fit" with one another, and with other parts of the inquirers' conceptual scheme and perceptual knowl-edge. The inquirers should end up with a coherent picture of how things would work if they put the solution into effect. Solutions in the form of vague ideas are clarified and rendered more relevant to the problem in this reasoning process. It is also important in terms of anticipating indirect effects. A solu-tion that solves one problem sometimes creates other problems; it must be evaluated in terms of its total effects (as much as could be anticipated). "When an activity and its consequences can be rehearsed by representation in sym-bolic terms, there is no . . . final commitment. If the representation of the final consequence is of unwelcome quality, overt activity may be foregone, or the way of acting be re-planned in such a way as to avoid the undesired outcome" (L12.63). Based on their reasoning, the inquirers select the best alternative and test it in the actual situation. If it works, the problem is solved; if not, the process of inquiry resumes with new information from the experiment with the selected solution. Even if a solution worked, there could nevertheless be unanticipated effects that could be problematic, and new inquiries, perhaps involving new participants, would be required.

The method of inquiry is inherently social. In science, "everything dis-covered belongs to the community of workers," and "every new idea and theory has to be submitted to this community for confirmation and tests" (L5.115). Communal participation is even more important in social inquiry. In the above simplified account, the inquirers are described as those involved directly or indirectly in the social problem; in fact, an ideal inquiry would have to be much more open, and participation much more extensive, involving a diversity of people. Possible solutions may involve people not affected by the original problems. Rather than involving these people (if they could be identified at that stage by anyone other than themselves) only when the issue arises in an inquiry, it would be better if the inquiry was open from the beginning so that anyone could judge for herself if she would be affected and whether she should get involved. This of course does not preclude the need to notify people who are going to be affected whenever possible.

The intelligence of an inquiry—the problem formulation, the alternative solutions proposed and selected, and so on—is social. It depends on how wide and minute observations are and on how imaginative and thorough the tracing is of specific connections between events. What one single individual lacks in any of these can be compensated by others in a *cooperative* inquiry, wherein the sharing of views, constructive criticism, and edifying discourse could lead to a more intelligent outcome than solitary thinking (M9.153). Furthermore, as far as Dewey is concerned, "*effective* intelligence is not an original, innate endowment"; it is social (L2.366). What we could do with our "innate endowment" depends on how it has been cultivated in the "embodied intelligence" of our sociocultural environment (L11.38–39, 48). This "nourishment" does not come only from our shared historical cultural legacies but also from the ongoing process of interaction with others, wherein there is free and open communication.

If we view the ideal community life as a process of cooperative inquiry, then two related characteristics stand out in avoiding the dangers of social and political oppression: its questioning, hypothetical stance and its open, extensive, and diverse participation. The first undermines oppression based on an individual's or a group's privileged claim to truth or wisdom. The need to adopt a questioning, hypothetical stance in inquiry means that we must anticipate, and even actively seek, differences of opinion. Part of the intellectual testing of hypotheses is to subject them to rigorous questioning and criticism, and this requires extensive and diverse participation and freedom of thought and therefore of speech, which ensure one's participation in directing events affecting one, and one's opportunities to contribute to social reconstruction.

A lack of participation leads to "the moral tragedy inherent in efforts to further the common good which prevent the result from being either good or common—not good, because it is at the expense of the active growth of those to be helped, and not common, because these have no share in bringing the result about" (L7.347). Participation is not only necessary to personal growth, but also critical to communal growth, and even communal survival. "Every new idea, every conception of things differing from that authorized by current belief, must have its origin in an individual" (M9.305). Since there is no knowing beforehand who would have the new idea or new conception needed to solve a problem, to limit participation would limit the chances of success. Open and extensive participation is critical for a community, because individuals, acting cooperatively, refashion social institutions and reconstruct social life to meet new challenges. "The direction, the quality of change is a matter of individuality" (L14.113). Without the ability to change deliberately, a community cannot grow; sometimes it cannot even survive.

Dewey shows us how a community built through cooperative inquiry would not oppress its members. To what extent could we incorporate cooperative inquiry into a Confucian community? While early Confucianism lacks a developed theory of inquiry that could be compared to Dewey's, there is enough common ground for an assimilation of cooperative inquiry in a reconstructed Confucianism. Confucius' example of undogmatic and flexible attitude to all issues renders it fairly easy for a Confucian to adopt a questioning, hypothetical stance toward specific social problems (*Analects* 9.4, 18.8). Nothing is beyond questioning, and certainly not social conventions and customs. Confucius "asked questions about everything" whenever he entered the Grand Ancestral Hall. Consequently, his knowledge of ritual practice was called into doubt. Confucius responded: "To do so is itself observing ritual practices" (*Analects* 3.15). It is not too far fetched to argue that the ideal Confucian community requires a questioning, hypothetical stance toward itself.

In its hypothetical stance, Dewey's pragmatism is oriented toward the future. "Experimental intelligence . . . liberates man from the bondage of the past, due to ignorance and accident hardened into custom. It projects a better future and assists man in its realization" (M12.135). For all of his melioristic emphasis on the future, Dewey does not reject the past entirely; it is a past "hardened into custom" that he rejects. For him, "man differs from the lower animals because he preserves his past experiences" (M12.80). "Ours is the responsibility of conserving, transmitting, rectifying, and expanding the heritage of values we have received that those who come after us may receive it more solid and secure, more widely accessible and more generously shared than we have received it" (L9.57). Experimenting does not mean "anything goes"— that would be mere caprice. Dewey's experimental method is rooted in the specifics of a situation, which is continuous with both past and future. The intelligence central to the experimental method is "the power of using past experience to shape and transform future experience" (M11.346).

Although Confucianism values tradition more, there is a difference of emphasis rather than total contradiction between its thinking and Dewey's pragmatism. The value of tradition for Confucius is not merely conservative but related to a concern with shaping the future. Confucius' "traditionalism" is more a concern with continuity than a conservatism that wants to preserve the past unchanged (which is impossible; if it is not improved upon, it deteriorates). Confucius does not equate the value of something with its age. He recommends the culture of the Zhou dynasty, because it built intelligently on what it had learned from the earlier Xia and Shang dynasties (*Analects* 3.14). If Confucius, in his modesty, did not see himself exceeding the achievements of the Duke of Zhou, then he was far from excluding the possibility of someone else doing so. "The young should be held in high esteem. After all, how do we know that those yet to come will not surpass our contemporaries?" (*Analects* 9.23). While there is a difference in emphasis in the ways Dewey and Confucius deal with continuity of the past with the future through the present, the difference is not as great as some are inclined to think. Combining the two, we should learn to emphasize past or present as appropriate to specific situations.

In comparing Confucian and pragmatic attitudes to tradition, Hall and Ames borrow G. K. Chesterton's "democracy of the dead" to highlight the importance of the past for the present and future in both philosophies.[61] Those concerned with individual liberty will find this notion not so much perplexing as dangerous. To whom or through whom do the dead speak? "Giving votes to the most obscure of all classes, our ancestors," could become a tool of oppression in the hands of those who have inherited, through birth, the most privileges in order to further entrench their interests. It also could be a stepping-stone to authoritarian power by those who set themselves up as "spiritual mediums" with a monopoly on the ability to receive and decipher the messages from the dead. The only way in which "a democracy of the dead" could fit into a Deweyan democracy is if everyone (who is affected directly or directly by an issue) gets to interpret the messages from the dead. "The best method humanity has discovered for combining the conservation of attained values with progress toward new goods is freedom of speech exercised in open, cooperative inquiry" (L7.361).

This brings us back to the importance of participation in cooperative inquiry—we are talking of the living here, for the dead, and the unborn too, only "participate" through the living. Participation brings together democracy and community in Dewey's philosophy. The idea of democracy "from the standpoint of the individual consists in having a responsible share according to capacity in forming and directing the activities of the groups to which one belongs and in participating according to need in the values which the groups sustain. . . . Regarded as an idea, democracy is not an alternative to other principles of associated life. It is the idea of community life itself" (L2.327).

How participative could inquiry be in a Confucian community? With the help of Dewey, one could construct a conception of Confucian inquiry that is also social. Among the cluster of concepts associated with thinking is *zhi* 知,

commonly translated as "to know," "to understand," but probably better rendered as "to realize," both in the sense of "coming to know" and "making real," one of the key ethical ideas in Confucianism. This character is absent in the scripts from the oracle bones and the bronzes, but *zhi* 智, the character for wisdom, is thought to be its earlier version. One may consider *zhi* 知/智 the result of inquiry, in that it solves problems; but given the conceptual elasticity characteristic of Chinese thought, it sometimes extends to the activity itself. It is because problems are solved with *zhi* that "the wise (*zhizhe* 知者) are not in a quandary" (*Analects* 9.29). A problematic situation creates perplexities; one is in a quandary (*huo* 惑), because one is faced with conflicting alternatives. *Zhi* as inquiry removes perplexities by reconstituting the situation. Confucius "was no longer doubtful (*buhuo* 不惑)" from the age of forty; this does not mean that he no longer encountered problems. His freedom from uncertainty in action results from a certain proficiency in problem solving, finding his way out of any quandaries that he might encounter.

Both 知 and 智 include "arrow (*shi* 矢)" and "mouth (*kou* 口)" in their composition. The latter is easily associated with communication. Confucius says that the wise (those who are *zhi*) know whom one should speak to, thereby neither wasting words nor letting people go to waste by losing an opportunity to improve them through communication (*Analects* 15.8). Hall and Ames suggest that the "arrow" component might indicate "casting" or "directionality."[62] There is a practice in ancient China of using an arrow as a token of command. In the Erya 爾雅 (ca. third century B.C.), "arrow (*shi*)" is glossed as "*chen* 陳, to display, to present" (*Erya* 1.25/7/7). The connotations of *zhi* are both communicative and performative. *Zhi* is "to realize" in the sense of knowing, understanding, as well as in the sense of making present, actualizing. Intelligence, knowledge, and wisdom all have an active element. Hall and Ames argue persuasively that *zhi* 知 "is a process of articulating and determining the world rather than a passive cognizance of a predetermined reality."[63] It is not simply a prerequisite for changing the world; it is an activity that changes the world. The theory of knowledge implicit in Chinese thought is pragmatic. As the result of inquiry or inquiry itself, *zhi* provides answers to the question, "What is to be done?" To know what to do in a problematic situation is know one's way (*zhidao* 知道); to know one's way is to reach a destination, to realize a goal, to make it real.

Several passages in the *Analects* make better sense when we recognize this active sense of *zhi*. A passage that commentators have difficulties making sense of is *Analects* 15.34. Waley translates it thus: "It is wrong for a gentleman to have knowledge of menial matters (*xiaozhi* 小知) and proper that he should be entrusted with great responsibilities (*dashou* 大受). It is wrong for a small man to be entrusted with great responsibilities, but proper that he should have a knowledge of menial matters."[64] Other translators usually have interpreted the exemplary person (*junzi* 君子) as the object of *zhi* and rendered the passage as saying that the exemplary person cannot be known, or appreciated, in small matters. For a better parallelism, Lau translates the contrasting *dashou* 大受 as "acceptable in great matters," but Legge and others translate it as "being entrusted with great concerns."[65] If we take into account the active aspects of *zhi*, instead of reducing it to something purely intellectual, then we can maintain the parallelism as well as retain the traditional understanding of *dashou* in a different translation: "Exemplary persons should not be given trivial assignments but can be relied upon for important responsibilities."[66]

The social, that is, communicative, characteristic of inquiry also is suggested by the composition of the character for "sage." The *Shuowen* lexicon gives the meaning of *sheng* as "to communicate (*tong* 通)."[67] Chen Ning argues that the *cheng* (manifest) component of *sheng*, which the *Shuowen* considers a phonetic component, but to which some scholars have attributed semantic weight, is a latter addition, no earlier than the Warring States period. Even in the Ma-wang-tui silk manuscript, *Lao Tzu* B, *sheng* (sage) is regularly written as a combination of "ear (*er* 耳)" and "mouth (*kou* 口)"—which, according to Chen, is similar to the Shang oracle bone inscriptions—that suggests communication. According to Chen, in the Shang oracle inscriptions, *sheng* was used to convey the meaning "to hear" and, by extension, "to listen to affairs of the state."[68]

The "ear (*er* 耳)" component associates the sage with "hearing (*ting* 聽)" and "keenness of hearing (*cong* 聰)." Confucius describes the process of his personal cultivation: "from sixty, my ear was attuned" (*Analects* 2.4). Keenness of hearing, indicating a more general sensitivity, is connected to intelligence; "intelligence" is translated into *congming* 聰明 in the modern language. To be intelligent is to be keen of hearing (sensitive), clear-sighted (perceptive), and bright. Linking "sage" to its homophone, "sound, to sound (*sheng* 聲)," suggests sensitivity and activity.[69] The *Analects* tells of a border official who, emerging from an interview with Confucius, informed the latter's students that "All under heaven has long since lost their way, and heaven is going to use the Master as a wooden bell-clapper"; the words of the sage, along with the mandate of heaven and the great person, should be held in awe, for he sends a message that can transform the world (*Analects* 3.24, 16.8).

Inquiry is social in the way it is carried out, as a cooperative activity involving a group rather than as a solitary endeavor. For Confucius, knowledge and wisdom are best gained in community, among authoritative persons (*Analects* 4.1). Inquiry is social in its consequences. Confucian inquiry would aim at the cultivation of persons in community; when effective, it changes a community through changing its members and their relations with one another. Like Deweyan inquiry, Confucian inquiry creates and sustains community. The wise devote themselves to what is appropriate for the people; they contribute to people's personal cultivation by promoting those upright in their conduct to serve as examples to others (*Analects* 6.22, 12.22). "The way of the sage is complete when he sets the world aright after having set himself aright."[70]

Confucius often associates *zhi* 知 with authoritative conduct (*ren* 仁), which is both person making and community making. "The wise enjoy water; those authoritative in their conduct enjoy mountains. The wise are active; the authoritative are tranquil. The wise find enjoyment; the authoritative find longevity" (*Analects* 6.23). In Chinese landscape paintings, mountains and waters interact to enhance each other's beauty and contribute to the overall aesthetic quality of a painting; *zhi* and *ren* are similarly related. Those with *zhi* are active, because it is the force of change within the process of social interaction; those with *ren* are tranquil, because it extends and strengthens their personal relations so that conflicts with others do not destabilize their lives. With *zhi*, one finds enjoyment as problems are solved, so that an indeterminate situation is reconstituted into a unified whole. With *ren*, one finds longevity as communal relations contribute to one's flourishing and ensure that one is remembered even after one's death.

The social nature of inquiry is revealed also in Confucian pedagogy. For Mencius, it is Confucius' commitment to communication in both learning and teaching that qualifies him as a sage "unsurpassed since humans have walked the earth" (*Mencius* 3.2/16/16). The *Analects* is a collection of conversations, questions, and answers between Confucius, his students, and others. They are records of social inquiries in which everybody participates according to their abilities rather than a one-directional transmission of knowledge, as witnessed in the reciprocity between learning and teaching. Though not always practiced with equal effectiveness, this method of acquiring knowledge persists as an ideal throughout the long history of Confucian domination of education in China. It also provides the model for public discourse. It is not surprising that schools have frequently become forums for the discussion of public issues, including criticism of rulers, from the time of Confucius to the present.

Wm. Theodore de Bary sees the private academies of the Song and Ming dynasties as arenas in which Confucians attempt to develop a civil society.[71] Western conceptions of "civil society" often imply a necessarily antagonistic relation between state and society, which is incompatible with Confucianism. Thomas Lee brings out this difference in philosophical assumptions about the relation between state and society in his discussion of the official sponsorship and suppression of the private academies.[72] Having said that, it is worth noting that the role of such educational institutions, in establishing the close association between education and public discussions of social and political issues, supports the argument that the inherently social nature of Confucian pedagogy implies that Confucian inquiry in areas other than education is social as well.

There is no lack of social inquiry in China's past, as Chinese rulers gathered the people to discuss important matters (as reported in the *Book of Historical Documents* and *Zuo's Commentary*), and rulers regularly discussed state affairs with their ministers. Despite taking the monarchical political structure for granted, Confucianism, philosophically, has never supported despotism in the sense of rule by the arbitrary will of one person. The model for political and social decision making is seen in the behavior of the sage kings, whose great wisdom lies in their *questioning* and *listening* attentively to others' views; the legitimacy of their decisions lies in their having taken relevant views of others into account.[73]

Historical examples of social inquiry often fall short of the kind of openness and extensive participation that Dewey envisages in an ideal community (as they regularly do even in Western liberal democracies today). Critics of Confucianism would point out that, apart from Chinese rulers falling short of ideal decision making, those who get to offer their views are limited to people with certain status in a strictly hierarchical society; there is an inherent, and not merely a historical, limit to participation. After all, Confucius says: "Do not plan the policies of an office you do not hold," and his student Master Zeng elaborates: "The thoughts of exemplary persons do not wander beyond their stations" (*Analects* 8.14, 14.26).

EQUALITY AND DIFFERENTIATED ORDERS

Scholars have regarded hierarchy as more than a contingent characteristic of Confucian societies; it is viewed as necessary for achieving harmony, which makes it a value in Confucianism. According to Benjamin Schwartz, Confucianism "accepts unblinkingly what it regards as the need for hierarchy, status, and authority within a universal world order." Confucius, Mencius, and Xunzi all assume the need for authority and hierarchy. Confucianism has consequently often been charged with being elitist. Hierarchy is supposed to be antithetical to democracy, which is "the constitutional rule of freemen and equals."[74] To those skeptical of the possibility of Confucian democracy, hierarchy unjustifiably limits political participation, because it denies the democratic value of equality.

One may be able to discern in past Confucian societies normative behavior comparable to Westerners' concern for the value of equality, but those societies lack an explicit acknowledgment of this value so central to Western liberal democracies. The language of equality is alien to Confucian discourse before the late nineteenth century. In contrast, it has occupied a prominent place in Western philosophical and political discourse since the Enlightenment. The value of equality is central to American democracy. What equality implies in terms of social and political action continues to be the main subject of public debate. Consensus on the meaning of equality itself remains elusive, and in the words of one writer, "the conflict over the meaning of equality is in reality a battle for the soul of America."[75] Continuing debates over the meaning of equality provide us with more room to construct a conception of equality appropriate to Confucian democracy.

Equality has been far from self-evident even among those who share the belief that men are created by God. Many thinkers in the Middle Ages accepted inequality as the fundamental characteristic of the created world, and maintained that existence and value issued from above in a "great Chain of Being." The very etymology of "hierarchy" associates it with religion: it is rule by a hierarch, a high priest, one who presides over sacred rites. Some hierarchical theories of authority attribute legitimacy, the right to rule, to a divine source. The belief in a natural, divinely ordained, hierarchical order in the cosmos was used to justify the divine rights of kings and a rigidly stratified society.[76] Those who describe Confucian societies as "hierarchical" often acquiesce consciously or unconsciously in these associations. David Keightley traces the concern for hierarchy in Confucian political culture to the practice of ancestral worship in the Shang dynasty. The nature and functioning of relationships that the Shang postulated as being basic in ancestral worship influenced the development of political culture in Zhou and later times. Keightley argues that "a natural acceptance of such a hierarchical yet nurturing relationship between generations legitimized superior and subordinate relationships among the living as well as the dead."[77] Many other scholars share the view that belief in a religious hierarchy justifies social hierarchy in Confucianism.

The Chinese religious hierarchy of the ancestors differs from the cosmic hierarchy of Judeo-Christian medieval religion. In the latter, the Creator is radically separate from the created hierarchy; the ranking principle is an external imposition and therefore not subject to change, unless the Creator himself changes it. The supreme Shang divinity, *di* 帝, for all of his power (and it is not clear if he is omnipotent), is not the divine creator.[78] The ranking of ancestors who were worshipped is a continuation, not just a projection, of actual social stratification among them when alive. The latter is simply taken for granted rather than justified by divine creation. The ranking principle is not fixed and externally imposed; it is contingent and subject to changes when the world changes. This applies even to the hierarchy among the ancestors or spirits whose respective ranks depend in part on their "performance," as witnessed in the achievements of their living descendents.

Beyond ancestor worship, scholars have argued persuasively that transcendence characteristic of Western cosmology is contrary to the correlative thinking of Chinese thought, and to a logic, embedded in the classical Chinese language, that "divides down" rather than "includes up." Individual things do not "exist"; rather, the world "has" them, and many nouns are mass nouns out of which particular things must be distinguished either grammatically or contextually.[79] There is one realm, not two, from which human discourse makes distinctions between the ideal and the actual, the human and the nonhuman, without separating them. These distinctions are made for specific purposes that do not imply metaphysical or ontological claims. Hall and Ames, Xu Fuguan, Tang Junyi, Xiong Shili, and Lao Siguang are among those who argue that *tian* 天, with important religious connotations, usually translated as "heaven," does not exist separate and prior to the human world; it does not create or unilaterally determine the human world.[80]

The traditional view of the cosmos as a stratified order includes a principle of spontaneous change; the cosmos is not ordered by a transcendent principle but is self-generating and self-sustaining (*ziran* 自然). This difference in religious and cosmological beliefs is among the reasons for eschewing the term *hierarchy* in discussing social stratification or inequality in Chinese thought. Without the same associations of transcendence, inflexibility of social stratification and persistence of inequalities are contingent rather than theologically or metaphysically necessary.

It is vital to the argument for Confucian democracy to offer an understanding of Confucian community that accommodates the differentiation required for its harmonious functioning without being necessarily anti-democratic. Such an alternative is available, and it includes a conception of equality that also could be found in Dewey's philosophy. Though some view equality as a conditional or an instrumental value in liberal democracy, Dewey considers equality one of the meanings of democracy (L7.148). But democracy does not preclude inequality of functional differentiation, or recognition of excellence and deference to it in any specific area. Ideal Confucian community, which is not to be identified with historical Chinese society, is not a hierarchical order but a differentiated order. This is not to deny that ranking, distinction between superior and inferior or between better and worse, or inequality of power is part of the differentiation required in such a community. What it denies is that such ranking has to be so totalistic that if one is superior, one is superior always and in all things, that it has to be so inflexible that one is born into a fixed place in the rigid social order and must live one's life as prescribed by one's position with no possibility of change. Both inequality and equality in the differentiated order of a Confucian community are relative rather than absolute. Such a community distributes respect, power, goods and services, and so on *proportional* to the degree that each individual meets the criteria ethically relevant to what is to be distributed.

In Europe, theories of natural/divine hierarchy, which abound from antiquity through the Middle Ages, coexist with theories of equality. Initially, equality often formed part of the myth of a lost Golden Age or Garden of Eden, or it was treated as an impossible ideal. From the fourteenth century, it began to be applied as a standard to evaluate institutions, and it came to justify a doctrine that based the legitimacy of authority on consent. As Nicolas of Cusa argued in *De Concordantia Catholica*, "if men are by nature equal in power and equally free, the properly ordered authority of one who is naturally equal in power can only be established by choice and consent of the others, and also law is constituted by consent." Later, original human equality became central to the classical liberal theory of government. For John Locke, "men being, as has been said, by nature, all free, equal, and independent, no one can be put out of this estate, and subjected to political power of another, without his own consent."[81]

On rare occasions, Locke allows for development in equality by admitting that children "are not born in this full state of *Equality*, though they are born to it," but the overall effect of his thought stresses equality as an original possession, part and parcel of an original, universal, and essential human nature. Locke's legacy remains in the continued attempts to ground arguments for equality as a moral norm on claims that human beings *are* equal in some sense. One of the building blocks of John Rawls's political liberalism, for example, is a conception of persons being free and equal in possessing two moral powers to the requisite degree.[82] To Dewey, such approaches are misguided, since human beings are not born with ready-made selves. Any qualities that a person possesses at birth become ethically significant only when they become part of her character through her interaction with the environment. Dewey's view of human nature as a product of experience leads him to reject the view of equality as an original possession. Equality is "moral, a matter of justice socially secured, not of physical or psychological endowment" (M13.299). In Dewey's view, equality "is not a natural possession but is a fruit of the community when its action is directed by its character as a community" (L2.330).

Given the similarity in understanding persons as always in the making, not ready-made, it comes as no surprise that the equality a Confucian democracy values would resemble Dewey's in being a product of experience rather than a natural possession. One discerns in Confucius' teachings a similar emphasis on what develops through experience instead of what one is born with. Confucius asserts neither an original human nature that justifies treating everybody the same nor innate differences that justify rigidly classifying people into masters and slaves, good or bad, capable or otherwise. *Xing* 性, usually translated as "human nature," is one of the subjects that Confucius seldom discusses with his students (*Analects* 5.13). The only passage in the *Analects* on the subject often has been cited as evidence that Confucius values equality: "Men are close to one another by nature; they diverge as a result of repeated practice" (*Analects* 17.2). But the passage only suggests that human beings resemble one another, not that they are the same. Close (*jin* 近) is not equal. More important, the emphasis is not on original endowment. *Xing* does not refer to some unchanging human essence; it is more "natural tendencies or dispositions" than "nature." Change is implied in its meaning. Natural tendencies are ethically significant only in conjunction with their development through practice. What interests Confucius more is what people become through practice, hence, his lifelong commitment to personal cultivation. He is more concerned with whether a person is doing her best to become better at any point in time than with what she was at birth.

After Confucius, *xing* became the subject of a persistent controversy in Confucianism. Confucius says nothing about whether *xing* is good or bad; Mencius insists that it is good, but Xunzi insists that it is bad. The Mencian theory often has been seen as claiming that men are equal in possessing moral potential.[83] To persuade rulers that it is not too difficult for them to govern ethically, Mencius insists that every human being has the beginnings of what constitutes ethical conduct: authoritative conduct (*ren* 仁), appropriateness (*yi* 義), ritual practice (*li* 禮), and wisdom (*zhi* 智) (*Mencius* 3.6/18/4). Does possessing these ethical beginnings make everyone *equally human*? Perhaps. But equality is not necessary for his purpose, thus all Mencius needs to argue is that everyone is capable of ethical behavior, not that they are equally capable, and not that this ability makes them ethically equal.

Even the claim that "All men can become a Yao or Shun" does not imply equality, except a purely formal one (*Mencius* 12.2/62/9). As Xunzi points out with his distinction between *ke* 可 and *neng* 能, there is a difference between "can" as a modal possibility and "can" as an actual ability, and Mencius' claim is plausible with reference only to the former.[84] When Mencius says that sages and the people are *lei* 類 (usually translated as "of a kind"), he is claiming a family resemblance (*xiangsi* 相似) rather than equality in the sense of sameness.[85] Besides all of these reasons for caution in attributing a claim of natural equality to Mencius, such a claim is also misleading, because even if it is valid, natural equality does not play the role that it plays in the Western discourse on equality: it does not justify treating everybody equally. Munro, who thinks that early Confucians believe in natural equality, points out that it does not imply evaluative equality.[86] People are treated according to the results of their personal cultivation and the probability of further improvement, which are not equal. It is difficult to persuade a Confucian that one whose conduct is unethical is nevertheless equal to another whose conduct is ethical (*Analects* 9.23).

It appears that Dewey's argument, that equality is a product of experience that is valuable, offers a better strategy when it comes to arguing for equality as a value in Confucian democracy. Equality has to be fostered deliberately by individuals acting together to change social arrangements so that they would produce equality. What kind of equality should be fostered? Radical egalitarians view all social inequalities as unnecessary and unjustifiable, and should be eradicated. Berlin points out that such an extreme doctrine requires that "everything and everybody should be similar as possible to everything and everybody else"; it is doubtful if anybody has seriously desired to bring about such a society, or supposed it to be possible.[87] There certainly will be inequalities in a Confucian democracy as in a Deweyan democracy.

A key difference in the meaning of equality in Dewey's philosophy and that in other traditional theories is how far equality implies sameness. Locke found "nothing more evident than that creatures of the same species and rank, promiscuously born to all the same advantages of nature, and the use of the same faculties should also be equal amongst one another without subordination or subjection." Sameness figures prominently in Locke's conception of human equality, and it continues to do so in subsequent conceptions as long as the idea of a universal and an essential human nature remains widely accepted. Some contemporary liberals prefer to tone down the claim to one of similarity, or possession "to the requisite degree" of certain characteristics. Others may still agree with Hugo Bedau, that not to recognize that equality (though different from identity requiring sameness in *every* respect) implies sameness in some respects would risk blurring the distinction between justifiable and unjustifiable inequalities—it would render the concept of equality so vague and ambiguous that it would be almost meaningless.[88]

Bedau singles out Dewey for using "equality" in a vague and an ambiguous way. According to Dewey, "Equality denotes the unhampered share that each individual member of the community has in the consequences of associated action" (L2.329). Bedau objects to this understanding of equality, because "unhampered shares" do not imply *equal* shares. If equal shares imply giving the same quantity of food to a hungry person and to one who is full, or giving the same pay to one who does a shabby job and to one who does an excellent job—then Dewey is definitely not advocating this kind of equality. Bedau separates the questions of what equality is and whether it is desirable or justifiable. In contrast, Dewey is approaching the question as one about the *value* of equality. He treats equality as normative in meaning. From this perspective, Bedau's understanding of equality is one of "mechanical identity," which Dewey explicitly rejects (L2.329).

However, their differences are not quite as great as first appears. Bedau distinguishes equal distribution from equal treatment, and he points out that unequal distribution can nevertheless be equal treatment. Bedau believes, mistakenly, that Dewey is talking about equality of distribution, when actually the value of equality in Dewey's ideal community lies not in equal distribution but in equal treatment: everyone's needs and capacities to utilize are treated equally, so where the needs and capacities are unequal, the distribution of goods to satisfy the needs and capacities would be correspondingly unequal.

Equality for Dewey implies not sameness but uniqueness (L7.346). Equality as a meaning of democracy should be based on individuality, since democracy "denotes faith in individuality; in uniquely distinctive qualities in each normal human being; faith in corresponding unique modes of activity that create new ends, and willing acceptance of the established order entailed by the release of individualized capacities" (M13.297). Dewey objects to both the equality and the inequality that reduce individuals to "creatures of a class, a quantitative class which covers up truly individualized traits" (M13.295). Democratic equality is "distinction made universal" (M13.300). "It denotes effective regard for what is distinctive and unique in each, irrespective of physical and psychological inequalities" (L2.329–30). Effective regard means equal treatment vis-à-vis the uniqueness of each person.

Equality based on unique individuality denies the existence of "common and quantitative standards." It therefore cannot be based solely on legal, political, and economic arrangements that are classificatory, concerned only with uniformities and statistical averages (M13.299). It may seem highly impractical to cater to an extreme degree of uniqueness, but the ideal as regulative serves to remind us of the imperfection of all existing social arrangements and the need for flexibility and constant improvement. The law is one such social arrangement. Dewey criticizes the traditional individualistic interpretation of equality as "equality before the law" which is, in his view, inadequate for genuine democracy (L7.335). But the remedy is not to do without laws altogether; laws and other social arrangements should be designed and used to secure substantive "equality of opportunity" which, according to Dewey, was the basis of the American democratic tradition (L11.168).

Dewey does not mean by "equality of opportunity" what contemporary philosophical and political discourse means by it. It is not equal access to the same jobs, same education, same health care, same protection by law, and so on. It means that each person has the opportunities that fit his or her unique set of needs and capacities; since people are different, the opportunities required in each case would be different rather than the same. A society fosters equality of opportunity by "establishing the basic conditions through which and because of which every human being might become all that he was capable of becoming" (L11.168). That is, democratic equality is equality of opportunity for growth (L11.219). In distributive terms, it means that resources and goods should be distributed based on needs and capacities that contribute to growth.

There is evidence of a comparable view of distribution in early Confucianism. In Confucius' view, a good ruler of a state or head of a household "does not worry that his people are poor, but that wealth is inequitably distributed (*bujun* 不均)" (*Analects* 16.1). Simon Leys translates *bujun* as "inequality." Other translations include "ill-apportioned" (Arthur Waley) and "uneven distribution" (D. C. Lau).[89] It is highly unlikely that Confucius would recommend equal shares (i.e., same quantity) and more likely that the shares should be proportional to some ethically acceptable criteria. One such acceptable criterion is need, since the first responsibility of a government is to satisfy its people's needs (*Analects* 12.7). "Exemplary persons help out the needy; they do not make the rich richer" (*Analects* 6.4). Confucius disapproves of the extravagance of the powerful at the expense of others (*Analects* 12.9). He goes so far as to disown his student, Ranyou, for adding to the coffers of the House of Ji, which was already richer than the Duke of Zhou.[90] In terms of educational needs, Confucius does not discriminate between the rich and the poor (*Analects* 7.7). His students include nobles and commoners. "In instruction, there is no such thing as social classes" (*Analects* 15.39). His only criterion for accepting a student is that the applicant be keen to learn. This does not mean, however, that his students all get the same education. It is quite clear from the *Analects* that Confucius varies his instruction according to the needs and abilities of the students.

Other than needs, distribution also is justified by abilities. Regarding the question, "Who should govern?," Confucius is seen as replacing an aristocracy of birth with a meritocracy of ethical achievement. Only one with the abilities to discharge the responsibilities of a position should be allowed to occupy it. Both Confucius and Mencius frequently reiterate the importance of appointing to political office those who are worthy of it.[91] Though for centuries, Confucians never explicitly questioned the hereditary monarchy, Mencius' discussion of how the sage-kings Yao and Shun both were not succeeded by their own sons because there was someone more worthy in each case is suggestive (*Mencius* 9.6/49/3). The meritocratic tendencies of Confucianism are most evident in its influence on the Chinese examination system. Though not without its imperfections, the imperial civil service examinations opened up a route to office by merit and contributed significantly to social mobility as well as assured imperial China of a civil administration that was the envy of the premodern world.[92]

Meritocracy and the absence of any beliefs in original nature determining one's merit imply that an ideal Confucian community must ensure that everyone will have a chance of rising to the highest office (the sage-king Shun himself was a commoner). Examinations may be useful in identifying those most fit for office, but they cannot replace actual participation in making decisions affecting the community. Each person participates in contributing to social inquiries according to her abilities and in benefiting from the inquiries according to her needs. An ideal Confucian community must therefore provide everyone with opportunities to participate, though not the same kind or same degree of participation.

Dewey's view of equality of participation is not entirely different. He believes that a person grows through participating in a community, in cooperative inquiries that construct common goods. What he says about school education and enlightenment may be applied to growth in general: "every individual becomes educated [i.e., grows] only as he has an opportunity to contribute something from his own experience, no matter how meager or slender that background of experience may be at a given time; . . . enlightenment [i.e., growth] comes from the give and take, from the exchange of experiences and ideas" (L13.296). As a process of education, of growth, democracy requires open and extensive participation, "without which individuals cannot come into full possession of themselves nor make a contribution, if they have it in them to make, to the social well-being of others" (L13.296). As a faith in individuality, democracy recognizes that growth, personal or communal, is uniquely distinctive in each individual. Hence, in participatory terms, equality of opportunity means that each should participate according to his needs and abilities that would contribute to his own and the community's growth; it does not mean having opportunity to the same type or degree of participation.

Philosophical similarities notwithstanding, in different practical contexts, significant differences emerge between the Confucian meritocratic view of participation and Dewey's democratic view of participation. Given a society that historically has been rigidly stratified, the language of meritocracy fosters elitist tendencies that more often than not underestimate both the needs and abilities of those in the lower social strata. In a society wherein the public ethos explicitly rejects historical social stratifications, the language of democracy, by requiring that any inequalities be justified rather than taking them for granted, is more favorable to participation by those from lower social strata. To compensate for its pernicious historical associations, Confucian democracy would have to be more self-consciously critical of existing inequalities to ensure that only those fulfilling its philosophical ethical standards are permitted; it also must avoid going to the opposite extreme of adopting a hostile attitude toward all inequalities, even deference to excellence.

If equality means distribution and participation based on needs and abilities, then as needs and abilities change, so should the distribution and participation. This is, however, only one aspect of the flexibility required for a social order to be differentiated rather than hierarchical. Dewey's democracy recognizes the need for inequality in terms of functional differentiation, of differentiated growth. It rejects rigid hierarchies that use a single set of fixed, and often arbitrary, qualities to determine all issues of distribution and participation. In a hierarchical society, who gets what always depends on a ranking system based on "an idea of abstract, universal superiority and inferiority," which Dewey considers an absurdity (M13.296).

Any judgment of superior and inferior must be specific to a situation. It is meaningless to ask if a person is superior or inferior without specifying superior and inferior in *what?* "One person is superior in one particular respect and inferior in some other to many others" (L7.346; M12.297). A superior business executive may be an inferior parent, or someone superior to you at tennis now may become inferior later if you improve your skill more rapidly than she. Empirically, superiority in one area is sometimes related to superiority in other areas. But this should be determined through empirical investigation, not asserted as some kind of a priori truth. Moreover, such relations are always contingent and subject to change. One's superiority in a specific area justifies one having more of some resources or goods only if such distribution contributes to growth (e.g., talent in mathematics and admission to a mathematics Ph.D. program). There is no superiority that justifies a higher entitlement to all resources and goods.

A Confucian meritocracy is a differentiated order based on ethical criteria. It is not a totalistic hierarchy in which distribution questions are decided by a single criterion: ethical accomplishment. The criterion of ethical accomplishment is not a unitary standard but should be flexibly understood according to the specific circumstances of each situation. Furthermore, although Confucianism considers the ethical perspective relevant to all areas of life, this should not be understood in either a reductionist or a totalistic manner. That the performance of a company president is not independent of ethical considerations does not mean that these are the only relevant considerations for evaluating her performance. Confucius is concerned specifically with government as an ethical endeavor; he seeks solutions to the related problems of "How should a person live?" and "How should people live together?" Living together harmoniously requires a differentiated order in which resources and goods should be distributed according to the needs and abilities relevant to each situation. That one should have more of something in one situation does not imply that one should have more of everything in every situation. The ethical criterion in a Confucian differentiated order functions rather like Dewey's criterion of growth: which needs and abilities are relevant to a distribution and participation question depends on the contribution to personal and communal growth.

In a Confucian meritocracy, the distribution of political power and social prestige, though based on merit, is not a reward for abilities. As Xunzi points out, social distinctions are made to prevent chaos that would be to everyone's disadvantage. The purpose of a differentiated order is to satisfy as many as possible, not to satisfy the capable more than others (*Xunzi* 9/39/11). The more capable does not, therefore, deserve more. One's position only entitles one to what is required to discharge one's responsibilities. Ritual forms of deference toward those in superior positions, for example, are not simply for personal gratification but have the communicative function of recognizing the authority of those positions and thereby subjecting the occupants to evaluation by making them more visible to others. One would be less concerned about how much better one's boss is if one is not expected to show deference. The greater the deference shown to an individual, the higher the standard she is expected to meet. In terms of material goods, those in higher positions are not automatically entitled to more because of their position. What is sufficient for the people should be sufficient for the ruler (*Analects* 12.9). Some Confucians take it farther. As Song Confucian Fan Zhongyan puts it so eloquently, an exemplary person must "be the first to worry over what worries the world, the last to enjoy what the world enjoys."[93]

EQUALITY IN HUMAN RELATIONS

We have been looking at equality in the context of societies and communities. We shall extend our exploration to the micro level of human relations. In human relations, equality does not mean that each gets the same thing in the same amount from the other. The parties in a relationship benefit from it more because of difference than sameness (L7.346). What a child needs and gets from her parent is different from what a parent needs and gets from her child. Dewey calls this equality "qualitative equality" in contrast to "quantitative equality". A comparison of quantity is relevant only when the same quality is in question. Since what the parties in a relationship give and receive are qualitatively different, the question of quantitative comparison does not arise. Qualitative equality involves a form of reciprocity. "When children are *active*, when they give as well as receive, the lives of parents are fuller and richer because of what they receive from their children as well as because of what they put forth" (L7.346). This reciprocity is not to be understood as "repaying" what one has received. What is given cannot be treated as repayment, because it is to be evaluated based on the current receiver's needs and capacity and on what would benefit her the most, rather than on the nature of what has been given before or what is expected in the future. Furthermore, the exchange should be spontaneous (but not necessarily unthinking) rather than calculative.

This kind of reciprocity has an important place in the Confucian view of human relationships. Instead of reciprocity, Hall and Ames prefer to speak of "parity" in Confucian relations: overlap of one's multiple relations enables one to give and receive comparable degrees of deference or benefits, since in some relations, one gives more than one receives, but the reverse is true in other relations. They argue that even Confucian friendship is "a one-directional relationship in which one extends oneself by association with one who has attained a higher level of realization."[94] We certainly should be wary of any comparison with equality in Western views of friendship that understands equality in terms of sameness. But in Confucian relations, there could nevertheless be qualitative equality, so that each benefits from the other in some respects appropriate to their different needs and abilities (i.e., reciprocity in the Deweyan sense). Confucius remarks that he expects a student, on showing one corner, to return with the other three (*Analects* 7.8). In doing so, a student, in learning, may teach the teacher something as well. In a friendship where one is ethically more accomplished than the other, there is reciprocity in that when one teaches, one also learns.

Critics of Confucian relations often single out the idea of the "three mainstays (*sangang* 三綱)" which, according to its harshest critics, had turned Chinese society into a society of the "three tyrannies" by rulers, fathers, and husbands. This idea, often interpreted as rendering absolute the inequality of power in the relations between rulers and ministers, fathers and sons, and husbands and wives undoubtedly had pernicious effects on Chinese society. However, this idea of Han origin deviates from early Confucian thought.[95] According to Yu Ying-shih, at least one Han thinker suggested that the Confucianism that Han Wudi 漢武帝 was so keen to adopt owed more to legalism than to early Confucianism. Subsequent practices that have been the targets of criticism were certainly close to the ideas in the *Han Feizi* 韓非子 of "three accordances (*sanshun* 三順)" and the "three services (*sanshi* 三事)," in which inequality is permanently fixed, so that relations are hierarchical in the sense of imposing an absolute inequality of power and prestige. "Ministers serve rulers, sons serve fathers, and wives serve husbands. When the three are in accord, the world is in order; when these three are reversed, the world is in chaos. This is the constant way of the world; even enlightened kings and worthy ministers will not change it. Even when a ruler is despicable, his minister will not dare go against him."[96]

Han Feizi's view differs from his Confucian teacher, Xunzi, who believes that there are occasions when rulers and ministers may "change positions" without bringing chaos, and that ministers who remonstrate and disobey their erring rulers should be treasured (*Xunzi* 8/27/23, 13/64/5). Xunzi views relations as reciprocal, as does Mencius. "If a prince treats his subject as his hand and feet, they will treat him as their belly and heart. If he treats them as his horses and hounds, they will treat him as a stranger. If he treats them as mud and weeds, they will treat him as an enemy" (*Mencius* 8.3/41/1). For Confucius, sociopolitical order requires that rulers behave like rulers, ministers behave like ministers; fathers behave like fathers, and sons behave like sons (*Analects* 12.11; *Xunzi* 9/39/6). For all parties in any relationship there are ethical requirements, albeit each has a different set of requirements. The absorption of yin-yang thought by Han Confucians tends to fix the superiority of yang (identified with rulers, fathers, and husbands) and the inferiority of yin (identified with ministers, sons, and wives), but the emphasis is still on their complementing each other in harmonious union. As de Bary argues, the "three mainstays" for Han Confucians signify bonding rather than bondage—the parties in each relation mutually support one another.[97] This is unlike legalist understanding, that the inferior must always obey the superior; the superior has absolute power, while the inferior has no ethical claims against the superior.

The *Book of Rites* considers the husband-wife relation fundamental (though not always of the greatest weight, should relations conflict), since it is the basis of the family, which is the basis of the state.[98] This relation is governed by gender differences mentioned in the *Mencius*: "between men and women, there are differences (*bie* 別)." This often has been interpreted as meaning that men are always superior to women, and many ritual norms adopted through the centuries reinforced the devaluing of women from birth to death. Julia Ching points out that women generally fared better in those ages when Daoism and Buddhism, rather than Confucianism, were dominant in China.[99] Gender inequality is one of the key concerns of the May Fourth movement in its rejection of Confucianism. It remains an important challenge in any reconstruction of Confucianism today.

There is no escaping the fact that Chinese society has propagated some of the worst discriminations against women, but one should not assume that all women have been helpless victims throughout Chinese history. Despite the belief that women belong to the "inner quarter" and men "the outer," women were not completely excluded from economic production and public life. As a study by Li Yu-ning shows, their contribution to the economy, the arts, the military, and even politics was far from negligible.[100] At all levels of society, some Chinese women wielded considerable power. However, part of persisting sexism is the way many Confucians and others ignore the contributions of women and reject their power as illegitimate, an offense against social and cosmic order.

There is no evidence that Confucius questioned the prevailing patriarchal order of his day. The few references to women in the *Analects* traditionally have been understood in ways detrimental to gender equality. Some later Confucians were more blatantly sexist. Even educated women who wrote texts to educate other women often appeared to support patriarchy. The most famous of such texts is Han dynasty Ban Zhao's *Admonitions for Women*. Though modeled on this earliest extant work of the genre, later educational texts do reveal changes in women's roles and aspirations. While the *Admonitions* advocate an apparently submissive role for a woman in the household she marries into, the Tang dynasty's *Women's Analects* devotes a section on how to manage the household, and it is less submissive in tone.[101]

The *Women's Classic of Filiality*, also from the Tang dynasty, goes farther to argue that a wife is not required to obey a foolish or bad husband. Just as remonstrating ministers and sons are valued, so should Confucianism value remonstrating wives. One could even point to the *Book of Rites* acknowledging that husbands' leading/commanding position is based on their wisdom. The Ming dynasty's Empress Xu argues that women too can become sages.[102] Given the Confucian belief that wisdom and other ethical attributes owe more to practice than to original nature, there is no philosophical reason within the core of Confucianism to continue denying women this ultimate aspiration.

Sexist discriminatory practices are not inherent to Confucianism as a philosophy. Rather, its historical sexist elements reflect Confucianism's pragmatic adaptation to its social milieu. In a different kind of society, the sexual division confining the women's activities to the "inner quarters" is neither necessary nor appropriate to Confucianism itself. Henry Rosemont points out that though sexist practices could not have persisted without some intellectual support, the sexism revealed in Confucian texts is characteristic only of gender structure (patterns of organization), not of gender symbolism or gender identity. This opens up possibilities for reconstructing Confucianism in ways that a great many feminist thinkers today might endorse.[103]

There is an increasing corpus of work reevaluating women's role in Chinese history and rereading Chinese texts to find less sexist messages for today. Some scholars have focused on Ban Zhao's argument about the equal importance of educating both genders in the *Admonitions*, or view the text as a "survival manual" to help married women negotiate the family politics of large aristocratic households instead of as an apology for patriarchy.[104] At the start of the twenty-first century, the authors of *The Sage and the Second Sex* attempt to revitalize Confucianism by finding within it the conceptual flexibility to embrace notions of male-female equality. In their contribution to this volume, Hall and Ames suggest that in valuing both feminine and masculine characteristics, and in some cases giving the former priority, Confucianism has something distinctive to teach us about how to achieve real gender equality.[105] I have nothing substantial to add to these works yet, though much remains to be done in this area. My own effort at ridding Confucianism of its sexist bias in this work is limited to using the feminine pronouns for exemplary persons, authoritative persons, and sages mentioned in Confucian texts as a test of how far we could reconstruct Confucianism in the direction of gender equality.

What kind of gender equality could a Confucian democracy accommodate? Our earlier discussion shows that any equality based on sameness would have no place in a Confucian democracy. The gender differences noted by Mencius should not be understood rigidly; they are functional differences that should vary according to contexts. In any situation, there could be tasks and roles more suited to one gender than the other. The distribution of tasks and roles according to gender should, however, be determined through cooperative inquiry in which both genders participate, and not dogmatically prescribed. This is where Confucian democracy differs from previous attempts to justify sexist practice by gender differences: what is most appropriate for a woman in any situation is determined neither by some essential female nature nor by others entirely; she has a say in the outcome. Nor should there be any preconceptions that just because experience in the past reveals a general match between certain tasks and one gender that that match would work in every instance and for every member of that gender. While one may generalize that women are more nurturing and more suited to caring for the young or the aged, there are nevertheless some women who are less nurturing compared to some men. Gender differences should be flexibly understood as part of individuality, which is presupposed by Confucian and Deweyan equality.

Some Western feminists have questioned the earlier strategies of trying to gain for women what men have in terms of rights and opportunities. What many women need and want is not to be able to act or live like men but to live fulfilling lives on their own terms, to influence the decisions of the community to reflect their views of human fulfillment as well as men's views. Added to this belief that gender differences should not be denied in the attempt to prevent them from being used to oppress women is a growing awareness among an increasing number of women in Asian societies that cultural differences also should have a place in their continued fight for freedom and equality. Elizabeth Croll notices that women's studies in China have begun to emphasize the specifically Chinese sociopolitical context of contemporary Chinese feminism and to demarcate its differences from Western feminism.[106] A Confucian democracy would have to include a Confucian feminism based not on equality as sameness but on equality as individuality.

Chapter 4

Ethico-Political Orders

The distinctive views of individuals and communities explored in the last two chapters have important implications for Dewey's and Confucius' conceptions of the relationship between ethics and politics. The inseparability of individual and social/communal means that ethics and politics also are inseparable. Ethics answers the question "How should one live?" Politics answers the question "How should we live together?" The questions may be distinct, but the answers involve one single ethico-political order in which individuals live together in harmony and personal fulfillment. This chapter explores how this view of ethics and politics differs from that in the "procedural republic" which, according to Michael Sandel, is characteristic of existing liberal democracies. A Confucian community, in deviating from the liberal ideal of political neutrality to conceptions of the good, is similar to a Deweyan community. Despite being different from existing liberal democracies, a Confucian community can be democratic in a Deweyan sense.

The Political Domains of Procedural Republics

In both Dewey's and Confucius' thinking, ethics has a critical role in politics, and vice versa. It is a belief reflected in the very way they live their own lives.[1] In contrast, the politics of a procedural republic need not, and should not, concern itself with "how a person should live"; instead, it should ensure that each person has an equal opportunity to live life as she chooses, as long as that particular form of life does not interfere with a similar liberty for others. The chosen form of life does not have to be good since, as John Stuart Mill puts it, "the only purpose for which power can be rightfully exercised over any member of a civilized community against his will is to prevent harm to others."[2] In a liberal democracy, a government should never impose a conception of the good life on its citizens.

The procedural republic asserts the priority of fair procedures over particular ends; its central idea is that government should be neutral toward the moral and religious views that its citizens espouse. In the deontological liberalism criticized by Sandel, this neutrality presupposes the primacy of justice (i.e., the right is prior to the good). Some might challenge this claim of neutrality on the grounds that liberalism already presupposes a particular moral view, and some ways of life require social conditions that are excluded by liberal frameworks of justice. However, this mistakes the nature of liberal tolerance. No society can include within itself all forms of life. As Berlin points out, "Some among the great goods cannot live together. That is a conceptual truth. We are doomed to choose, and every choice may entail an irreparable loss."[3] The most that could be hoped for is to minimize such losses, and liberalism, so its supporters argue, offers the best chances of doing so by accepting that there could be a large number of valid conceptions of the good instead of insisting on the validity of only one.

Rawls strengthens liberalism's claim to neutrality by arguing for a political liberalism centered on a political conception of justice. Conceptions of the good, moral or religious, belong not to political doctrines but to comprehensive doctrines. Political conceptions do not presuppose any one comprehensive doctrine, which "includes conceptions of what is of value in human life, as well as ideals of personal virtue and character, that are to inform much of our non-political conduct (in the limit of our life as a whole). . . . by definition, for a conception to be even partially comprehensive, it must extend beyond the political and include non-political values and virtues."[4] As a political conception, justice as fairness can be the focus of an overlapping consensus among diverse, reasonable, comprehensive doctrines. I shall argue that the separation of the political from the nonpolitical is tenuous at best; moreover, it is undermined by Rawls's requirement of an overlapping consensus instead of a *modus vivendi*.

Rawls identifies the political domain by two special features: it is neither voluntary, such as associations of various kinds, nor "affectional," such as the personal or familial.[5] It is the domain of what Kant described as man's "unsocial sociability," which binds him to those "whom he cannot bear, yet cannot bear to leave."[6] As an abstraction in political philosophy, it is undoubtedly possible to distinguish the political from the nonpolitical, but what is at issue is not the possibility of abstract distinction but how much experience can escape the constraints of a political conception of justice. How could we resolve the problems of political life effectively when we exclude the question of what constitutes a good life?

In Rawls's political liberalism, the political involves more than the institutions and procedures of government; it concerns social and economic, as well as political, institutions—that is, the basic structure of society, "understood as the way in which the major social institutions fit together into one system, and how they assign fundamental rights and duties and shape the division of advantages that arises through social cooperation. Thus the political constitution, the legally recognized forms of property, the organization of the economy, and the nature of the family all belong to the basic structure." If what makes the basic structure the primary subject of justice is because it "shapes the way the social system produces and reproduces over time a certain form of culture shared by persons with certain conceptions of their good," and is the source of "the inequalities in life prospects between citizens that arise from starting social position, natural advantages, and historical contingencies," then little falls outside of this domain.[7]

One may argue on Rawls's behalf that just because an institution, the family, for example, is part of the basic structure it does not preclude bonds of shared interests, aims, and affection from contributing to its functioning; what makes it part of the basic structure is the need for limits set by public conceptions of justice in the event that common interests, aims, and affection could not provide a solution to problems. But might setting such limits not undermine the importance of those bonds of community? When issues in a family could not be resolved based on shared interests and aims, and bonds of affections, the political conception of justice provides the most obvious tool to solve the problem; its solutions would not, however, repair those broken bonds. On the contrary, they blind the parties to alternatives that could reconstitute the family as something more than a system of fair cooperation, more than a unit expressing our unsocial sociability. Even without the breakdown of communal bonds, a concern with justice could undermine those very bonds themselves. The likelihood of this happening increases with Rawls's claim of the priority of political values over nonpolitical ones. Given the great weight of political values of justice, even when shared interests and aims, or bonds of affection, exist, if the two conflict, it would seem right to follow the course of justice. "A reasonable and effective political conception may bend comprehensive doctrines toward itself."[8]

Rawls does not advocate pluralism per se but pluralism of reasonable doctrines. For a comprehensive doctrine to be reasonable in a democratic society, its political values must be liberal, since it is only by endorsing "a family of reasonable *liberal* conceptions of justice," one of which (or a mix thereof) effectively regulates the basic structure, that comprehensive doctrines can share an overlapping consensus. Reasonable liberal political values that sustain an overlapping consensus presuppose a political conception of the person as free and equal, and a political conception of society as a fair system of cooperation. These conceptions differ from those in comprehensive liberalism only in their scope, which excludes the nonpolitical.[9]

Is it possible to restrict these conceptions to the political domain and maintain different (e.g., communitarian) conceptions of person and society in the nonpolitical domains? According to Rawls, the liberal political conceptions of society as a fair system of cooperation and of citizens as free and equal are implicit in the existing political culture of liberal democracies. It is questionable how far a liberal political culture can be sustained if the wider background culture is not liberal. Rawls claims that "political democracy depends for its enduring life upon the *liberal background culture* that sustains it."[10] On a few occasions, however, he also links the "background culture" to comprehensive doctrines in contrast to the political. We may overlook these minor textual inconsistencies if not for the fact that Rawls's account of the development of an overlapping consensus also undermines the separation of the political from the nonpolitical.

Rawls uses three comprehensive doctrines in his model of an overlapping consensus: a religious doctrine with an account of free faith leading to principles of toleration, a comprehensive moral doctrine such as Kant's or Mill's, and a partially comprehensive doctrine, where values in different areas of life are not systematically unified but balanced either in groups or singly, in particular cases. Rawls distinguishes an overlapping consensus from a modus vivendi. The latter lacks the moral force and depth of the former, in which "those who affirm the political conception will not withdraw their support of it should the relative strength of their view in society increase and eventually become dominant."[11] Contra Rawls, the political conception by the first and last kinds of doctrines can be no more than modus vivendi if the nonliberal, nonpolitical values are to survive in the long term. Furthermore, the more likely scenario would be for the liberal political values and presuppositions to undermine the nonliberal, nonpolitical values and presuppositions and recast the latter in their own image, if the political has the kind of moral breadth and depth that Rawls claims.

Religions support liberal political conceptions of justice, because this allows their believers the greatest room to practice their religion freely under conditions of conflicting religious beliefs. From a religious point of view, there is nothing inherently valuable or right about such political conceptions; were it possible to convert everyone without violence and bloodshed by adopting some other political conceptions, a religious believer would consider it right to do so. W. H. Auden remarked, "The only reason the Protestants and Catholics have given up the idea of universal domination is because they've realized they can't get away with it."[12] The support for liberal political conceptions is thus a compromise born of the inability to convert everyone else to one religion without violence and a fear of being converted by force. Some might argue that religious tolerance goes farther and is rooted in the recognition that genuine religious conversion cannot be achieved by force (hence, the link between *free faith* and tolerance). This view, which places individual will and conscience at the center of religious belief, is itself distinctly liberal, linking reason and thought to individual autonomy and valuing actions only insofar as they are autonomous.

Where religions lack such liberal underpinnings, their support for liberal political arrangements is based on the knowledge that it is not advantageous to violate the political arrangements under current circumstances, but should conditions change, they would pursue their goal at the expense of other religions and consider it morally right to do so. The agreement to support the political conception is therefore only a modus vivendi. Rawls thinks otherwise, only because he implicitly shares Kant's view that morality, in terms of the right, must come before religion, whereas in most religions, even tolerant ones, morality is derivative and secondary. Therefore, the only religions that would support liberal political conceptions to the extent required for an overlapping consensus are those that have among their basic tenets a belief in the liberal doctrine of individual autonomy.

In Rawls's account of how a modus vivendi may develop into an overlapping consensus, with a constitutional consensus as an intermediate stage, the partially comprehensive doctrine (i.e., a pluralist view) plays an important part, since a "certain looseness in our comprehensive views, as well as their not being fully comprehensive, may be particularly significant" in the process.[13] The looseness in the way different kinds of values fit together allows liberal political values to be combined with nonliberal, nonpolitical values, but contrary to Rawls's belief, this "looseness" is not only required initially, it is a necessary condition to sustain the "combination," forcing on us a growing compartmentalization in our experience. There is a limit to how far we could compartmentalize our lives without undermining our mental health, let alone our moral perspective. If liberal political values also are moral values—and Rawls claims that they are—then they must be made coherent with nonpolitical moral values.

Rawls recognizes the need for values in a pluralist view "to be balanced . . . in particular kinds of cases." To talk of balance gives the impression that which values have greater weight depends on the particular case. However, this does not appear to be so given Rawls's claim that political values are supposed to override other values when there is conflict; it seems more likely that liberal political values are dominant values that set the order for other values. Reflective resolution of moral conflicts is part of a broader ethical reflection that tends to encompass "the whole of life." When asking myself what I should do in a particular situation where both political and nonpolitical values are relevant, I do not simply take the perspective of what kind of citizen I am, even if I give overriding importance to the political; the very apportioning of relative moral weights to the political and nonpolitical raises the question of how being the kind of *citizen* I am fits into being the kind of *person* I am.

Our nonpolitical values cannot but be transformed after being tested in conflicts with political values, given sufficient frequency and intensity of such conflicts. Because of the tendency in ethical reflection to find a coherent perspective for the whole of life, beyond a certain point, the overriding moral weight given to the political will affect the nonpolitical, even without any direct conflicts. Assigning a pregiven dominance to certain values restricts ethical reflection; only when there is the possibility of the mutual modification of political and nonpolitical values would ethical reflection be adequate.

For communitarians, political liberalism remains as problematic as comprehensive liberalism. We have discussed communitarian dissatisfactions with the liberal conceptions of the person and society; these conceptions cannot be restricted to the political domain, given the tenuous nature of the proposed separation of the political from the nonpolitical. Attempting such separation leads people to compartmentalize their lives, thereby disintegrating their experience. It also engenders a sense of helplessness, and it may eventually give way to despair, given the widespread consequences that the political has on each person's life and on the lives of local communities. To avoid unraveling the moral fabric not only of communities but also of personal experience without the state imposing a unitary morality on everybody from the top down, a more integrated approach toward the relation between politics and ethics is required. We shall find such an approach in the thought of Confucius and John Dewey.

ETHICO-POLITICAL ENDS

Dewey does not understand the political primarily in terms of structures that "assign fundamental rights and duties and shape the division of advantages that arises through social cooperation."[14] These structures are relevant only insofar as they affect the process of human beings living in association, which is Dewey's starting point and focus. In associated living, human acts have consequences, some of which are perceived. Their perception leads to subsequent efforts to control action to secure some consequences and to avoid others. Whenever two or more persons interact, so that communication occurs and reflection becomes possible, we have a social situation. Politics is a subset of the social domain. It is concerned with the control of a specific kind of consequence: extensive, enduring, and indirect. A consequence is indirect when it affects those not directly involved in a transaction and is not taken into consideration by those who are involved.

Indirect consequences can sometimes become direct consequences, for example, through negotiation, so that those involved in the original transaction take those consequences into consideration, thereby expanding the scope of the transaction to include those affected. Solving the problem of indirect consequences in this way becomes more difficult and at some point practically impossible as the consequences become more extensive. When indirect consequences cannot be dealt with directly and require regulating by other means, they become political issues. A common interest in regulating such indirect consequences calls a public into existence, and the organization of a public forms a state. By "state," Dewey does not mean a sovereign nation-state but rather social arrangements with positions of authority, in which some issue commands that others view as legitimate and then obey. Those who issue legitimate commands are representative officers who comprise a government. "A public articulated and operating through representative officers is the state; there is no state without a government, but also there is none without the public" (L2.277). Politics comprises the activities of organizing and organized publics, the activities of states.

What Rawls calls the "basic structure" is not irrelevant to Dewey's view of political domain, but Dewey eschews an overemphasis on structure in his understanding of the political, because in his view, such an approach is too preoccupied with form at the expense of content and mistakes contingent products of history for essential forms. This is one of Dewey's criticisms of theories of *political* democracy. "Politically, democracy means a form of government which does not esteem the well-being of one individual or class above that of another; it is a system of laws and administration which ranks the happiness and interests of all as upon the same plane, and before whose laws and administrations all individuals are alike, or equal. . . . But political democracy is not the whole of democracy. . . . It can be effectively maintained only where democracy is social—where, if you please, it is moral" (M10.137; L7.348). It is the way human beings live in association that gives content to political forms. Associated living becomes human only when it becomes reflective, when it is guided by intelligent inquiry and regulative ideals. For democracy to have content as well as form, it has to become social and ethical.

For Dewey, democracy is the ideal in politics; at the same time, it is an ethical ideal. Politically, it guides our answers to the problem of how the common interest of the public in controlling extensive, enduring, and indirect consequences of transactions might be taken care of. This problem must be solved experimentally, and the formal criteria for evaluating the success of various experiments are the degree of the organization of the public attained and the degree in which its officers are so constituted as to perform their functions of caring for public interests (L2.256). These formal criteria are, however, insufficient on their own to evaluate political experiments. How are the public interests to be defined? How do we decide which indirect consequences need controlling through public action? What alternative consequences are desirable? What is needed is an ideal of practice that would provide ends-in-view for the public organizing itself experimentally. To find this ideal, we examine the formless, unorganized public.

Before any political organization, there are just human beings living in association. To organize, to form themselves into a public, a state, they need a shared ideal of associated living. "From the standpoint of an individual, it consists in having a responsible share according to capacity in forming and directing the activities of the groups to which one belongs and in participating according to need in the values which the groups sustain. From the standpoint of the group, it demands liberation of the potentialities of members of a group in harmony with the interests and goods which are common" (L2.327). This ideal of democracy, which is the ideal of community, answers not only the political question of how to organize the public but also the ethical question "How should one live?"—which is inseparable from the question "How should we live together?" Ethics is inseparable from politics, for it provides the content of political forms (L7.348).

Growth is the end in ethics and in politics. It provides the criterion for distinguishing the ethical quality of an act. The question finally at stake in any ethical situation is: What shall the agent become? (M5.194) Reflective morality broadens the scope of the ethical to include (potentially, at least) *all* actions. "Morals is not a theme by itself, because it is not an episode nor department by itself. It marks the issue of all the converging forces of life" (L5.275). A person's growth cannot occur in a social vacuum; her relations with others, social conditions, affect it, for better or for worse. "Individuals are free to develop, to contribute, and to share, only as social conditions break down walls of privilege and of monopolistic possession" (L7.348). Politics determines, in part, the nature of social conditions. All political institutions and political action determining social conditions should aim at contributing to the all-round growth of every member of society (M12.186). General well-being, the good life for all, which is the concern of politics, "demands the full development of individuals in their distinctive individuality. . . . Only when individuals have initiative, independence of judgment, flexibility, fullness of experience, can they act so as to enrich the lives of others and only in this way can a truly common welfare be built up" (L7.348).

Politics, when practiced well, and ethical living (i.e., a life of intellectual and moral growth) proceed together. Dewey's language may mislead us into thinking that he is claiming a mutual necessity that is a vicious circle: if politics is not practiced well, then one cannot live ethically. If one is not living ethically, then one cannot practice politics well. If this is what Dewey means, he contradicts himself when he insists that growth is possible, even when politics is far from good, "in the midst of conflict, struggle, and defeat" (M14.226). Individuals, starting from where they are, could change society as they change themselves. "We are not caught in a circle; we traverse a spiral in which social customs generate some consciousness of interdependencies, and this consciousness is embodied in acts which in improving the environment generate new perceptions of social ties, and so on forever" (M14.225).

Dewey sometimes refers to one thing being the "necessary condition" of another when "they are two names for the same fact" (L7.185). The most obvious interpretation would take this to be a case of logical entailment: politics practiced well and ethics are not two phenomena but one, so that one could say each is necessary for the other (one logically implies the other, and vice versa). However, more than logical entailment is at stake. The earlier objection of vicious circularity is based on an understanding of causality as an external relation; this is not in tune with Dewey's understanding of the continuity of experience. Politics practiced well and ethics are related, as are means and ends in *praxis*. Means are sometimes constitutive of ends, and viewed from different perspectives, means may become ends, and vice versa. It is in this practical sense that politics practiced well and ethics, like means and ends, "are two names for the same reality."[15]

Political participation is part of personal growth. A person grows when she becomes better at intelligently finding and using means to direct consequences, at reflecting critically on the nature of her ends-in-view, the meaning of her ideals—making them more inclusive, more enduring. Ends-in-view include regulating indirect consequences, and the means of achieving them often are political ones. A person functions better (i.e., grows) when she attains better control over, interacts better with, her environment—political participation is an important part of this endeavor. Ethical ends unify and expand a person's powers and interests, and Dewey argues that such ends are social ends (which includes political). "Human nature is developed only when its elements take part in directing things which are common, things for the sake of which men and women form groups—families, industrial companies, governments, churches, scientific associations, and so on" (M12.199). A person who focuses solely on her own needs and wishes is ethically stunted, since she fails to recognize the sociality of human beings, to reflect on the values and claims of this sociality.

The *kind* of self formed through action faithful to relations with others will be a fuller and broader self than one cultivated in isolation from or in opposition to the purposes and needs of others (L7.302). To grow ethically means making one's ends-in-view and ideals more inclusive of the well-being of others. What can be achieved in this regard by individual action, in private

transactions, is extremely limited in scope and in some cases totally ineffective. Dewey cites Jane Addams: "To attain personal morality in an age demanding social morality, to pride oneself upon the results of personal effort when
the time demands social adjustment is utterly to fail to apprehend the situation."[16] This failure is due to the fact that "the subject matter of moral inquiry
has been increasingly pushed out of the range of the concrete problems of economic and political inquiry" (L15.232). Excluding questions concerning conceptions of the good from the political domain renders both ethics and politics
inadequate and associated living unfulfilling for all.

DEWEY ON POLITICS IN ANCIENT CHINA

Given the resonance between Dewey's idea of growth and the Confucian idea
of personal cultivation, one would expect a fairly strong parallel in the roles of
these ideas in their views of the relation between politics and ethics. Before
we explore Confucian ethico-political ends and their resemblance to Dewey's,
we need to consider a potential obstacle in our comparison. In *The Public and
Its Problems*, while searching for the limits of the state, Dewey describes the
association in ancient China as too "narrow, close, and intimate" to be political (L2.262). His suspicion that China is a society without a state arises from
the belief that China has no middle ground between "the intimate and familiar propinquity group," the family, and "the remote and theocratic state." Traditionally, Western societies draw a clear distinction between the private and
the public along the line that separates the family from what lies outside of it.
(Locating the private/public division along the individual/social boundary is a
more recent development.) What is considered "family" has varied over time
and in different societies, with a tendency toward a narrower definition.
Though theories may hold up family relations as the ideal for other relations,
as in the brotherhood of man, the family/society divide remains clear in day-
to-day dealings.

In Chinese thinking, though *jia* 家 includes the Western "family," it has
never been restricted to that as we have seen in our earlier discussion of the
elasticity of the idea. Though their practice may be as far from the ideal as
Western practices from the "brotherhood of man," the Chinese idea of "the
world as one family (*tainxia yijia* 天下一家)" has much greater force, because
of the inherent porosity of *jia* as a group, and the less salient distinction
between the metaphorical and the literal and between the ideal and the practical. Philosophically, the various Confucian relations are closely integrated by
the Confucian ethical vision, but it is an exaggeration to think that "all virtues
are summed up in filial piety," even if it is an understandable claim, given the
overwhelming weight given to that particular virtue from the Han dynasty

onward. The Confucian idea of the five primary relations makes it clear that the claims the parties have on one another are different in each relation, even though comparisons may be made between nonfamily and family relations. It is interesting that Dewey mentions only four of the five cardinal relations in Confucian thought, leaving out the one that is overtly political, between rulers and ministers (L2.262). Political obedience in imperial China was not replaced by but built on personal loyalties and deference to elders (especially fathers). To justify imperial authoritarianism, state orthodoxy prescribes paternal authoritarianism which, however, is not part of Confucius' teaching. Xu Fuguan argues persuasively that Confucian familism, centered on love and concern for others, does not support authoritarianism, and that in practice it has even mitigated some of the excesses of Chinese authoritarianism; later distortions of Confucian thinking, due mostly to legalist influence through the *Classic of Filiality*, made familism a tool of despots.[17]

If we look at the political as being concerned with the regulation of extensive, enduring, and indirect consequences of actions, then there is no lack of the political in ancient China. Such consequences can occur at the level of the *jia*, which often is more of a clan than a family understood in modern Western terms, at village or town levels, as well as the entire country. While resorting to the law is a disgrace as it signifies a breakdown of ethical relations and an inability to repair it by ethical means, there is, historically, no lack of litigation in China. Confucius admits the need for penal codes, administrative injunctions, and courts to resolve disputes—however much he might wish for a community that could do without them—the means deliberately adopted to control those indirect consequences that call forth a public.[18]

The "state" during Confucius' time was smaller and therefore less remote than the imperial state that Dewey is talking about. Even after unification, it is doubtful if the Chinese state is quite as remote as Dewey implies. For many local Chinese communities, "the mountains are high and the emperor far away." What happened in the imperial capital might have little impact on the remote villages on the margins of the Chinese empire, but the imperial bureaucracy had more impact on the people's lives than Dewey recognizes. Officials appointed by the imperial government were sent to the remote areas. Even though they had a considerable amount of autonomy in the day-to-day running of their administration, they were ultimately answerable to the authority in the capital. Officials are not merely law enforcers. The magistrates, at least, also would collect taxes, initiate and supervise public works, play a leading role in certain communal rituals, and participate or preside over various other communal activities. They would report natural disasters and apply for aid from the central authorities and dispense the relief granted. If "officials are known but only to be shunned" completely, then it is because they do a poor job of taking care of what Dewey calls "public interests."

The state, "whose value lies in what it does *not* do," (L2.262) may be found in the notion of *wuwei* 無為 and, according to Confucius, this is how the sage-king, Shun, governed (*Analects* 15.5). Not even in Confucius' time, and certainly not since then, had such an achievement been repeated. Some would go farther and say that Shun himself is a myth, though an important myth in terms of establishing Confucian ethico-political norms. A *wuwei* state would still qualify as a state, despite its rare political form. Sometimes Dewey himself seems insufficiently aware of the potential of his reconstructed conception of the political. He remains too attached to the political forms familiar to him.

According to Peter Manicas, Dewey is hampered by the connotations of "states" as "legally defined entities claiming sovereignty and a monopoly of legitimate force. Each circumscribes an extended territory and a very large population."[19] In contrasting those who rule with those who are ruled, government usually implies dominion, legitimate domination of the rulers over the ruled. Dewey, however, takes "government" to mean "representative officers"—one holds a public office whenever one represents the public, when the public acts through a person. In this sense, a citizen-voter is an officer of the public, and part of government (L2.282). Dewey's concept of government undermines the traditional division between the rulers and the ruled. The function of public officers sanctions no legitimate domination. Coercion is not a required feature of Dewey's conception of the "state." Manicas argues that Dewey's liberalism and democratic philosophy are "more anarchist than communist *or* liberal," where anarchism means *anocracy*—government without domination.[20]

To fully appreciate Dewey's conceptual reconstruction, the political forms of social and ethical democracy are not to be equated with specific modes of government as we know it. Even assuming that democratic forms of government have to be "systems of laws and administration" might be allowing what *is* too much constraint over what *can be*. This is no mere utopian claim; the awareness of such a possibility is a safeguard against the facile assumption that the solution to every political problem must be some law or government agency or action. Dewey insists on the plurality of political forms, and he repeatedly cautions readers against prejudging which political forms would work best. Systems of laws and administration, governments as we know them, may appear necessary now, but that does not mean that they will always be necessary. "As far as political arrangements are concerned, governmental institutions are but a mechanism for securing to an idea channels of effective operation" (L2.325).

In Dewey's view, a frequent mistake of critics of democracy, such as Reinhold Niebuhr and Walter Lippmann, is taking the existing political form of democratic states as being somehow "essential," whereas for Dewey, it is to be transformed in an experimental process guided by a regulative ideal. To recover our sense of the promise and danger of democracy, we need to discard any fixation about current and known modes of government, something that

Dewey's philosophy attempts to do. "Possibly one can better gauge the effort required [for this recovery] if one tries the experiment of replacing "democracy" throughout Dewey's writing by the word 'anarchism.'"[21]

A Confucian *wuwei* state shows us an alternative political form that can realize Dewey's political ideal of anocracy: government without domination. In most Western views, political power is coercive, and laws are the most common means of controlling indirect consequences. According to Dewey, laws function as "dikes and channels so that actions are confined within prescribed limits, and in so far have moderately predictable consequences" (L2.268). For Confucius, ritual practice (social habit) would be a much better way of achieving the same objective. Political power need not lie in the hands of those who make and enforce laws; it functions better in the hands of those who, through their excellence, show the way to "taking others' concerns as one's own." Dewey considers "objective regulation" necessary for one to be reasonably sure of the effects of one's action on others besides those closely associated with us. In Confucius' view, the authoritative person performs this function. Her accomplishment in "taking others' concern as her own" is not purely affective, it also is cognitive.[22] A *wuwei* state is an organized public that has acquired the power (*de* 德) to use specific means (*li* 禮) to achieve specific ends of controlling indirect, extensive, and enduring consequences, so that there is ethico-political order. Not only is politics for Confucians far from being "submerged in morals," the ideal society, the Confucian community, is not an ethical achievement devoid of politics, it is an ethico-political achievement.

THE SAGE-KING: AN IDEAL IN QUESTION

Any misgiving that there is too drastic a difference between their conceptions of the political for a comparison of Dewey's and early Confucian views of the relation between ethics and politics is unwarranted. We shall see that there is remarkable resonance between Dewey's philosophy and early Confucianism in this respect. Discussions of the inseparability of politics and ethics in Confucianism often revolve around the notion of the inner-sage-outer-king (*neisheng waiwang* 內聖外王). This term is not of Confucian origin but comes from the *Zhuangzi* 莊子 (*Zhuangzi* 91/33/14). The Confucian appropriation of the notion appears to be widely accepted by the Song dynasty. According to the *Song History* and the *Records of Song and Yuan Scholars*, the prominent Song Confucian scholar, Cheng Hao (程顥, 1032–1085), praised another Confucian scholar, Shao Yong (邵雍, 1011–1077), for showing the "way of the inner-sage-outer-king." The association of sagehood and kingship, however, is of much older vintage. We find the term "*sage-king*" (*shengwang* 聖王) in the

Mencius (6.9/34/30). Ching traces this sage-king paradigm, uniting divine wisdom with human (especially political) efficacy, to the shamanic kings of antiquity (third or even fourth millennia b.c.), before the Shang and Zhou dynasties.[23]

Interpretations of how sagehood and kingship are related in Confucianism vary. A common view is that kingliness is the "outer manifestation" of sagehood. Sagehood must first be achieved, and then kingliness follows. Chen Xiyuan, analyzing the *Great Learning* passage regarding the process of ethical cultivation and bringing about sociopolitical order, argues persuasively that such an interpretation limits cultivation efforts to the first stage of the process of investigating things and events (*gewu* 格物) alone, with the rest following automatically in a kind of "domino effect." The process then becomes oversimplified and highly implausible. A more adequate interpretation is to view the ethical cultivation of the person as requiring "actualization" in terms of sociopolitical order at each stage and level of political engagement—family, state, and the world.[24]

Is sagehood necessary, sufficient, or both necessary and sufficient for kingship? The least demanding interpretation would be to claim that sagehood is necessary but not sufficient for kingship. This gets around the objection that sages are not always kings, but it still faces the obvious objection that kings are not always sages. One way of countering this is to differentiate between actual rulers and "true kings." While this distinction could be explicit in translating *wang* 王 as "true king," where the context indicates normative connotations, the ambiguity between descriptive and normative uses remains in the Chinese language, and it has undoubtedly contributed to the de facto ruling powers' appropriating the sage-king paradigm to convey normative prestige on a political domination they hold through coercive power rather than ethical excellence. Claiming that sagehood is necessary but not sufficient for kingship—and, furthermore, that kingship refers not to actual political rule but to normative fitness to rule—preserves the ideal while conceding the overwhelming difficulties involved in its realization. Just what is sufficient for kingship, and for sagehood, for that matter, no one has ever given a satisfactory answer that could withstand the test of history, but perhaps the mistake lies in trying to find necessary and sufficient conditions.

The significance of the sage-king paradigm lies in its claim that only sages are *fit* to be kings. The paradigm has served an important purpose: it provides a norm by which to judge and criticize those in power, and it is not entirely without beneficial impact in the course of Chinese history.[25] However, Li Zehou considers the inner-sage-outer-king ideal obsolete, applicable only in a tribal society with a clan government. Between the collapse of the Zhou feudal system and the Song dynasty with its "moral metaphysics," there were many (Confucians?) with admirable political achievements who had no claims to sagehood. Li attributes the political failures of Confucians from the Song dynasty onward to their attempts to subordinate politics to their "pan-ethicism." Ching, while not rejecting the sage-king paradigm as no longer practical, agrees that there is an increasing divergence in the inner-sage and the outer-king, with the inner winning over the outer during the Song and Ming dynasties. She also points to a pernicious aspect in the sage-king ideal: preoccupation with it is in part responsible for the political apathy of the Chinese people, so that for centuries they "never expected more than a benevolent monarchy, or perhaps we should say, a benevolent despotism."[26]

If one claims unity rather than mere relatedness between sagehood and kingship, then the existence of one implies the existence of the other not simply in a logical sense but also in Dewey's "practical" sense. If there has been no true king in Chinese history, then there has been no sage either, and vice versa. The problem with realization, and hence the practicality of Confucianism in this respect, could be dealt with not by simply redefining *wang* but also by refocusing the discourse on the whole process of the ethico-political development of an entire community instead of one person's ultimate achievement. At each stage of this process, and ethical cultivation and political participation mutually reinforce each other, and ethical achievement and political achievement imply each other, but the progress from one stage to the next is contingent. Too often, objections regarding the divergence of the political and the ethical confuse different stages of the process, or they mistake part of the process for the entirety—for example, people being honored as sages for achievements that, however worthy, fall short of the sage-king ideal.

While ultimate success in terms of the appearance of a sage-king cannot be guaranteed, that should not be the criterion for judging Confucianism's practicality or success. In judging any one Confucian's attempt to unite politics with ethics, one needs to remember that success is not a matter of all or nothing; every life, every career, political or otherwise, and every person, whether king or peasant, is a mixture of successes and failures. As with Dewey's regulative ideal, the sage-king ideal may be impossible to realize, but that would not make it impossible for any person to unite ethics and politics in a meaningful way and to be successful at least some of the time, at the stage of ethico-political development appropriate to herself. This suggested approach is grounded in the *Analects* itself.

EXEMPLARY PERSONS: ETHICO-POLITICAL ENDS-IN-VIEW

If the sage-king paradigm in Chinese politics has contributed to "the siren-call of the strong man"—the preference for authoritarian government among some Confucians—then it is certainly not Confucius' fault. The term *sage-king* is not found in the *Analects*, and "sage" appears in only six passages, four attributed to Confucius himself. His only characterization of the sage is one "who is broadly generous with the people and is able to help the multitude," hardly a recommendation of authoritarian government (*Analects* 6.30). Later Confucians, from Mencius on, much less reticent with regard to the sage, not only see Yao and Shun as sage-kings but also elevate Confucius and others to sagehood. But Confucius himself denies that he is a sage and claims that even Yao and Shun have trouble making the standard (*Analects* 7.34, 6.30). The *Analects* not only supports shifting the focus of the discussion about the unity of politics and ethics away from the sage-king paradigm but also shows the way to do so.

In the *Analects*, ethical living is an extremely complex issue and could not be captured in any simple formula. But as a beginning, one might look at Confucius' account of his own life (*Analects* 2.4). An ethical life begins with learning, which for Confucius is first and foremost learning to be an exemplary person (a *junzi* 君子). Confucius laments that he would never get to meet a sage, but he would be content to meet an exemplary person (*Analects* 7.26). The sage may be the highest ideal, but it is so difficult to achieve that Confucius, with his usual practicality, did not set that as the goal for his students. While sagehood is always in the background as a regulative ideal, Confucius taught more about what may be called ends-in-view, which vary from one student to the next. This accounts for the different answers to the same questions (What is an exemplary person, an authoritative person, good government?) asked by different persons. Each particular answer aims at what the interlocutor specifically has to do to achieve his own end-in-view.

There are various models of living ethically: the scholar-official (*shi* 士), the good person (*shanren* 善人), the worthy person (*xianren* 賢人), the great person (*daren* 大人), and the consummate person (*chengren* 成人). These are not mentioned as frequently, nor have they the same importance, as the exemplary person (*junzi* 君子) and the authoritative person (*renzhe* 仁者) in the *Analects*.[27] In early Zhou texts, *junzi* refers to "the Lord's son(s)." Peter Boodberg points out that *junzi* probably refers to those who, though of noble birth, could never become real lords for one reason or another and are therefore perennial "Lords' sons."[28] If the term did in fact refer to the *declassé*, then it strengthens the case for expanding the focus of uniting politics and ethics beyond those with ruling power. Most commentators pay more attention to the denotation of nobility of rank and birth rather than to the "*declassé*" connotation of *junzi*, which also could be the diminutive form of *jun*, a lord, one who does have political power.

Hall and Ames show how the character for "exemplary person" is associated with personal order that expands through political participation.[29] Regardless of the actual power of the *junzi* before and during Confucius' times, the model of the exemplary person in Confucius' teaching renders political participation and the quest for personal ethical progress practically concomitant. In transforming a title denoting social/political rank into an ethical model, Confucius has not stripped the term of its political connotations. Many aspects of the exemplary person's way mentioned in the *Analects* (5.16, 14.42, 19.10, 20.2) are sociopolitical. Political participation is part of the process of learning to live ethically (*Analects* 1.7).

Both Confucius and Mencius spent a significant part of their lives trying to find a ruler who would accept their advice on governing. The ethical requirement to take office remains a perennial theme in Confucianism. Both the *Analects* and the *Mencius* are preoccupied with the art of effective and ethical political engagement. Engagement must occur under appropriate circumstances; one must not accept just any kind of political office. Confucius implied that he was waiting for "the right price," an appropriate appreciation of his talents (*Analects* 9.13). When the Duke of Qi showed himself to be interested only in his own pleasures, uncaring about good government, Confucius promptly left Qi (*Analects* 18.4). Mencius tended to take a more pragmatic attitude. He allowed being treated with respect as a reason for staying in office, even when one's advice was ignored, and in desperate circumstances, "to ward off starvation," one could even accept charity from a ruler who ignored one's advice (*Mencius* 12.14/66/30).

In general, the only good reasons for not taking up political office are inadequate ability or if the political situation of the time renders taking office an ineffective way to bring about sociopolitical order.[30] "Qu Boyu was indeed an exemplary person! When the way prevailed in the state, he gave of his service, and when it did not, he rolled it up and tucked it away" (*Analects* 15.7). Withdrawal from the public life is not just to preserve one's life and limb. The point is to serve only where one could make a difference. The Confucian tradition is full of praise for those who not only risk, but even sacrifice, their lives attempting to influence bad rulers for the benefit of the people (*Analects* 18.1).

In the *Analects*, we see a build up of the pressure for participation in government. Initially, Confucius seemed content for his contribution to be made through the immediate circle of family and friends (*Analects* 2.21). Later, he was prepared to offer his counsel even to rebels and to one whose character was questionable (*Analects* 17.5, 17.7). When commenting on those ancients who retired from government to preserve their ideals and integrity, he considers himself as different in not having "presuppositions about what may or may not be done" (*Analects* 18.8). While Confucius advises that "one should remain hidden" when the way does not prevail (*Analects* 8.13), we find Zi Lu, presumably with Confucius' support, asserting that one must do one's best to reconstitute the situation instead of simply withdrawing, even when the way does not prevail. "To refuse office is to fail to do what is important and appropriate (*yi* 義). If the differentiation between young and old cannot be abandoned, then how could one think of abandoning what is appropriate between ruler and subject?" (*Analects* 18.7).

Previous chapters examined how the ethical process brings together the growth of a person and the building of community. This personal-communal growth may be understood as *ren* 仁, authoritative conduct. Liang Ch'i-ch'ao remarks that Confucian thinking on ethics and politics is rooted in the notion of authoritative conduct. Hsiao Kung-chuan also argues that *ren* in Confucius' thinking brings together politics and ethics, oneself and others, and family and state. Chan Wing-tsit, among others, suggests that authoritative conduct is a general virtue under which all particular virtues can be subsumed.[31] Chan might have gone a little too far, but ethical qualities such as wisdom or intelligence and courage often are associated with authoritative conduct, and there is little doubt that whatever other qualities an exemplary person must acquire, acting authoritatively is central to exemplary conduct. "Wherein do the exemplary persons who would abandon their authoritative conduct warrant that name? Exemplary persons do not take leave of authoritative conduct even for the space of a meal. When they are troubled, they certainly turn to it, as they do in facing difficulties."[32] The *Analects* uses "authoritative person" and "exemplary person" interchangeably and often describes them in strikingly similar terms.[33]

Authoritative conduct takes others' concerns as one's own. "Authoritative persons establish others in seeking to establish themselves and promote others in seeking to get there themselves" (*Analects* 6.30). The key to establishing (*li* 立) others and oneself is ritual practice (*li* 禮): "if you do not study the *Rites*, you will be at a loss as to where to stand (*li* 立)" (*Analects* 16.13). Confucius highlighted his ability to take a stance, to establish himself, which required a mastery of ritual practice as a key stage in his life, which he achieved from age thirty. It is through ritual practice that one becomes authoritative. If for a day one is able to conduct oneself authoritatively through self-discipline and ritual practices, then "those near at hand are pleased, and those at a distance are drawn to him," and over time "the whole empire would defer to this authoritative model" (*Analects* 12.1, 13.16). The authoritative person participates effectively in politics. "Through disciplining oneself and ritual practices one becomes authoritative in one's conduct" (*Analects* 12.1) is given an explicitly political import in *Zuo's Commentary*, where Confucius is reported to have blamed the political troubles of King Ling of Chu on his failing to live up to this.[34] Following the *Analects*, the *Mencius* further strengthens the link between authoritative conduct and government with frequent discussions of "authoritative government" (*renzheng* 仁政), while the *Xunzi* reinforces the link between good government and ritual practices.

Authoritative conduct through ritual practices is the ethical construction of human relationships that constitutes a person. The term *lunli* 倫理 often is used to refer to ethics. *Lunli* is "the proper pattern of key relationships." Following Hall and Ames, I have chosen "pattern" instead of the more philosophically loaded "reason," "rationality," or "principle" (their compatibility with pre-Qin Chinese thinking is questionable). Qualifying "pattern" with "proper" registers the normative aspect of *li*—although I hasten to add that the fact-value dichotomy cannot be imposed indiscriminately. Nevertheless, not just any configuration would qualify as *li*. *Li* is proper pattern, or patterning that embodies order. The five key Confucian relations of ruler-subject, father-son, husband-wife, elder-younger brothers, and friends are referred to as *wulun* (五倫). Ethics as *lunli*, the proper patterning of key relationships, would be a matter of how to relate to one another to generate and sustain harmony in a community.

Understood in these terms, ethics is inseparable from politics. This inseparability is also evident in another Chinese term for ethics, *daode* 道德. The term *way* (*dao* 道) is associated with "to lead" (*dao* 導). The "way of the true king" (*wangdao* 王道) has long been a major topic in Confucian discourse. Political legitimacy, encapsulated in the concept of *tianming* 天命 (usually translated as "heaven's mandate"), is associated with excellence (*de*) since Zhou times. Confucius says, "Governing with excellence can be compared to being the North Star: the North Star dwells in its place, and the multitude of stars pay it tribute" (*Analects* 2.1). Ethical ends are political ends, and vice-versa, in early Confucianism.

The characters in modern mandarin used to translate "politics," *zhengzhi* 政治, also occur in ancient Chinese texts. *Zheng* 政 usually refers to the political activity of governing, while *zhi* 治 usually refers to the order achieved. According to Confucius, "Governing well is doing what is proper (*zheng* 正)."[35] The criterion for what is "proper" is contribution to the development of ethical character and communal harmony. *Zhengxin* 正心—which Hall and Ames translate as "attuning hearts-and-minds," and Lau translates as "rectifying the hearts"—is a critical part of the ethical cultivation of the person (*xiushen* 修身) and ultimately brings peace to the world.[36] Mencius considers acting appropriately (*yi* 義) "the proper human path (*zhenglu* 正路)" (*Mencius* 7.10/37/21). For Xunzi, making the person "proper" by ritual practices is central to personal cultivation (*Xunzi* 2/8/1).

An exemplary person is one who would "repair to those who know the way and find improvement (*zheng* 正) in their company" (*Analects* 1.14). According to Confucius, if a ruler leads by doing what is proper, then no one would dare do otherwise (*Analects* 12.17, 12.19). At its best, politics is leadership by example. "When you personally are proper in your conduct, the world will turn to you" (*Mencius* 7.4/36/21). Confucius also describes governing well as a situation in which "the ruler rules, the minister ministers, the father acts like a father, and the son like a son" (*Analects* 12.11). Politics practiced well brings order through construction of proper human relations. To live a good life, one must participate in politics properly; to participate in politics properly, one must contribute to others' ethical growth, even as one cultivates oneself. Political and ethical achievement are two sides of the same coin.

People As Basis (*MINBEN* 民本)

Through different routes, Dewey and Confucius could arrive at the same conclusion, that ethics and politics are inseparable. Though different, their paths are nevertheless marked by some significantly similar signposts: a conception of personal ethical development premised on the sociality of individuals, an emphasis on the ethical in politics, a view of community and of ethico-political order constituted by the development of every individual member, and a "bottom-up" emergent sense of ethico-political order. In exploring their similarities, I reconstruct Confucianism to widen the scope of politics beyond the activities of rulers. Early Confucian views regarding politics and ethics in terms of political participation go beyond the conventional understanding of governing, but what is the nature of this participation, and how widespread could it be? For Dewey, the ideal ethico-political order has a "government of the people, by the people, for the people."[37] Could we say the same of Confucian ethico-political order?

In 1919, Chen Duxiu 陳獨秀, a leader of the May Fourth movement, declared that "In order to advocate democracy, we are obliged to oppose Confucianism." In their conviction that "Confucianism and monarchy were indissolubly bound," May Fourth radicals did not distinguish Confucianism as the philosophical tradition based on Confucius' teachings and Confucianism as state orthodoxy.[38] Confucians might have taken the monarchical political structure for granted, but monarchy is not a necessary part of Confucianism. Chen admitted in the 1930s that the May Fourth slogan, "Down with the Confucian Shop," while serving an important purpose in their political struggles was less than fair to thinkers such as Confucius and Mencius. This distinction between Confucian philosophy and the imperial state orthodoxy is recognized by moderates such as Hu Shih (even though he played a key role in popularizing that anti-Confucian slogan), who suggested that ideas and institutions may be found in Confucianism that could provide the basis for establishing democracy in China.[39]

While conservative Confucians resisted change and opposed democracy, some members of the Chinese intellectual elite at the beginning of the twentieth century who visited countries such as England and the United States were impressed by their democratic institutions and compared them to "the

Golden Age of Ancient China." K'ang Yu-wei 康有為, through a reinterpretation of Confucian texts, concluded that Confucius was a most enthusiastic advocate of democracy. This new paradigm dominated classical Confucian scholarship until the May Fourth period; even K'ang's political opponents adopted it. Republican Confucians such as Liu Shipei 劉師培 and Zhang Binglin 章炳麟 attempted to trace the origins of democratic ideas in China to ancient Confucian texts. The founder of the Chinese Republic, Sun Yat-sen, also cited passages from classical texts that emphasized the people's welfare as the purpose of governing and their right to revolt against rulers who failed to take care of their welfare as evidence of democratic ideas in ancient China.[40]

It is a futile anachronism to attempt to turn Confucius or Mencius into a democratic theorist. What is worth considering is that Confucian texts could have cultural resources hospitable to democracy. As Ambrose King notes, Confucian ethics and values are still a living cultural force for East Asian societies, and if they are going to develop democracy fully, then the idea of democracy has to come to terms with Confucianism.[41] For Confucians who believe in democracy, it is vital to find an interpretation of Confucianism that is compatible with democracy. New-Confucian scholars contend that the development of democracy in Confucian societies is not something externally imposed on them but rather a natural direction of their cultural development.

In "A Manifesto on the Reappraisal of Chinese Culture", issued in 1958, five of these New-Confucians argued that the Confucian ethico-political ideal requires every person to participate in politics, and that "the establishment of a democratic government is necessary for the development of China's culture and history." They were "certain that Marxist-Leninism will be discarded eventually and the spiritual life of the [Chinese] nation will press forward toward the establishment of a democratic government."[42] Marxist-Leninism may have been discarded, at least in substance if not in rhetoric, but there is little reason for complacency, or any certainty about the democratic direction of the Chinese state. The path to democracy will not be smooth, and its aspired end is by no means guaranteed. Establishing compatibility between Confucianism and democracy will not guarantee the historical inevitability of democracy in China or in any Confucian society, but the belief that a Confucian democracy is possible and worthy of our best efforts will foster a commitment to work for its realization.

Confucian promoters of democracy have made extensive use of the notion of "people as basis (*minben* 民本)." According to King, the *minben* tradition captures the main themes of Chinese political thought throughout the ages, but Andrew Nathan argues that promoting democracy in the language of "people as basis" involves a radical extension of the original idea in which the people's only claim on the government is for welfare—it "had never meant people's rights (*minquan* 民權) or people's rule (*minzhu* 民主)." (*Minzhu* is the term currently used to translate "democracy.") The background against which Nathan criticizes Chinese democracy is an understanding of democracy in terms of the American political system with "[its] emphasis on individual rights, [its] tolerance for the expression of conflict and antagonism in politics, [its] acknowledgment that the political process can legitimately be used by individuals and groups to try to force the state to serve their selfish interests, and [its] system of judicial review."[43] This is the political democracy that Dewey considers uninspiring. While his emphasis on individual rights and his realist conception of democracy render his approach incompatible with our current project, Nathan nevertheless highlights some of the serious limitations within the Chinese tradition which, even if it is not part of the Confucian ideal, have to be dealt with efficaciously if there is to be a Confucian democracy in China.

Nathan is not alone in believing that *minben* falls short of democracy as "government by the people." Liang Ch'i-ch'ao credits the concept with capturing "government of the people, for the people," but not "government by the people." Hsiao Kung-chuan, commenting on Mencius' interpretation of the concept in the form of "the importance of the people," distinguishes it from modern democracy: "it merely commences with the idea of 'for the people,' and proceeds toward that of 'of the people.' Both the principle of 'by the people' and the institutions necessary to it are things of which [Mencius] had never heard." Liu Shu-hsien argues that the Confucian concept of *minben* is inseparable from virtuous government and quite compatible with an undemocratic, monarchical polity.[44]

It is of serious concern to those who would like to root democracy in Confucian soil whether we could extend the idea of *minben* to include "government by the people." According to the *Routledge Encyclopedia of Philosophy*, "Democracy means rule by the people, as contrasted with rule by a special person or group."[45] Dewey also emphasizes "*by* the people" in borrowing Lincoln's formula of democracy. Dewey is highly skeptical of the possibility of any government being for the people for any long period rather than for a governing clique or bureaucracy if it is not government *by* the people (L17.474). As far as China's history goes, government often has been for the benefit of governing cliques more than for the benefit of the entire people. And it is arguably because China did not have government by the people that its Confucian commitment to "government for the people" has borne such meager fruits.

However, this must be put into perspective by asking just how many states through the ages could claim to have done better in terms of putting the people before the governing cliques. One could argue that the political system of the United States is so dominated by interest groups that it is questionable whether there is government "for the people." Some Asian critics of liberal democracies argue that Asian governments have been able to benefit their people more without a liberal democratic political system. Some seventeenth- and early-eighteenth-century European thinkers such as Leibniz and Voltaire believed that China's despotism was remarkably enlightened and benefited the Chinese people more than the European autocracies of the time.[46] When Louis XIV declared, "L'état, c'est moi," he was claiming his divine right to do as he pleased with the state and, hence, the people, but when Chinese emperors claimed the Chinese world as his "family/estate" (*jiatianxia* 家天下), it is justifiable from a Confucian perspective only as a claim of responsibility, not of right. This is not denying that, in practice, too many Chinese rulers have betrayed that responsibility and behaved as autocratically as the French king.

Confucian views of the ruler's normative relationship to the people owe much to the idea of *minben*. The term *minben* is traced to the *Book of Historical Documents* 尚書.

The people are the root [basis, *ben* 本] of the state,
The root is firm, the state is at peace.[47]

Though this passage is in a chapter believed to be a later forgery, the idea also could be found in the *Book of Songs* (dated between 1,000–600 B.C.), which describes the ruling aristocracy as "parents of the people." King Wen, the father of King Wu and the founder of the Zhou dynasty, is the subject of praise in various songs in that text, and the benefits he brought to the people are central to his excellence.[48] Whether or not it predates Confucius, the idea of "people as basis" of the state has a strong presence in the *Analects* and is more explicitly developed into a claim of the priority of the people over the ruler in the *Mencius*: "The people are of supreme importance; the altars to the gods of earth and grain come next; last comes the ruler" (*Mencius* 14.14/74/14). In Xunzi's view, the people do not exist for the sake of the ruler; the ruler exists, *qua* ruler, for the sake of the people (*Xunzi* 27/132/19).

The importance of the people places a heavy responsibility on the ruler whose *raison d'être* is to take care of the people. Both Mencius and Xunzi elaborate on Confucius' view that good government, the true king, should act authoritatively, love the people, and put their needs and concerns first. Mencius sees authoritative government as "compassionate government based on a heart-and-mind sensitive to the sufferings of others" (*Mencius* 3.6/18/4). For Xunzi, a ruler is "one who brings people together . . . bringing people together means being good at providing a living for the people and caring for them, bringing about ethico-political order, guiding them according to their better dispositions, constraining their faults, and refining them" (*Xunzi* 12/59/11). Mencius' conception of a good, that is, an authoritative, government is an extension of Confucius' recommendation of providing for their material welfare and edu-

cating them.[49] While Xunzi disagrees with Mencius about some methods of
bringing about the Confucian ethico-political ideal, his interpretation of the
ruler's normative relation to the people does not depart from the Confucius-
Mencius axis. Xunzi gives more credit to laws than either Confucius or
Mencius, but the laws that he promotes are those of the true king, which "are
the means of nourishing the people" (*Xunzi* 9/38/9). This also is one of the
reasons he emphasizes the rulers' establishing ritual practices, which "means
that which nourishes" (*Xunzi* 19/90/5). Xunzi's idea of "nourishing the people"
also revolves around "enriching them, educating them."[50]

Only a government for the people could achieve ethico-political order; it
also is the only stable and enduring government. One who takes care of the
people's welfare will gain their confidence, and "he who gains the confidence
of the people will be the son of heaven."[51] Unless a government is for the
people, the people would not support it—which will eventually lead to its collapse. "If the people do not have confidence in their leaders, the community
will not endure" (*Analects* 12.7). Xunzi provides a vivid metaphor for this. "The
ruler is the boat, the people water; it is water that sustains the boat, it is water
that capsizes the boat" (*Xunzi* 9/36/7, 31/147/6). According to Mencius, a
ruler who fails to achieve ethico-political order deserves to be removed from
his position, like "a Marshal of the Guards [who] was unable to keep his guards
in order," or rejected, like a friend who has broken his promise (*Mencius*
2.6/10/280). Taking "people as the basis" of the state is the key to political
legitimacy in Confucianism.

THE ROLE OF THE PEOPLE IN *TIANMING* 天命

Confucian political legitimacy lies in ensuring that people live well both
materially and ethically. This link is already present in the concept of *tianming*
天命, usually translated as "heaven's mandate," used by the Zhou kings to
justify their overthrow of their Shang overlord. The *Book of Historical Documents* repeatedly cites the failures of the last Shang ruler, King Zhou 紂, in
terms of the misery of the people under his rule and the disorder in his realm,
as the cause of a "change of *tianming*," which justifies King Wu 武 of Zhou
deposing him.[52] The concept of "people as basis," understood as "government
for the people," tells us how to decide who is fit to rule from a Confucian perspective, but it does not tell us who should decide, and how to enforce the
decision. The answers to the last two questions would indicate if there is "government of the people, by the people." The idea of *tianming* would indicate
that it is *tian*, rather than the people, who bestows the world on the ruler, but
there is a complex relationship between *tian* and the people. According to
Mencius, the world does *not* thereby become the ruler's personal property—

he does not have the right to "give" it to whomever he chooses. All a ruler can do is recommend his choice of successor to *tian* and the people, who then accept or reject the proposed candidate based on the candidate's performance. If the sacrifices made by the recommended successor are accepted by the various deities, then *tian* has approved the choice; if the successor's handling of the affairs of state proves efficacious, and the people live well as a result, then he has been accepted by the people (*Mencius* 9.5/48/7).

Does the world belong neither to the ruler nor to the people but to *tian*, a separate entity who bestows legitimacy based on the performance of rulers assessed in terms of the people's welfare? One might conclude from the exchange between Mencius and Wan Zhang that *tian* and the people *together* decide "who governs?"—assuming that the distinct existence of the two could be established (*Mencius* 9.6/49/3). This assumption of separate existence does not stand up well under closer examination. The separate mention of *tian* could be attributed to Mencius making an allowance for existing religious practices in his desire to win over new adherents to Confucianism, but his appropriation of the existing vocabulary also involves reinterpreting it to serve Confucian purpose.

Robert Eno argues that both the "prescriptive" and "descriptive" uses of *tian* in the *Mencius* are part of a self-conscious political rhetoric that reduces *tian* to *min*, the people.[53] How do we know that "the deities have enjoyed/accepted" any sacrifice made? An affirmative answer seems to be in the "blessings" bestowed on the one who made the sacrifice, that is, the success of that person's undertakings in the world—*tian*'s acceptance of a recommended successor to the throne boils down to the same criterion for acceptance by the people, his ethico-political efficacy. Before further discussion of the role of the people in conferring political legitimacy on a government, we should perhaps sketch in the background controversy about the concept of *tian*, and its implications for political legitimacy.

One obstacle to replacing *tian* with *min* is the claim that *tian* is transcendent. Roger Ames and Henry Rosemont, in their philosophical translation of the *Analects*, choose not to translate *tian*, because they believe that its conventional English rendering as "Heaven" is overburdened with Judeo-Christian theological and philosophical baggage that obscures rather than illuminates. Historically, translation of *tian* as "Heaven" can be traced to the Jesuits, who first translated the Confucian classics (the *Analects*, the *zhongyong*, and the *Great Learning*) into Latin. The 1687 *Confucius Sinarum Philosophus* suggests that the Chinese understand by *tian* nothing other than the true God. The presentation of ancient Confucianism as a natural religion—its belief in and worship of *tian* as a monotheistic tradition—is a chief component of Matteo Ricci's accommodationist strategy. The claim came to be accepted by many among his audience, both in China and Europe. Since then,

Confucian discourse has been dogged by two questions regarding *tian*: Does it signify an anthropomorphic deity (the Chinese term is *rengeshen* 人格神, translated as "personal deity," i.e., one with characteristics of a person) like the Christian God? Is it transcendent?[54]

Hou Wailu and Ren Jiyu argue that Confucius views *tian* as a deity with a will.[55] It is difficult to decide how much of the anthropomorphic language surrounding *tian* is merely pathetic fallacy and how much indicates that *tian* retains in early Confucianism personal characteristics attributed to a deity. There is textual evidence showing that the Zhou rulers, after their conquest of Shang, identified their indigenous notion of *tian* with the Shang personal deity, the Lord-on-High (*shangdi* 上帝)—the two are used interchangeably in parts of the *Book of Historical Documents* and the *Book of Songs*—and it is probable that the Zhou rulers claimed *tian* as their ancestor, as reflected in the Zhou ruler's title, "son of *tian*." Notwithstanding the Zhou rulers' claim of *tian* as royal ancestor, an impersonal sense of *tian* persists and gains importance in Confucianism.

Eno observes, "a consensus has emerged which characterizes Hsün Tzu's [Xunzi's] position on T'ien [*tian*] by stressing that he saw T'ien not as anthropomorphic god, but as an impersonal force of Nature, or as natural or universal law." Both Eno and Edward Machle challenge the view that Xunzi's understanding of *tian* is devoid of ethical significance; Machle goes farther in maintaining that *tian* in the *Xunzi* is not only ethical but religious, without being anthropomorphic.[56] Discussing Confucius' "realizing *tianming* from fifty," Xu Fuguan argues that *tianming* is not religious but ethical. In general, Confucians discern in *tian* an ethical dimension, as evidenced in the description of the ethical way of life as the way of *tian* (*tiandao* 天道), the distinction between the nobility of *tian* and the nobility of humans (*tianjue renjue* 天爵人爵), and the ethical importance of knowing and serving *tian*, which is the source of the human heart-and-mind and its ethical predispositions.[57]

As a realm of ethical ideals, *tian* imposes demands on us that could be experienced as *external* to ourselves; as the sum total of existence, *tian* includes conditions and possibilities not within human control.[58] Some see this relative distance between *tian* on the one hand, and the natural or social order and human desires and endeavors, on the other hand as involving transcendence. Heiner Roetz, who sees Mencian ethics as heir to the "religion of Heaven," argues that Heaven, "as an embodiment of moral norms," is transcendent. Its distance from the realm of mundane authorities allows Mencius to attack the ruling elites and provide "the Archimedean point to move the world" which, according to Max Weber, is entirely missing in the immanent Chinese order. Benjamin Schwartz also believes that, in Confucianism, "the transcendental element is undeniably present in the sense of the yawning abyss between the ideal social order and the actual state of affairs." Some Chinese scholars, such as Mou Zongsan, also argue along the same line as Schwartz, though they tend to be influenced by Kant's account of morality.[59] But the ideal need not be radically separate from the actual; Dewey, for example, views it as "the tendency and movement of some thing which exists carried to its final limit, viewed as completed, perfected" (L2.328).

Liu Shu-hsien claims that "Heaven is transcendent in the sense that it is an all encompassing creative power which works incessantly in the universe. It is not a thing, but it is the origin of all things. . . . Heaven is also immanent in the sense that it penetrates deep in every detail of the natural order, in general, and the moral order of man in particular."[60] Though Liu maintains that Confucian philosophers see transcendence and immanence as interdependent rather than contradictory concepts, others question the very coherence of claiming transcendence and immanence at the same time. Chad Hansen understands transcendence as involving dualism rendering the interaction between two elements or realms problematic. Responding to Roetz's criticism of his naturalist interpretations based on a pragmatic approach for "demeaning Chinese thought" by denying the autonomy of moral norms, he argues that there is moral transcendence—neither actual social practice nor nature determines morality—without religious or metaphysical transcendence in Chinese thought.[61] Probably the most radical opponents of attributing transcendence to Chinese thought, Hall and Ames are of the view that transcendence is required by neither the ethical nor the religious characteristics of *tian*. They define transcendence in terms of a strict foundational dualism: "A principle A, is transcendent with respect to that, B, which it serves as a principle if the meaning or import of B cannot be fully analyzed and explained without recourse to A, but the reverse is not true."[62] Thus A and B could be related, but such a relationship tends to be inherently problematic.

What is at stake in the transcendence debate for political legitimacy? A transcendent *tian* would imply a strict external triadic relation, while a non-transcendent *tian* would allow internal and dyadic relations in the workings of the mandate to rule. The different ways in which the *tian*-people-ruler relations play out have significant implications for the question of whether the political legitimacy of *tianming* could support government by the people. In a triadic relation, *tian* decides who rules, based on how the people fare under a particular ruler. The people's role may be that of *tian*'s representative—articulating *tianming*—or that of the signs by which gifted individuals (who may be rulers, but certainly sages) may decipher *tianming*. The first appears to be Mencius' view, "*Tian* sees as my people see, *tian* hears as my people hear," to elaborate on what "acceptance by *tian*" means (*Mencius* 9.5/49/1). Does *tianming* become known only as *the people's* mandate?

The term *minming* 民命, which could mean "the people's mandate," appears in the document of "Pan Geng 盤庚" of the *Book of Historical Docu-*

ments, but it usually has been translated, legitimately, as "the people's lives." The reason for this translation is because the term occurs in the context of the Shang ruler, Pan Geng, admonishing those among the people who opposed his proposed move to Yin—which seems to indicate a typically paternalistic situation, rather than the ruler following "the people's mandate." However, if *min* 民 is an indefinite collective noun that could refer to either everyone who counts as "the people" or to some among them, then it would still be possible to view the move according to "the people's mandate," even if some people are against it. This seems to be supported by Pan Geng reproaching those against the move for suppressing the views of the poorer classes and spreading disaffection. Though the chapter "The Great Declaration 泰誓" with the statement found in the *Mencius* on *tian* seeing and hearing as the people see and hear is probably a Han forgery, which makes it more likely that it was borrowing from *Mencius* than the other way around, the "The Counsels of Gao Yao 皋陶謨" chapter takes a similar stand, in different words: "Heaven hear and see as our people hear and see; Heaven brightly approves and displays its terrors, as our people brightly approve and would awe."[63]

Some scholars have tried to find a principle of accountability of the government to the people, even of popular consent in Mencius' defense of King Wu's "removal of the mandate" from the last Shang King. Fung Yu-Lan, in the new edition of *A History of Chinese Philosophy*, calls this the Confucian "right of revolution (*gemingquan* 革命權)." Julia Ching calls this "a grand deception." In her view, the people never had any real power in the dynastic system, and none of the "revolutions" in China transferred power to the people. Hence, "prior to modern times, China knew only rebellions but not a revolution, as the new governments ushered in resembled too much the ones that they replaced."[64] Even if revolution or rebellion could be seen as an exercise of choice of government on the part of the people, a theory of justified elimination of tyrants (*baojun fangfa lun* 暴君放伐論) still would not qualify as "a seed of democracy." If the people's representation of *tian* is effective only in revolutions, then it certainly would not amount to "government by the people." Revolution is a desperate measure; it cannot be part of normal political practice. One of the advantages of democracy is that it provides a way to change government without violence or too much suffering by the people. This is patently not the case, even in successful revolutions; the cost of failure in revolutions often is the participants' lives.

The interpretation of *tianming* being known only as articulated by the people runs into a problem because for much of Chinese history, the people lacked a voice in politics without anyone believing that *tianming* was unknown or unknowable as a result. This consensus should not be taken too much for granted, as the "Pan Geng" document, for example, seems to indicate that the common people at some time had more direct access to the ruler—and therefore they could speak for themselves and on behalf of *tian*—than became the norm in later times. But de Bary's view reflects the majority opinion: "What failed the Confucians repeatedly . . . was not the lack of a prophetic voice but the lack of an articulate audience—the absence of a political and social infrastructure that would have given the people themselves a voice." Many scholars believe that, though not lacking in democratic ideas such as equality and government by popular consent, China failed to develop democracy because of the lack of institutions that could actualize those ideas, institutions that would give the people a say.[65]

One might draw a parallel between the problem of the Chinese people and what Dewey perceives to be the problem with the Great Society: an eclipse of the public. In doing so, one would be less sanguine about the assumption that China would realize the democratic ideas in its ancient traditions if it adopts Western democratic institutions. Even for his own country, Dewey wondered if the political institutions and their legal accompaniments inherited from the founders were in fact democratic for his time (L13.151). If a political democracy is to survive the challenges that constantly confront it, then it must "become part of the bone and blood of the people in daily conduct of its life" (L11.225). Given their different ways of life, the political forms that would realize democracy in Confucian societies would probably be different from Western ones. Ritual practices are likely to have a greater role than laws in a Confucian democracy. This can be an advantage. Part of the difficulty of bringing about democracy as "a way of life," as urged by Dewey, is an overly narrow understanding of culture and how people interact. The Confucian emphasis on ritual practices draws attention to something that some sectors of Western societies are sorely in need of, which Western scholars have gestured at with words such as "civility," "courtesy," and "trust." In this area, Confucianism may suggest new possibilities in the quest for a Deweyan democracy.

Whatever the political forms appropriate to a Confucian democracy, Dewey's discussions about the public highlight a problem that must be solved if there is to be a democracy. The public must be organized to inquire into its common interests and to communicate its views to others. In Confucian terms, unless the people organize themselves to give voice to their views, they cannot speak on behalf of *tian* in conveying its mandate; the people would, at most, through the conditions and quality of their lives, provide the signs by which the mandate could be deciphered. The people may see and hear on behalf of *tian*, but they do not *speak* on its behalf. When the people are living well, it is a sign that *tian* is pleased and would bestow its mandate on the reigning king. The mandate is bestowed on the government *for* the people; whether or not government *by* the people is desirable depends on whether or not it is the best way to bring about government *for* the people. Chen Daqi suggests that "Who governs?" is not the chief concern of Confucius, who is more interested in the results of government.[66] The answer to the question "Who governs?," as well as the question of which political forms to adopt, will depend on who and what best serve the purpose of the people's material well-being and ethical growth. It is not entirely clear that giving the people a voice is the only or best way of governing *for* the people. Even if the people have a voice, they may not be in the best position to interpret the signs of *tian*'s mandate and decide what should be done.

While acknowledging that there is some difficulty in ascertaining whether the people are living well, even though "the feelings of the people can for the most part be discerned," the "Announcement to the Prince of K'ang 康誥" in the *Book of Historical Documents* appeals not to the people's voice but to the ruler's sincerity—which is said to be "assisted by *tian*"—and his conscientious "use of all his heart-and-mind."[67] The idea that only sages are fit to rule in itself inclines toward the view that a select minority knows best what is in the people's interests and could best take care of those interests. Knowing *tian* is a sagely achievement, and though Mencius believes that "everyone *can* be a sage," even his staunchest defender would concede that, in reality, sages, and even near-sages, are extremely rare. In a triadic relation in which the people are relegated to the role of signs, the key link in political legitimacy is between the ruler and *tian*—a link established by ancient shamanic kings and reinforced by the sage-king paradigm. There is little democratic content in this view of the *minben* tradition. If *tian* is transcendent, then what China had, and not just in its historical institutions but also in its ideas, is closer to the "divine right (or, rather, responsibility) of kings" than "government of the people, by the people."

A dyadic relation of political legitimacy is only possible if *tian* is non-transcendent and identifiable with either the people or the ruler. We mentioned earlier Eno's argument that the *Mencius* reduces *tian* to the people. Eno distinguishes this view of *tian* from that of the early Zhou, which identifies *tian* with the ruler.[68] The latter is problematic, as the possibility of *tian* removing its mandate from a particular ruler is central to the Zhou idea of political legitimacy—when the Shang ruler lost *tian*'s mandate, did he (as identified with *tian*) deprive himself of the mandate for the sake of the people? Whatever the actual beliefs of the early Zhou period, the dependence of the mandate on the people's welfare is undeniably a central tenet in Confucian political philosophy. The Confucian development of the idea of *minben* makes the identification of *tian* with the people more plausible than that of identification with the ruler. If *tian* is reducible to the people, then the argument that the ruler, or even the sage, knows *tian* better than the people (as a whole rather than any one individual) do would carry less force because of the elevated status of *tian*.[69] The sage knows *tian* only as well as the entire people, because his authoritative conduct extends to include relations with the entire people—his perspective is one that incorporates all of the people. This strengthens the argument that the political legitimacy found in the mandate of *tian*, as interpreted by Mencius, is some form of popular consent and, hence, democratic in idea, even if the above-mentioned problem of how consent is expressed and enforced in political practice remains.

There is another nonreductionist and, in my view, better way of understanding political legitimacy in the Confucian tradition—with its emphasis on "people as basis" and the dependence of *tian*'s mandate on the people—which allows us to argue that Confucian ethico-political order, and how it is achieved, contains the cultural prerequisites for democracy. Even if *tian* is nontranscendent, it is not necessarily reducible to the people. Instead, a nontranscendent *tian* includes the people, and the realm of *tian* is inseparable from human experience. In this case, the internality of the relations is more important than whether we view the relations as dyadic or triadic. Problems occur when internal relations are mistaken for external ones, so that confrontation replaces cooperation. While reducing *tian* to the people is not as implausible as reducing it to the ruler, there are good reasons to avoid the reductionist approach to the relations between *tian*, the people, and the ruler.

Whether descriptively or prescriptively, *tian* does appear to be *more* than just the people. The term *min* is used to describe those under the rule of a particular ruler; it has no ethical connotations. Such groups of people are limited in space and time; *tian* has no such limitations. Descriptively, *tian* is the entire field of existence, without fixed spatial boundaries, with neither a beginning nor an end, including past, present, and future. It is both nature and culture, of which past human contributions constitute significant parts. It is a context within which the lives of particular individuals are played out. A people constitute a focus (of varying quality) of this field. In turn, a people constitute a field focused variously by each individual member in it, and exemplary persons and sages are the best among these foci. Prescriptively, *tian* is the emergent order of the field; its realization involved transforming the quality of the various foci to achieve harmony.

For any single person, *tianming* is never a one-to-one relation; many others mediate it. The knowledge of *tianming* is found through the people. "A person should not use water as his mirror; he should find his mirror in the people."[70] One might use the *Analects*' association of wisdom with water to extend Xunzi's metaphor of water for the people: a ruler depends on the people not only for the security of his position but also for the wisdom of his rule. Not every individual is wise, but there is an important link between the people and wisdom, especially wisdom in terms of knowing *tianming*. Metaphors of water and mirrors in ancient Chinese texts function differently from Western metaphors of the mirror in which the subject and object are radically separated.[71] The Chinese mirror metaphor, when the mirror is water, plays on the copresence of both reflection and transparency to elucidate a view of knowledge and wisdom in which subject and object are not radically separated but bound together in transactions. Such knowledge is transformative. Whether one knows another and, consequently, how one affects her and vice versa, depend on how one interacts with her. Since *tian*, as a field, is focused in the people, the quality of a person's wisdom, her knowledge of *tian*'s mandate, lies in the quality of her interactions with the people—how well she acts as a focus with transformative power for the people—in her authoritativeness, which requires putting herself in the people's place.

Nontranscendent *tian*, as the unfolding process of existence, becomes known through human interpretation, and this interpretation affects both how the world is and how it would become. Knowing *tian* as descriptive is inseparable from realizing *tian* as prescriptive. Anyone could, and should, realize *tian*, both in terms of knowing the field of existence and bringing about the emergent order, though the quality of that realization varies. The exemplary person and, ultimately, the sage, emerge—but they are never completely separated—from the people by distinguishing themselves in realizing *tianming*. One who does not realize *tianming* can only be a petty character, never an exemplary person. Knowing *tianming*, exemplary persons hold it in awe, because its realization is of great import—it is the realization of authoritativeness, of ethico-politcal order, of sagehood (*Analects* 16.8). The relation with *tian* is not limited to rulers in both the *Analects* and the *Mencius*. Confucius claims to know *tianming* at age fifty; I do not believe that he was aiming for the position of the "son of *tian*" (*Analects* 2.4, 16.8). Knowing *tianming* is knowing how one should act, given what one knows of how the world is and how it should be. Insofar as everyone, in acting, has a capacity to be guided by a desire to become better and to make the world a better place, *tianming* is a call to self-realization through communal participation.

To know, to understand the people, an exemplary person needs to take into account people's own self-interpretations and their views of their world. More important, to bring about order, she needs to transform these as a constitutive means of transforming people. The exemplary person, and certainly the sage, is wiser than the average person, yet in political action, what people believe, how they feel and think, no matter how foolish or even deluded, cannot be ignored. Acting authoritatively toward people requires helping them become wiser, hence, the importance of education as a responsibility of authoritative government. The transformation of people requires their participation; one cannot transform them entirely from without.

People constitute both the problem and the solution in effecting ethico-political order in Confucianism. Insofar as people's self-interpretations and their views of the world determine what the political problems are, and their transformation is required for enduring solutions, people have to participate actively if politics is to be efficacious. Unless everyone affected has a say in what a problem is, and how it could and should be solved—unless there is government by the people—there would be no adequate solution, and there would be no government for the people. In Dewey's words, "If there is one conclusion to which human experience unmistakably points, it is that democratic ends demand democratic methods for their realization" (L14.367).

There is at least one way of interpreting Confucianism and its notion of political legitimacy so that government by the people is a constitutive means of government for the people. This should not be mistaken for the kind of instrumentalist defense of democracy that Andrew Nathan criticizes when he accuses twentieth-century Chinese political thinkers and leaders of treating democracy as merely a means to an end—an attitude that he believes is encouraged by the primacy of "government for the people" in the idea of "people as basis."[72] His criticism assumes that means are somehow inferior to ends, that means can be shunted aside easily and require no commitment. This criticism is valid if the means are external to the ends and dispensable once the ends are achieved or some better means are found, but it carries no weight with constitutive means, which are not dispensable. "Democratic means and democratic ends are one and inseparable" (L11.299). Dewey believes that government by the people is a constitutive means to government for the people. Democracy is not an end-in-itself; there is no such thing. It would be foolish to insist on democracy—or liberal political rights, about which Nathan is more concerned—if the consequences of having such are not believed to be good for the people.

ARE PEOPLE GOOD ENOUGH FOR SELF-GOVERNMENT?

I have been defending Confucianism against critics who believe that even if it advocates government for the people, it does not believe in government by the people, by arguing that its advocacy of government for the people implies advocacy of government by the people. Whether or not the belief is part of early Confucianism, for Confucianism to be a viable, practical philosophy in current historical contexts, it can and must be reconstructed to advocate government by the people. However, this position also has to be defended against critics of participatory democracy in Western political thought who have challenged the very possibility of government by the people, never mind its effectiveness in governing for the people. Otherwise, even if the reconstruction of Confucianism to accommodate government by the people rescues Confucian democracy from being an oxymoron, it may turn out to be a lost cause.

One criticism against democracy is that most people are simply not interested in governing themselves. Low election turnouts have been a favorite among evidence cited of people's political apathy. Dewey himself identifies some of the chief causes of such apathy: people have been systematically miseducated, propagandized, alienated in their working lives, and exploited in their economic relations, so that they come to believe that whatever they do will not make much difference regarding what happens in politics, and they prefer to seek solace in their families or in mindless distractions. Dewey acknowledges that such apathy poses serious problems for democracy, but he believes that it could be overcome if people's "discontent and unrest" could be directed and organized (L6.189). One way of doing this in the United States, Dewey suggests, is organizing political parties that are issue oriented and would provide a voice for people's concerns as an alternative to the power-oriented two-party system. Another is to provide more opportunities for people to work in voluntary associations that address social problems directly so that they will discover from personal experience the compelling nature of participation—that an individual, through participation in a group's activities, may make a difference in whether and how problems that affect others besides herself are solved.

For people to even try to govern themselves, it is important that they believe they have a chance of succeeding. It is this belief that Walter Lippmann attacks. (Lippmann's work, *The Phantom Public*, is the context of Dewey's *The Public and Its Problems*.) Not only is "a public which directs the course of events" in democratic politics "a mere phantom" but, given the size and complexity of modern states, people are incapable of governing themselves. Democratic theory is guilty of a "mystical fallacy," a belief in the "omnicompetence" of every individual in a state. People are simply not intelligent enough to govern themselves. According to Lippmann, the government "enforces some of the working rules of society. It interprets them. It detects and punishes certain kinds of aggression. It presides over the framing of new rules." All of these, which the government does specifically and in great detail, the public cannot do except "crudely, by wholesale, and spasmodically." The democratic conception of the public "is false because it fails to note the radical difference between the experience of the insider and the outsider; it is fundamentally askew because it asks the outsider to deal with the substance of a question as the insider. No scheme of education can equip him in advance for all the problems of mankind; no device of publicity, no machinery of enlightenment, can endow him during a crisis with the antecedent detailed and technical knowledge which is required for executive action."[73]

In Lippmann's view, governments do not express the will of the people; they do not, cannot, and should not act in response to public opinion *continually*. "Public opinion is a reserve of force brought into action during a crisis in public affairs." The people cannot govern, but "by their occasional mobilization as a majority, people support or oppose individuals who actually govern." The role of the people in a democracy should be "to support the Ins when things are going well; to support the Outs when they seem to be going badly." Furthermore, the people cannot judge the government's performance based on any thorough understanding of the substance of policies. Their "judgment will necessarily be made on the basis of a sample of behavior, an aspect of a situation, by very rough external evidence. With the substance of the problem [the people] could do nothing usually but meddle ignorantly and tyrannically." Not only is government by the people impossible in the current state of affairs, it will never be possible—no education, information media, or public debate would make it possible. It is not even desirable to try to bring it about. This "false ideal of democracy can lead only to disillusionment and to meddlesome tyranny." It is better if we recognize that government is safest and best in the hands of an educated elite, "the insiders," so that "each of us may live free of the trampling and the roar of a bewildered herd."[74]

Dewey agrees with most of Lippmann's criticisms of contemporary institutions of political democracy without viewing them as necessary to democracy as an ideal. He believes that what Lippmann calls the "pseudo-environment" of facts and dreams, illusions and prejudices, and casual opinions could be improved significantly by cooperative inquiry. The people's current performance in self-government is not a good reflection even of their current abilities, precisely because their environment is perverted by defective practices. "Until secrecy, prejudice, bias, misrepresentation, and propaganda as well as sheer ignorance are replaced by inquiry and publicity, we have no way of telling how apt for judgment of social policies the existing intelligence of the masses may be" (L2.366). Neither are the people's current abilities a good indication of whether they are good enough at democratic participation—they may not be good enough now, but they can become better at it. And if the present generation can never achieve the ideal in the limited time it has, then there is always hope for future generations; the chances of future generations to fulfill that hope depend in part on what the present generation does.

Dewey's ideal of democracy does not, as Lippmann implies, "pervert the true possibilities of its subject, like a fat man's ideal to be a ballet dancer."[75] For one thing, we should never be too dogmatic about what is possible and what is not; a person's possibilities are not fixed but expandable, to some extent. Most important of all, democracy is not just about oneself or even one's own generation—as an ideal of community, it is more about the human species than the human individual. This does not mean that the present generation would not benefit from an attempt to realize democracy; on the contrary, any such attempts would be beneficial even without full realization of the ideal.

Dewey agrees with Lippmann that the public is in eclipse, but he disagrees with Lippmann's elitist conclusion. His recommendation is to work

harder and more intelligently at providing the conditions necessary for bringing the public out of its eclipse—among them are a radical reform of education and the revitalization of the local community. Dewey has been criticized
for not making clear what political forms would be required for his ideal
democracy and therefore failing to counter criticism such as Lippmann's effectively.[76] Any theory of political forms, for Dewey, would have to be rooted in
practice. Perhaps he was never satisfied enough with the results of his political activism to recommend specific political strategies or political institutions,
or he felt that this was a question best answered within specific situations by
those actively engaged in reforming political institutions. If we are so inclined,
we could certainly reconstruct—from Dewey's own involvement in the
Thought News project, the League for Independent Political Action, the movement to outlaw war, the Commission of Inquiry into the Charges Made
against Trotsky in the Moscow Trials, to name only a few of his projects—
some political practices and institutions that Dewey would consider contributing to "government by the people." In any such undertakings, however,
one should always remember that in Dewey's philosophy, historical contingencies render any theoretical certainty a delusion.

Lippmann assumes that if the people were to govern effectively, then they
would have to be a mass of equally qualified super-executives "with the appetite
of an encyclopedist and infinite time ahead of [them]." This is a mistaken view
of government by the people. Each individual among the people need not
"have opinions on all public affairs" but only on issues that affect her. And in
a less than ideal world, where issues affecting one may exceed what one could
deal with, one prioritizes and participates most actively in those of greatest
concern to oneself. As different individuals would almost certainly have different sets of priorities, there would be a "division of labor," so that hopefully
one would be adequately represented by others who share a common interest
(in being similarly affected indirectly by certain actions) in issues in which one
is not actively participating. Government by the people means that all should
be participating actively in something, as much and as well as each can manage;
it is not "the theory that everybody was doing everything."[77]

Neither is it necessary for a democracy that one should be an expert in
any and every issue in which one is actively participating. The whole point of
cooperative inquiry is that a community of inquiry could attempt and have a
better chance of solving problems that would defeat any of its members individually. Nor does Dewey romanticize the possibilities of intelligence. Our
problem-solving abilities, even when we pool our resources, do not make us
omnipotent. "All action is an invasion of the future, of the unknown," and "[we]
always build better or worse than [we] know" (M14.10, 143). There would
always be problems that are beyond our current abilities to solve, and the best
that we could attempt to do is accommodate ourselves, hope that future gen-

erations would have a better chance of solving them, and improve their chances of success if within our power. Even when we solve some problems, this would not necessarily reduce the number of problems in the world, for "problems will recur in the future and in a new form or on a different plane" (M14.197). For Dewey, "when all is said and done, the fundamentally hazardous character of the world is not seriously modified, much less eliminated," and our world remains a "precarious and perilous" place (L1.45). While he believes that democracy will give us the best life possible in this precarious and perilous world, Dewey does not promise an end to all troubles if we attain it, nor does he promise a smooth path to a guaranteed destination.

Defenders of democracy are confronted not only by claims that people are not intellectually good enough to govern themselves, but also by claims that people are not *morally* good enough to govern themselves. Dewey often has been criticized for overlooking "the stark reality of evil" in human nature, "the capacity of human beings *en masse* to commit heinous crimes against other human beings."[78] Such criticisms find easy sympathy among a generation with the images of Auschwitz burned into their brains, superimposed by more recent ones of the carnage in the dismembered former Yugoslavia, of inter-tribal massacres in Africa, the slaughter of innocents in East Timor, escalating international terrorism . . . the list gets longer every day. Among critics of Dewey who take this route, Reinhold Niebuhr is one of the most influential.

For Niebuhr, politics is not so much about interpersonal as it is about intergroup relations—his understanding of society is based on Marxian class analysis. Government is the exercise of power by dominant groups in society over the powerless. The gulf between the governing and governed cannot be crossed, and politics is always coercive. In politics, conflict is inevitable, and power can be countered only by power—cooperative inquiry as a method will not work in politics, as it is based on a false conception of human collective behavior. For Niebuhr, "the limitations of human imagination, the easy subservience of reason to prejudice and passion, and the consequent persistence of irrational egoism, particularly in group behavior, make social conflict an inevitability in human history, probably to its very end."[79] According to this view, Dewey's democracy is not only impossible to attain, but the methods he proposes offer little promise of attaining any ethical social improvement, which for Niebuhr means reducing the inequality of power and privileges.

Niebuhr's view is rendered more plausible, because he does not claim that man is inherently evil and nothing else. "Human nature is not wanting in certain endowments for the solution of the problem of human society. Man is endowed by nature with organic relations with his fellowmen; and natural impulses prompt him to consider the needs of others even when they compete with his own." But "there are definite limits in the capacity of ordinary mortals which make it impossible for them to grant to others what they claim for themselves." For Niebuhr, despite his recognition of human social impulses, egoism is at the root of man's inability to conform his collective life to his individual ideals. "The force of egoistic impulse is much more powerful than any but the most astute psychological analysts and the most rigorous devotees of introspection realize." Egoism is the driving force of group behavior. "The group egoism of a privileged class is . . . the sum and aggregate of individual egoisms," and "the man in the street, with his lust for power and prestige thwarted by his own limitations and the necessities of social life, projects his *ego* upon his nation and indulges his anarchic lusts vicariously."[80]

At times, Niebuhr suggests that even apparently unselfish behavior may be a disguised form of selfishness. For example, even a person's sociality expressed in his most intimate relations, such as the family, "is also a projection of his own *ego*. . . . every immediate loyalty is a potential danger to higher and more inclusive loyalties, and an opportunity for the expression of a sublimated egoism." On other occasions, unselfishness enables individuals to devote themselves to groups, and the resulting loyalty and fervor work against reason, undermining the critical attitude of individual members toward the group and its enterprises. The unqualified character of devotion to the group, most evident in patriotism, is the very basis of a group's power and its freedom to use the power without moral restraint. Thus unselfishness of individuals makes for the group's selfishness. "A combination of unselfishness and vicarious selfishness in the individual thus gives a tremendous force to national egoism, which neither religious nor rational idealism can ever completely check."[81]

Niebuhr is scornful of the belief that education can solve the problem of politics. "It is sentimental and romantic to assume that any education or example will ever completely destroy the inclination of human nature to seek special advantages at the expense of, or in indifference to, the needs and interests of others." He is skeptical of both the revolutionary zeal of Marxian proletarians and the parliamentarian tactics of evolutionary socialists. "The future peace and justice of society therefore depend upon, not one but many, social strategies, in all of which moral and coercive factors are compounded in varying degrees. So difficult is it to avoid the Scylla of despotism and the Charybdis of anarchy that it is safe to hazard the prophecy that the dream of perpetual peace and brotherhood for human society is one which will never be fully realized." What Niebuhr's tragic vision of the human predicament leaves us is a much more modest goal than Dewey's ideal democracy: it is not the creation of an ideal society in which there will be uncoerced and perfect peace and justice, but "a society in which there will be enough justice, and in which coercion will be sufficiently non-violent to prevent his common enterprise from issuing into complete disaster."[82]

Insofar as Niebuhr elides description and prescription in his criticism of democratic society, Dewey's response to him would be similar to his response to Lippmann: existing democratic states are not embodiments of ideal democracy. While Niebuhr's social criticism is perceptive and powerful, his criticism of the moralists finds no purchase where Dewey is concerned. Even a cursory read of *Individualism Old and New*, let alone the other millions of words in social criticism that Dewey had written throughout his long career, reveals that Dewey is far from unappreciative of "predatory self-interests" and the covert manner in which powerful interests in society operate against the interests of the majority and obstruct the path to a better society. Our earlier discussion of egoism and altruism gives us some idea of what Dewey's response would be to Niebuhr's claim about "stubborn egoism." Egoism that is morally problematic is, for Dewey, an acquired character. Changing a person's environment could prevent it.

Niebuhr does not mistake the results of pathological social conditions for some kind of human essence; like Dewey, he recognizes how strongly our environment affects our character. He differs from Dewey in believing that intelligence and education are powerless when in comes to changing an environment dominated by coercive power. Dewey is politically much less naïve than Niebuhr makes him out to be. He acknowledges that "intelligence has no power *per se*," and it contributes to social reconstruction "only as it is integrated into some system of wants, of effective demands" (L9.110). In terms of practice, as Westbrook points out, by the 1930s Dewey was not arguing for "social intelligence" as an alternative to politics but for a radical politics that incorporated intelligence.[83] Dewey is cautious but not squeamish about power, or even the use of force. He does not plead with the oppressed to abandon the effort to match power with power in favor of only reasoning with "dominant economic interests"; he appeals to them to wage their struggles intelligently.

To Niebuhr, "Life according to [Dewey's] school is energy; and its dynamic character provides that it will move forward. If reason cuts straight and broad channels for the stream of life, it will flow in them. Without reason life spends itself in the narrow and tortuous beds, which have been cut by ages of pre-rational impulse, seeking immediate outlets for its energy." This grossly oversimplifies and distorts the extremely complex relations between impulse, habit, and intelligence in Dewey's philosophy. On the few occasions Niebuhr mentions Dewey by name, his attack appears to be aimed not so much at Dewey as at straw men.[84] Dewey is not the kind of "rationalist" Niebuhr attacks. Though Niebuhr treats intelligence and reason as though they are interchangeable, his view of reason is frequently one opposed to passions and can only be the latter's slave, and only infrequently does it involve the broader "reasonableness." Whatever Dewey may have inherited from the Age of Reason, his view of intelligence is much more complex and nuanced than Niehbuhr implies. For one thing, it is based on the continuity of feeling and thinking, and in no way is it self-sufficient. Moreover, Dewey has no delusions about the "omnipotence" of intelligence.

Niebuhr often criticizes "the moralists" as though they are all certain that their ideals will eventually be realized in every detail. Such certainty breeds absolutism, and "societies risk the welfare of millions when they gamble for the attainment of the absolute. And since coercion is an invariable instrument of their policy, absolutism transmutes this instrument into unbearable tyrannies and cruelties." Idealism may be productive of good in individual conduct, but in politics it is pernicious to the extreme. Niebuhr also objects to those who acknowledge the impossibility of full realization but still claim that the ideal is worth pursuing—these people exchange moral potency for rationality. We are caught between fanaticism and apathy. "The inertia of society is so stubborn that no one will move against it, if he cannot believe that it can be more easily overcome than it is actually the case. And no one will suffer the perils and pains involved in the process of radical social change, if he cannot believe in the possibility of a purer and fairer society than will ever be established. These illusions are dangerous because they justify fanaticism; but their abandonment is perilous because it inclines to inertia."[85]

An ideal need not be proven to be fully realizable in order to have consequences for social practice. One need not be an absolutist for ideals to play an important role in improving one's life. Dewey would argue that having ideals, which push to the limit our imagination the values we find in experience, ensures that we would spare no effort in getting closer to that limit— the point is not whether one actually reaches the limit but to get as close to it as possible. Niebuhr's recommendation of a more modest goal may end up making us satisfied sooner than we should be. It seems unduly pessimistic to limit the possibilities, other than Niebuhr's resignation to a more modest goal, to either apathy or fanaticism. Dewey and Confucius, both in their philosophy and in their lives, are among those who show us another alternative. They do not underestimate the great difficulty of even approximating to any significant degree their ideals, but neither do they give in to despair and forsake their commitment. Their perseverance in working for their ideals is greater precisely because they do not delude themselves that the ideals are easy, or even necessarily possible, to achieve. There is perspicacity without despair, courage without fanaticism.

FAITH IN PEOPLE

The only true idealism, for Niebuhr, is religious. It requires a "sublime madness" that secular imagination is incapable of supplying.[86] Dewey would agree that idealism draws its strength from the spiritual. "It involves a radical venture of the will in the interest of what is unseen and prudentially incalculable" (M5.371). It is this "attitude which the will takes toward the facts, the vital personal setting of the soul which is faith" (L17.16). As William James points out, "we cannot live or think at all without some degree of faith."[87] In "Creative Democracy—The Task before Us," which was written for a celebration of his eightieth birthday in 1939, Dewey discusses democracy as a faith in various guises: "Democracy as a way of life is controlled by a working faith in the possibilities of human nature, . . . faith in the capacity of human beings for intelligent judgment and action if proper conditions are furnished . . . a personal faith in personal day-by-day working together with others . . . faith in experience and education" (L14.226–9; L11.219). Democracy as an ideal requires faith, not in its inevitable realization but in the possibility of ever-closer approximation. It is a faith that is a willingness to try, to take a chance on failure while hoping for success. Such faith is a tendency toward action, rooted in "the dumb pluck of the animal" but capable of inspiring us to greatness (M14.200).

For Dewey, "faith in the power of intelligence to imagine a future which is the projection of the desirable in the present, and to invent the instrumentalities of its realization, is our salvation" (M10.48). Unlike Niebuhr, for whom salvation and the kingdom of God (which is the only perfect society) are only possible "though the intervention of God," Dewey places the responsibility of salvation and the task of improving society squarely on the shoulders of human beings themselves, without any guarantee of success. He is not "naively optimistic" about democracy, but he is a meliorist. He firmly believes "that the specific conditions which exist at one moment, be they comparatively bad or comparatively good, in any event may be bettered" (M12.181). He has faith in people's capacity for self-government if the proper conditions are provided, not by divine intervention but through human efforts at social reconstruction.

Can Confucianism share Dewey's democratic faith? Faith as "a tendency to action," a willingness to try without guarantee of success, a positive attitude to the unknown and uncertain, is very much part of Confucius' worldview and practical philosophy. In his attitude to *tian*, we discern a belief similar to Dewey's, that "there is in things a grain against which we cannot successfully go"; like Dewey, he would "insist that we cannot even discover what that grain is except as we make this new experiment and that fresh effort" (M11.50). In his ethico-political quest, Confucius' willingness to try is such that one refers to him as "the one who keeps trying although he knows that it is in vain" (*Analects* 14.38). Does Confucius' faith extend to the ability of the people to govern? There are many historical reasons for him to draw conclusions similar to those of Western political realists such as Lippmann and Niebuhr.

One passage in the *Analects* has been singled out as advocating that the people should be given only the role of "followers" in any ethico-political undertaking: "The common people can be induced to travel along the way, but they cannot be induced to realize it" (*Analects* 8.9). Liang Ch'i-ch'ao argues that—despite the ambivalence of *ke* 可, which can mean either "can" or "should," or both—the passage is concerned with what can be done rather than with what should be done. He concedes that the people probably are not capable of understanding the reasons for "following the way," or the nature of the way itself. As the *Mencius* observes, "The multitude can be said never to understand what they practice, to notice what they repeatedly do, or to be aware of the path they follow all their lives" (*Mencius* 13.5/67/26). The people may not be as bewildered as Lippmann describes those of modern societies, but they are a herd nevertheless.

We could attempt to rescue the text by noting that it speaks not of the people's possibilities directly but of the possibilities of "inducement." The character *shi* 使 is glossed in the *Shuowen* lexicon as "command." One might argue from this that knowledge, realizing the way, requires voluntary cooperation and active participation of the people; unlike mere compliance, it is not something that can be commanded or coerced, which they can be "induced to do." But *shi* in the *Analects* is also used to mean "to cause something to happen" or "to employ," and these uses do not always involve force or command. A more significant obstacle to this rescue attempt is the meaning and connotations of *min* 民 itself. Hall and Ames have explored in detail the associations of *min* with "blindness and confusion."[88] There are other classical Chinese terms that could refer to "the people"—among them, "multitude" (*zhong* 眾), "many people" (*shuren* 庶人), and "the hundred surnames" (*baixing* 百姓). These have importantly different connotations, even though sometimes they also are used interchangeably with *min*. They seem to share one difference from *min* in that while they all suggest an assembly of discrete persons, or at least discrete clans, *min* would seem to connote the people as an undiscriminated and undiscriminating mass.

Some have read the passage in the *Analects* "when the way prevails in the world, the common people do not debate affairs of the state" as being against the people's participation in politics,[89] but one also could understand it to mean that one cannot expect the people to suffer in silence if government fails in its responsibilities. It is not the common people debating matters of the state that leads to the way not prevailing in the world but the other way around. As *Mencius* 6.9 shows, it would be better if there is no need for "disputation," but it becomes necessary when the Confucian way does not prevail in the world. Who should do the disputing depends on the quality of the disputation, not on the social status of the disputers. If there is a problem with the "debate" of the common people from a Confucian point of view, then it is the common people's lack of learning that renders their "debates" no more than grumblings of discontent.

From a Deweyan point of view, one would point out that one does not have to be "learned" to engage in an inquiry, that on the contrary one becomes learned through such inquiry. There are reasons—which will be considered in greater detail in the next chapter—to believe that Confucius would not believe that every and any kind of debate would be beneficial, either for the individuals involved or for the state. And even for Dewey, one must also acknowledge that not just any kind of discourse qualifies as an inquiry, let alone an inquiry that would result in the solution of problems. If the people, as an ignorant and a disordered mass, debate affairs of the state only in terms of the unfocused airing of opinions, an unguided release of emotions, then even Dewey would have to admit that there is no inquiry, and that such debate is not going to solve any problems.

The significance of the "benightedness" of the common people for Confucians is not that they should be kept out of active politics or treated like sheep, but that they require education. An important Han text compares them to "sleeping eyes that need to be awakened." Hall and Ames point out that while Confucius distinguishes between people as the ignorant masses (*min* 民) and people as distinctive particular persons (*ren* 人), he also believes that "edification permits one to move from the indeterminate masses to the expression of one's particularity and, ultimately, to the expression of one's authoritative humanity (*ren* 仁)."[90] Democracy will not succeed if the people are "benighted," but insofar as Confucius has faith in education, in the possibility of the people being awakened and therefore becoming capable of self-government, then Confucians could have faith in democracy. As Dewey points out: "Faith in democracy is all one with faith in experience and education" (L14.229).

Though Confucius admits the possibility of people who are born wise, or who acquire knowledge because of a greater natural propensity for it, the majority of people gain wisdom through learning, and he counts himself among the latter (*Analects* 16.9, 7.20, 7.28). One learns in order to participate effectively in ethico-political practice (*Analects* 19.7). In learning, Confucius does not believe that there is anyone who fails because of a lack of ability; even the least able could always improve if he or she tries—one should not prejudge what one is capable or not capable of. Even when it comes to authoritative conduct, though its full realization is difficult, and perhaps impossible, Confucius has never met anyone who lacks the strength to embark on the path (*Analects* 4.6). When a student excuses himself from learning Confucius' way on the grounds of "a lack of strength," Confucius exposes him. "Those who do not have the strength collapse somewhere along the way. But with you, you have drawn your own line before you start" (*Analects* 6.12). In having the ability to learn, one has the ability to think for oneself—one who learns, on being shown one corner, is able to come back with the other three (*Analects* 7.8). Confucius would agree that, though people's abilities vary, everyone has enough intelligence to contribute something to sociopolitical order. All would benefit from more extensive participation.

Lack of faith in the possibilities of human nature is not characteristic of early Confucianism. On the contrary, a persuasive case can be made that Confucians should have faith in people: they are capable of democratic participation if they are provided with appropriate conditions. It is the role of a good Confucian government to provide those conditions. A Confucian ethico-political order could be a Confucian democracy.

Chapter 5

Authoritative Freedom

While Dewey does not simply equate democracy with freedom, there is no doubt that freedom is a central democratic value. "Democracy as a moral ideal is thus an endeavor to unite two ideas which have historically often worked antagonistically: liberation of individuals on one hand and promotion of a common good on the other" (L7.349). "The task of democracy is forever that of creation of a freer and more humane experience in which all share and to which all contribute" (L14.230). In turn, "the permanence of the democratic political order depends upon the energy and sincerity with which we devote ourselves to maintenance of the moral foundations of a free society" (L15.174). Dewey counts himself among those who "took it for granted that the values and purposes of a free society provided the core of the definition of civilization, and the measure of our collective moral advance" (L15.170). The ideal of associated living is one of ordered richness, wherein freedom is valued as "the secure release and fulfillment of personal potentialities which take place only in rich and manifold association with others: the power to be an individualized self making a distinctive contribution and enjoying in its own way the fruits of association" (L2.329). Freedom is "the most practical of moral questions" (M14.8).

I have tried to show that although Confucianism has advocated government for the people but not government by the people, government by the people is not incompatible with Confucianism, and it is actually necessary to government for the people. Moreover, Confucius and later Confucians have the "faith in the possibilities of human nature" that Dewey argues is central to the democratic ideal. I shall further elucidate this faith by comparing Dewey's and a Confucian understanding of freedom and authority, the conditions required for a person to be free, and how a free, yet ordered, society might be achieved. The answers to the questions of whether freedom has an important place in the Confucian ethico-political ideal and whether and how a Confucian society might be a free society will take us a step farther in ascertaining whether Confucian democracy is possible.

Negative and Positive Freedoms

Since Isaiah Berlin's 1958 seminal work, "The Two Concepts of Liberty," the distinction between negative and positive liberty has been the subject of many philosophical discussions of freedom, and the terms have since become part of the common vocabulary of Western political philosophy. Berlin's distinction raises an issue that is critical for the following discussion: are Dewey's and Confucian conceptions of freedom the kind that could be easily perverted into justifying its opposite, so that authoritarian government might justify "forcing people to be free"? According to Berlin, positive conceptions of freedom have led to such results historically. He defends the negative sense of freedom, more suited to pluralism, as a "truer and more humane ideal."[1] Dewey, writing before Berlin, also speaks of "negative" freedom and "positive" freedom—while "negative" freedom means largely the same thing for Dewey as it does for Berlin, there are significant differences in their conceptions of "positive" freedom.

Dewey traces the importance given to the negative sense of freedom in politics—absence of interference from others—to John Locke, to the classical liberalism born in a revolt against tyrannical government and religious intolerance. Negative freedom views government as the greatest threat to individual liberty and focuses on limiting the area in which a government may interfere with individuals' lives. Born in a struggle against the oppression of arbitrary political power exercised from a distant center, it is not surprising that the founders of the United States identified freedom with negative freedom.

Even more than political freedom, early America valued the "freedom of opportunity" that sustained the "American Dream": all individuals who put forth the required effort would have a chance to succeed. This opportunity often was understood narrowly as economic opportunity that is material and pecuniary. The conception of negative freedom became "the equal right of every individual to conduct business and make money free from social restraint, so long as he broke no law on the statute book [which] coincided with the notion that government is the chief source of oppression."[2]

Dewey recognizes that negative freedom contributed significantly to the liberation of many on both sides of the Atlantic (L3.99). His criticism is that those who continue to defend it overlook the historical relativity of freedom. "The conception of liberty is always relative to forces that at a given time and place are increasingly felt to be oppressive" (L11.35). The oppression might have come mostly from governments at one time, but for his time and place, it comes from "material insecurity and from the coercions and repressions that prevent multitudes from participation in the vast cultural resources that are at hand" (L11.36). Ensuring those who suffer from such "oppression" an equal "space" guaranteed by the law to do as they like is not going to make them free. In Dewey's view, liberals, by failing "to distinguish between purely formal or legal [i.e., negative] liberty and effective liberty of thought and action," have failed to achieve the true goal of liberalism: a social order in which individuals are not merely freed from external constraints but shall have the conditions required for their individuality to flourish, to remake themselves and their world through effective action. Since socioeconomic conditions may restrict, distort, or even prevent the development of individuality, the goal requires positive social and political action rather than merely leaving people alone (L11.23–40).

Dewey sees the purely negative view of freedom as "the root of the defects in our so-called individualism" (L15.181). He insists that liberty, thought of as "independence of social ties, . . . ends in dissolution and anarchy" (L2.329). For him, "liberty does not mean the removal of the checks which nature and man impose on the life of every individual in the community, so that one individual may indulge impulses which go against his own welfare as a member of society" (M8.297). Negative freedom focuses too much on freedom of *action* as overt and public—on the opportunity to act—and neglects "the importance of freed intelligence which is necessary to direct and to warrant freedom of action" (L11.220). It assumes that people are able to act, and it believes that it does not, or should not, matter what it is that they would choose to do within the area free from interference, as long as they do not harm others or deny a similar liberty to others.

Dewey believes, on the contrary, that "the democratic idea of freedom is not the right of each individual to *do* as he pleases, even if it be qualified by adding 'provided he does not interfere with the same freedom on the part of others'" (L11.220). Unintelligent actions result in confusion and disorder; they have no value. The mental process that issues in action is critical to the value of freedom, and Dewey is concerned with freedom as a value rather than as something that may or may not have value depending on circumstances. "If a man's actions are not guided by thoughtful conclusions, then they are guided by inconsiderate impulse, unbalanced appetite, caprice, or the circumstances of the moment. To cultivate unhindered, unreflective activity is to foster enslavement, for it leaves the person at the mercy of appetite, sense, and circumstance" (L8.186).

Dewey does not reject negative freedom completely. He considers it part of a more important freedom. "For freedom from restriction, the negative side, is to be prized only as a means to a freedom which is power: power to frame purposes, to judge wisely, to evaluate desires by consequences which will result from acting upon them; power to select and order means to carry chosen ends into operation" (L13.41). Dewey distinguishes three important elements in genuine freedom: (1) efficiency in action, ability to carry out plans, the absence of cramping and thwarting obstacles; (2) capacity to vary plans, to change the course of action, and to experience novelties; (3) the power of desires and choice to be factors in events. Dewey's conception of freedom as power goes beyond the question that Berlin's negative freedom answers: "What is the area within which the subject—a person or group of persons—is or should be left to do or be what he is able to do or be, without interference from other persons?" But is it a positive conception that is concerned with the question "What, or who, is the source of control or interference that can determine someone to do, or be, this rather than that?"[3]

Rather than "what or who," Dewey is more concerned with "how" actions are controlled. This draws our attention to the different psychology underlying the various conceptions of freedom. The psychology underlying negative freedom conceives of the individual self as something given, complete in itself, with a given human nature anchoring the claim to freedom. Such a conception of the individual leads to the view of "liberty as a ready-made possession of the individual, only needing removal of external restrictions in order to manifest itself" (L11.290). In contrast, in Dewey's psychology, a person is not a fixed, ready-made self but "something achieved, and achieved not in isolation but with the aid and support of conditions, cultural and physical: including in 'cultural,' economic, legal, and political institutions as well as science and art" (L11.291). Dewey substitutes "culture" for "human nature" as the locus of the problem of freedom in *Freedom and Culture*. Instead of "separation" and "independence" of the individual from nature and other individuals, we find "interaction" between a person and her environment. Intelligence, on which free actions depend, is not a faculty "in" a person, a higher self, or a social entity; it is a way in which a person or a group interacts with the environment (L11.47).

For Dewey, freedom is achieved in the growth of individuality through ethical living. A person living ethically is constantly growing; she grows with the aid and support of others, acting together. Such freedom is not "an original possession or gift. It is something to be achieved, to be wrought out," not in isolation but in a community (L2.61). Freedom is not "a personal problem, capable of being decided by strictly personal choice and action" (L13.103). For Dewey, social action beyond removing external constraints is necessary to secure freedom for individuals.

Some of those who hold conceptions of freedom that Berlin classifies as "positive" share the assumption of the isolated, fixed, and given self of negative conceptions. Immanuel Kant, whose conception of freedom in terms of autonomy is concerned with "Who governs action?" rather than the area in which one can act without interference, is an example. But in contrast to the empirical self in negative freedom, Kant's autonomous subject is transcendent, beyond the realm of natural causality.[4] Other positive freedom proponents, however, see the free self as the culmination of a developmental process. Among these are thinkers Dewey calls "institutional idealists"—in the tradition represented by Spinoza and Hegel. They contend that "freedom is a growth, an attainment, not an original possession, and it is attained by idealization of institutions and law and the active participation of individuals in their loyal maintenance, not by their abolition or reduction in the interests of personal judgments and wants" (L3.103). There are significant similarities between Dewey's positive freedom and that of the institutional idealists, but there also are important differences.

Institutional idealists are as guilty of a "separatist" psychology as are the defenders of negative freedom. The defenders of negative freedom, and of positive freedom of the Kantian variety, reserve their concern for the agent; the institutional idealists reserve their concern for institutions. Positive conceptions of freedom assume an "either, or" between the free self and others when it comes to control over action. The higher self capable of freedom is perceived of as a completely separate "other" to the unfree, empirical self. For Kant, heteronomy and autonomy are mutually exclusive—either the self acting under laws of nature or the self acting according to laws of reason is in control at any one time. For Hegel, despite the claims of organicism in his philosophy, the higher, perfectly rational self, in its organic unity with the social entity, becomes separate from and "other" to the empirical, imperfectly rational self. It is as an *other* that the higher self gains control over and subdues the empirical self. The participation of the empirical self is deliberately excluded from free actions.

In contrast, both agent and environment (including, but not restricted to, institutions) are important in Dewey's interactionist psychology. The question of control over action is not a matter of either "completely mine" or "completely others'." Freedom does not lie in complete control over action, in excluding the participation of lower selves or others, or excluding the contribution of external conditions to one's action; it has to do with how the various factors of a situation—whether internal or external, pertaining to an agent or others, though these would amount to no more than abstract heuristic distinctions for Dewey rather than metaphysical categories—are integrated in the quest for a satisfactory outcome.

In the positive conceptions that Berlin objects to, freedom consists in realizing the higher self, or its rule over the empirical self. The higher self is frequently identified with some social entity. "This entity is then identified as being the 'true self' which, by imposing its collective, or 'organic', single will upon its recalcitrant 'members', achieves its own, and therefore their, 'higher' freedom."[5] Thus positive conceptions of freedom have led to the defeat of negative freedom. Dewey is no stranger to the vocabulary of the higher self: "the higher self is that formed by the step in advance of one who *has* been living on a low plane. As he takes the step he enters into an experience of freedom" (L7.308). However, Dewey does not separate this "higher self" from the empirical present self—the two are joined by a process of growth. Capacity for growth, "to become different, even though we define freedom by it, must be a present capacity, something in some sense present" (L3.111). The process joining a present self and its "higher self" is directed not by the higher self but by the present self acting intelligently, employing its insight and foresight to organize the means to bring about the higher self. The higher self is not defined by a predetermined ideal but is shaped with reference to the present self. There is no question of the higher self "ruling" the present self.

Furthermore, Dewey does not understand the "higher self" in a perfectionist sense—it is only one, not the final, stage in the process of personal growth. A self "higher" relative to an earlier self could always grow further into some other even higher self. The conception of self associated with Berlin's positive sense of freedom, in contrast, is perfectionist, and freedom lies in the realization of a perfect self, higher than the empirical self in a final sense, as part of a perfect social or cosmic order. Perfectionism implies that there is "a final solution" to all problems, that there exists one and only one correct answer to any question, that there is only one right way to live. It is this very perfectionism that renders positive freedom so pernicious historically. This perfectionism is fundamentally contrary to Dewey's philosophy in which the possibility of freedom means "a universe in which there is real uncertainty and contingency, a world which is not all in, and never will be, a world which in some respect is incomplete and in the making, and which in these respects may be made this way or that according as men judge, prize, love, and labor" (M11.50).

FREEDOM AS GROWTH

Dewey identifies "the essential problem of freedom" as "the problem of the relation of choice and unimpeded effective action to each other" (L3.104). Intelligence is the key to this relation. "The only freedom that is of enduring importance is freedom of intelligence, that is to say, freedom of observation and judgment exercised in behalf of purposes that are intrinsically worth while"

(L3.39). While he often stresses the primacy of freedom of *thought*, thought is free only as it can manifest itself in action.[6] Action is free only as it is *thoughtful*, the manifestation of a specific kind of thinking, of choice. Dewey does not locate the significance of choice in the freedom of the will, in the antecedents of choice. The significance of choice lies instead in its consequences and the progress from antecedents to consequences.

A current situation in which a choice is required is a nexus between what has been and what may yet be. Both past and future render the situation indeterminate. The future does so because it is an open, infinite field of possibilities. The past does so because there are infinite ways of understanding past events that may have an impact on the future, and because one's life history is so complex that there is always the possibility of continuing diversification of behavior (L3.96). The significance of choice for freedom lies in the possibility of action making a difference regarding how the past will affect the future through the present. "To foresee future objective alternatives and to be able by deliberation to choose one of them and thereby weight its chances in the struggle for future existence measures our freedom" (M14.214). Intelligence means framing our purposes and organizing the means for achieving them through insight into experience and foresight of possible consequences of actions. Choice, therefore, requires intelligence, "the power of using past experience to shape and transform future experience" (M11.346).

The relation between intelligence and freedom is spiral rather than linear, something that commentators have sometimes misunderstood. An example of such misunderstanding is Boyd Bode's claim in *Progressive Education at the Crossroads*: "According to Dewey, freedom is achieved through the exercise of intelligence, whereas the less discriminating of his disciples understand him to mean that intelligence is achieved through the exercise of freedom."[7] Both Bode and "the less discriminating of [Dewey's] disciples" overlook the importance of Dewey's views about means and ends being internally related, creating a kind of spiral mutual enhancement—either freedom or intelligence could be the starting point in this process. Which is emphasized, which is treated as the end and the other as the means, depends on the situation in question.

One does not have to be intelligent before one can be free. This is important if one is to defend Dewey against distortions of his views that deny freedom to those considered "unintelligent" or defend the idea of "forcing people to be intelligent." Freedom to think, to experiment, is required if one is to develop a potential into actual intelligence, to increase intelligence, but unless one acts intelligently, the initial freedom remains a negative condition, an opportunity missed, a freedom of little significance. Both freedom and intelligence are relative concepts for Dewey. We all begin with a little of both, and we are unlikely to achieve the maximum of either in a lifetime, but a flourishing life, a life of growth, is one in which intelligence and freedom mutually enhance each other.

"What men actually cherish under the name of freedom is that power of varied and flexible growth, of change of disposition and character, that springs from intelligent choice" (L3.111). Intelligent choice contributes to growth—the only moral end for Dewey—by framing purposes that develop one's individuality and contribute to the making of community and by organizing the means of realizing these purposes (M12.181). An intelligent choice "enlarges the range of action, and this enlargement in turn confers upon our desires greater insight and foresight, and makes choice more intelligent" (L3.104). A child may play truant to gratify the immediate desires of having fun, or she may go to school. The former, while giving immediate satisfaction, has consequences (not only limited to being punished by adults) that limit future satisfactions. By going to school, satisfaction may be postponed, but the child will have access to a much wider range of enjoyments in the future—partly by being better at acquiring more material resources (usually but not always the case) and partly by developing more capacities (e.g., the ability to read, to understand and therefore to benefit from modern technology, and to appreciate the arts). Developing one's capacities also enables a person to compare and discriminate among different enjoyments and to choose intelligently.

Developing one's capacities will not rid one of all troubles and sufferings in life, even though it helps one avoid some of them. Moreover, being capable of more enjoyment might involve developing sensitivities that also give one's sufferings a keener edge. Without entering into a prolonged argument to show that pain and suffering could make one a better person, I would point out that among the capacities that people develop are those that would enable them to understand their suffering better and, when it could not be avoided, to endure suffering in such a way that it might still enrich their experience instead of being a totally negative factor.[8] Being freer does not necessarily make us happier. What the development of capacities does is increase one's range of future choices and actions, so that intelligent choice and intelligent action are related in a widening spiral that constitutes the process of growth.

"Freedom for an individual means growth, ready change when modification is required" (M12.198; L7.305). It is "the secure release and fulfillment of personal potentialities," the making of our future selves (L2.329). It also is the making of our future world, for our selves do not grow in isolation but in interaction with the environment. This does not imply complete control over either self or world (M11.50). In the struggle for future existence, we could only choose among "objective alternatives" and "weight its chances."[9] Even with one's best efforts, one's chosen course of action may be defeated, but to the extent that one's act is truly a manifestation of intelligent choice, one learns something. With freedom of intelligence, one can turn frustration and failure to account in one's further choices and purposes (L3.105). "Freedom consists in a trend of conduct that causes choices to be more diversified and flexible, more plastic and cognizant of their own meaning, while it enlarges their own range of unimpeded operation" (L3.108). Therefore, freedom is to be sought in "something which comes to be, in a certain kind of growth; in consequences, rather than in antecedents. We are free not because of what we statistically are but in as far as we are becoming different from what we have been" (L3.108).

Various factors beyond our control enter into not only the outcome of a choice but also the choice itself. Others could have played a crucial role in the alternatives available, in our understanding of the alternatives, and in our very selection of one rather than another of the alternatives. If one does not have complete control, then what makes a choice and its resulting action free rather than unfree? What kind of interference from others would not infringe on a person's freedom? The answer lies in the integrative functions of intelligence, the organic unity of growth. We cannot be forced to act intelligently, to grow, because coercion alienates us from the ends of our action, so that the result is apathy and disintegration of experience and personality. In growth, experience is consummatory; it achieves an organic unity. In an unfree action, one acts to realize not one's own end but another's. Taking "the power to frame purposes" as an important constituent of freedom, Dewey agrees with Plato, who "defined a slave as the person who executes the purposes of another" (L13.43).

An end is not one's own not because one is not its *original author* and not because it is not entirely one's own creation, but because there is a lack of organic, internal relations between the end and one's other ends and between the end and one's means. In an intelligent action, a free action, the means and the end are internally related, so that the end not only constrains and provides the standards of adequacy for the means, but the means, as the agent comes to know them, will refine and enlarge the end. Furthermore, an intelligently chosen end is in turn internally related to other ends that a person may have, so that each enhances the meaning of the others, and ideally they form a harmonious whole. The purposes on behalf of which "freedom of enduring importance" is exercised are "intrinsically worthwhile," not as "ends-in-themselves" but as being intrinsic (i.e., internally related) to a person's life, to what she has been and what she could be. Internal relations do not come into being through coercion; they emerge within a person's experience as she lives it. An action is unfree without a person's participation, which is a function of her unique life history and intelligent integration of means and ends. Regardless of its origin, if one manages to establish such organic internal relations, then an end becomes one's own, and the action to realize it is free, regardless of contributions that others may have made to the choice and action. In the absence of such internal relations, a person's choice and its resulting action are not free, even if the end originated with her.

An end is my own when my judgment of its value emerges from my experience: I perceive it as a constitutive means toward how life should be lived, toward a better world, a better "I"—as my experience has led me to understand both self and context. Such an end is revised according to what a new experience reveals to me. This flexibility, the key to efficient interaction between my environment and me, is missing in an unfree action, wherein the end is not mine. In an unfree action, the end is external and fixed for me by another. Any variation would have to come from, or be permitted by, the source of coercion. I am unable to refine or enlarge the end, even if my experience warrants it. Not only flexibility but also initiative and effort would be affected when actions are not free. My own ends command a personal commitment that manifests itself in the initiative and effort that I put into organizing the means to realize that end. Though more obvious in the momentous decisions of one's life, this model is applicable more generally to all actions.

When an end is not my own, my interest in the outcome decreases dramatically, and so do initiative and effort. The problem with forcing a person to do something is that all too often one has to tell her exactly what to do at every stage. She cannot be relied on to complete the task on her own, or do an excellent job, either through lack of understanding and/or commitment to the end. This is frequently overlooked, because discussions of unfree action usually deal with actions that are simple, one-step actions. With a simple action, the question we need to ask is how it is connected to the rest of a person's actions—we will find that the coerced person will attempt to minimize its effect on her life. In contrast, with a free action, an intelligent person attempts to maximize its effect, to make as many connections as possible with other ends and actions.

Imagine a situation where, having been forced to take up a subject of study that was not her original choice, a student nevertheless takes the initiative and effort, even in the absence of supervision and continued coercion, in advancing her course of study. I would argue that the initiative and effort, to the degree that it develops and becomes motivated by real interest in the subject, indicate the extent to which she has made the end her own so that an initially unfree action has become free. However, "supervision and continued coercion" could take many forms. There may be no one constantly looking over her shoulder, but there could be serious penalties awaiting failure. In that case, her initiative and effort may not be an indication of her having truly appropriated the end (of studying that particular subject) and reauthorized it, thus making it her own, but in pursuit of a very different end of her own, (i.e., avoiding those penalties of failure).

If her end was merely to avoid the penalties of failure, then she would do the minimum necessary, and if there were an easier way of avoiding the penalties (e.g., cheating at exams without being caught), then she might do so. If the end of studying the subject has become her own end, then she would see the skills and knowledge to be acquired as contributing to a better life, to her growth; then cheating would be self-defeating. Furthermore, the two scenarios are different in terms of the flexibility in revising the end. When she has appropriated the end as her own, she may find herself studying other related subjects, not because it is *necessary* to the first subject, but because experience has enlarged the end, or she may stop studying the subject if experience shows that it has lost its value vis-à-vis some new end or the rest of her ends. If her study remains coerced, then she would not do the former, and she could not do the latter.

Dewey's view of freedom, therefore, could be defended adequately against infiltration of the authoritarian doctrine of "forcing people to be free." Given the similarities between Dewey's conception and the constructed Confucian conception of the person, and Dewey's criticism of negative freedom, we would expect freedom in a Confucian democracy to take a positive form. Learning from Dewey's understanding of freedom, I shall attempt to construct a defensible account of positive Confucian freedom.

CONFUCIAN POSITIVE FREEDOM

The modern Chinese characters that translate "freedom" (*ziyou* 自由) did not appear before the Han dynasty, and even then they did not have the meaning of the modern usage. Taken separately, *zi* 自 and *you* 由 occur fairly frequently in the pre-Han texts, meaning "self" and "from," respectively—their combination indicates the self as the source of thoughts and acts. Despite their differences, there is enough continuity between the classical language and modern mandarin to make the choice of translating "freedom" as *ziyou* interesting in this discussion. It suggests that Chinese thinking has been more interested in the question "Who governs?" rather than the question "What is the area in which one can do as one pleases?" Ching renders *ziyou*'s "literal" meaning as "self-determination."[10]

The term *ziran* 自然, "self-so-ing," or "spontaneity," often is considered the closest equivalent to "freedom" in the classical language. Traditionally, Daoism, much more than Confucianism, has been concerned with *ziran*, with the interaction between nature and human beings. One could, however, argue that Confucianism is not as unconcerned with nature as has been made out, especially if we take into account an understanding of *tian* 天 to include both nature and culture. And in Daoism, *ziran* also is relevant to interpersonal relationships. Nevertheless, there are probably stronger contenders when it comes to a concept of freedom in early Confucianism. Zhang Dongsun claims that "the Chinese from ancient times has nothing like the western concept of freedom," but he allows that "getting it in, by, or for oneself (*zide* 自得)" bears some resemblance to freedom. The Confucian concept of *zide* and the western concept of freedom have different starting points, different meanings, but they come close in terms of attitudes. Others are prepared to make much more of this "resemblance." De Bary, focusing on neo-Confucianism, finds an entire Chinese liberal tradition based on *zide* and related notions.[11]

Zhang is not arguing that the concept of freedom has no place in Confucianism today—quite the opposite. He considers developing a free, democratic, yet still Confucian culture in Chinese society the most important task facing his generation. He suggests that this is best done by learning from Western cultures, but not in slavish imitation. For him, freedom is a cultural value so that where it is realized in a particular society, its actual content would always be specific to the historical and cultural circumstances of the society. He understands the Western concept of freedom to be a mixture of negative and positive aspects (if we apply Berlin's distinction retrospectively), with different aspects being emphasized at different times and in different societies, according to their specific historical and cultural needs. The Western concept, in his account, comes closest to Confucianism in its connection to morality and reason, that is, in its positive dimensions. What he perceives to be lacking in Chinese culture—a lack that could be compensated by understanding and selectively learning from Western cultures—are the negative aspects of freedom, which he argues are necessary to positive freedom.[12]

Even if the ancient Chinese have no actual concept of freedom, Xu Fuguan contends that the sense of freedom became important as early as the beginning of the Zhou dynasty, when it was argued, as a significant philosophical issue, that one's life—one's fortune or misfortune, success or failure—is related to ethical or unethical conduct rather than resulting solely from *tianming* (heaven's mandate). Whatever their differences when it comes to the presence of a concept of freedom in past Confucian thought, commentators who see Confucianism as a viable way of life today generally agree that it is compatible with freedom, and some go so far to say that its ideals could not be achieved without freedom, whether or not this was recognized by earlier Confucians. Though they disagree on the detailed contents, there is a fair amount of consensus that the freedom compatible with Confucianism cannot be purely negative; negative freedom is at best only a supplement to positive freedom in Confucianism.[13]

Xu Fuguan defends a "self-mastery (*zizuo zhuzai* 自作主宰)" conception of freedom. Mou Zongsan's conception of freedom is explicitly Kantian. The strong influence of German idealism, in particular the philosophies of Kant and Hegel, is evident also in Tang Junyi's and Carsun Chang's conceptions of freedom. He Xinquan argues that these New Confucian conceptions of freedom could lead to democracy only if they combine both positive and negative conceptions of freedom, and that the New Confucians do this by limiting their positive conceptions to personal ethics and applying only the negative conception of freedom in politics. Among the evidence that He Xinquan cites in support of his view is Xu Fuguan's argument that in pre-Qin Confucianism, one could detect a significant difference in what one could legitimately demand of oneself in cultivating one's own person and what one could demand of others in governing them.[14] However, this is problematic, given that early Confucianism is distinguished by the inseparability of politics and ethics. Xu's distinction between personal cultivation and governing people should not be confused with a separation between ethics and politics; it is a distinction made within Confucian politico-ethics. Nor could we apply positive freedom to oneself and negative freedom to others in Confucian contexts. Despite the differences, early Confucian texts have ample evidence that we could not limit our concern for others' freedom to negative freedom, any more than we could do so in our own case. We require an alternative path to a Confucian positive freedom that would be democratic and not fall prey to justifications of "forcing others to be free."

A search for equivalents of "freedom" in the *Analects*—*ziyou* (自由), *ziran* (自然), or even *zide* (自得)—would come up empty. But is Confucius not claiming a kind of freedom when he tells us that "from seventy, he could follow what his heart-and-mind desire without overstepping the boundaries"? (*Analects* 2.4). This is not the ready-made freedom of the negative conceptions assuming a fixed and given self. It is a positive freedom that is achieved only after a long, arduous process of cultivating the person, in which the person or self, far from being fixed and given, changes for the better over time. In this process, we see a parallel to Dewey's conception of freedom as growth, which also is freedom of intelligence. The personal cultivation process begins from the time Confucius was fifteen, "setting his heart-and-mind on learning." Learning, conducted well, always involves reflection (*si* 思), and this combination of learning and reflection is aimed at answering the question "What is to be done?" It is similar to intelligence in Dewey's philosophy—observing, reflecting on past experience to shape the future by determining the present situation, and selecting a course of action. As with intelligence, learning and reflecting, for Confucius, operate through one's interaction with the environment.

To interact well is to find, or cocreate, a proper place for oneself in a wider-emerging scheme of things. This is done through ritual practices, with its combination of constraint in the form of self-discipline and creativity in endowing each act with personal significance. From age thirty, Confucius achieved some success in this when he "took his stance." Having some sense of one's place in a wider scheme of things means greater coherence in one's experience. One can make better sense of what is happening and thereby find one's way forward without being "beset by doubts," as Confucius did from age forty onward. His virtuosity in interacting with his environment continued to increase—" he realized *tianming*" from age fifty, and "his ear was attuned" from age sixty— until he reached the freedom of "following what his heart-and-mind desire without overstepping the boundaries." Freedom is present not only at the end of this process. There is freedom in "setting his heart-and-mind on learning" but relatively less in scope and quality than the freedom he achieved from age seventy. Freedom is a relative concept for Confucius, as it is for Dewey. As one successfully cultivates oneself and grows ethically, one's freedom increases.

While the similarities traced above give us some confidence that a strategy similar to that adopted by Dewey might be successful too in preventing Confucian positive freedom from falling victim to authoritarian perversion, we need to set out the actual defense in greater detail. Since similarities do not make them identical, there might be criticisms against one that do not apply, or not with equal force, against the other. In his criticism of positive freedom, Berlin identifies a strand of it as "self-abnegation in order to attain independence." To avoid being crushed by external constraints, whether laws or accidents of nature or the deliberate malice of others or unintentional effect of their acts and human institutions, one liberates oneself from desires that one knows or fears one cannot realize.[15] This is the freedom of Epictetus, who claims that he, a slave, is freer than his master. This conception of freedom aids authoritarianism by relocating the problem from others imposing constraints—whether they are justified—to the agent herself. It is only the agent, not the world, who must change if she is to be free. Is Confucius' freedom such a case of "internalizing" external constraints—is he a man who grew to love his chains?

Though Confucius does not subscribe to a dualism of desires versus reason or ethical nature and conduct (e.g., he speaks of "desiring authoritative conduct"), he praised Meng Gongchuo for "lacking desires (*buyu* 不欲)" (*Analects* 14.12). In the absence of an absolute opposition between desires and ethical conduct, what matters is the distinction between ethical desires and unethical ones. One should liberate oneself from greed, from any kind of *excesses* in gratifying one's own physical appetites, which is unethical. Avoiding such unethical desires would rechannel one's energy into ethical desires. A closer look at the use of *buyu* 不欲 in the *Analects* itself substantiates this. Confucius considered Meng Gongchuo qualified to be household steward to the Zhao or Wei families (*Analects* 14.11). A greedy man in such a position would easily succumb to corruption or misappropriation. Meng Gongchuo's lack of greed, his "lacking [excessive] desires," made him eminently qualified for that post. Another instance where *buyu* 不欲 is understood as the lack of greed is in the case of Master Jikang—whose family was "richer than the Duke of

Zhou"—worrying about thieves, and Confucius said to him, "If you were not so greedy (*buyu* 不欲), the people would not steal even if you pay them" (*Analects* 11.17, 12.18). Master Jikang's greed was at the expense of the people, making them so poor and desperate that they resorted to thefts.

Confucius' freedom is not self-abnegation in the sense of getting rid of all desires. Contrary to the self-abnegation that Berlin criticizes, one liberates oneself from some desires not because one *cannot* realize them but because one *should not* realize them. In the former, "internalization" takes place regardless of the ethical nature of the external constraints. In the latter, the ethical or unethical nature of the constraints is of paramount importance to one's action. While it involves evaluating desires and avoiding some in favor of others, Confucius' freedom is not a case of "reducing the area of one's vulnerability" to external factors. The "pruning" of desires, instead of stultifying oneself, would help one grow better. It is an open question whether that reduces or increases one's vulnerability to the world. Even though efficacy is as important in Confucian freedom as it is in Dewey's conception—since the consequences of cultivating the person may be seen in terms of *de* 德, which I have translated as "excellence," but which also suggests *virtus*, potency—Confucius does not see the world as being completely within one's control, even if one is a sage. It is quite possible to find more of one's desires frustrated with greater positive freedom; being able to follow one's desires without overstepping the boundaries is no guarantee that the desires will be fulfilled. In a degenerate world, when the way does not prevail, it might be easier to gratify unethical desires than to fulfill ethical ones.

The boundaries that Confucius from age seventy no longer overstepped are those between ethical and unethical desires. They are the boundaries of his way of ethical living (*dao* 道). The freedom to be found within these boundaries does not posit oneself in opposition to others as negative freedom does; the Confucian way brings self and others together in achieving harmonious community. Confucian values, such as authoritative conduct (*ren* 仁), appropriateness (*yi* 義), ritual practice (*li* 禮), wisdom (*zhi* 智), and keeping one's words (*xin* 信), are understood in interpersonal terms. The one thread that runs through Confucius' teachings is the concept of deference or reciprocity (*shu* 恕). "Do not do to others what you yourself do not desire" (*Analects* 4.15, 15.24). The "Great Learning" calls this "the way of the try square (*jieju zhi dao* 絜矩之道)": "What I detest in those above me, I do not do to those below me; what I detest in those below me, I do not do when serving those above me" (*Book of Rites* 43.2/166/3). The character for a "try square," *ju* 矩, is that which is translated as "boundaries" in the above *Analects* passage on Confucius' freedom from age seventy. A try square marking out the boundaries of what qualifies as a square is a metaphor for the ethical standards of sagely conduct exemplifying the way, marking the boundaries between the ethical and the unethical (*Mencius* 7.1/35/29, 7.2/36/10). The boundaries marked out by this metaphorical try square Confucius did not overstep.

This try square metaphor may mislead us into thinking that the ethical boundaries are external standards, so that if freedom is found therein, one can be forced to be free through the external imposition of these standards. A square is objectively determinable, since the standard is intersubjective and transcultural. However, "objectivity" in ethical standards is not absolute but revisable over time through the cumulated actions of individuals. At issue are the concrete standards that are dependent on the instruments that vary in accuracy rather than abstract definitions. Moreover, when a try square should be used always depends on the artist's judgment or sensibility. What is important about the try square is not its externality (its given physicality) but how a craftsperson uses it. The "what," as a relatively stable form, may be external and relatively fixed, but the "how," governing the particular content of each use, is unique to each situation in which it is used. Moreover, the instrument may be improved over time, through the experience, the experiments, of particular individuals, so that even external physicality changes—it does not matter that we may no longer call it a "try square"; it is the function that the instrument fulfills that is important.

Therefore, the way is not a fixed standard of conduct, a perfectionist ideal. It is something that emerges from one's personal experience, albeit an experience that always involves others with whom we interact; it cannot bring ethical success if imposed from without. "It is the person who is able to broaden the way, not the way that broadens the person" (*Analects* 15.9/44/3). Such "emergence" of the *dao*, like freedom of intelligence in Dewey's philosophy, requires an organic integration of one's actions with the rest of one's experience, which precludes coercion as a means. Coercion results only in external compliance. For example, one may force another to follow a way, but even if she complies, she cannot be coerced into "realizing the way."[16] Realizing (*zhi* 知) a Confucian way requires integrating it into one's experience through learning and reflecting, just as intelligence integrates past and future through present action in Dewey's philosophy. Confucian freedom lies in realizing a way, not in following one—it cannot be forced.

A further examination of the process of personal cultivation—the path to freedom—also reveals why "forcing people to be free" would be self-defeating in Confucianism. "Becoming authoritative in one's conduct [i.e., personal cultivation] is self-originating; how could it originate with others?" (*Analects* 12.1). We are not talking about absolute origins here, but rather the origin that is important within the given context. Others may contribute to one's personal cultivation, but it is one's own efforts that make the achievement a realization of oneself rather than the making of an automaton that follows orders (however wise) efficiently. To illustrate this, we may borrow Mencius' story of the man from Song, "who pulled at his rice plants because he was worried at their failure to grow"—he thought he was "helping the rice plants grow" when he actually was killing them (*Mencius* 3.2/16/4). Plants sometimes grow better with human interference—watering when rain is insufficient, digging trenches to drain the soil when rain is too abundant, fertilizing, weeding, pruning, and so on—but pulling at them is not one of the ways to help them grow. Others may help us cultivate ourselves—by deliberately teaching us, providing an examplar or unintentionally providing a model or an example of what not to do, providing various needed economic and social conditions—but coercion is not one of the ways to help us become cultivated. Coercion will not make us free.

In *Analects* 12.7, Confucius says that if circumstances do not allow a government to achieve its three goals of security, material sufficiency, and the people's trust (*xin* 信), then a government should sacrifice first security and then material sufficiency before giving up trust. Some scholars have read this as simply another plank in the platform elevating ethical considerations above material ones. After all, "exemplary persons do not look for full stomachs when eating, nor seek comfort and contentment in their lodgings" (*Analects* 1.14). And, "for resolute scholar-apprentices (*zhishi* 志士) and authoritative persons, while they would not compromise their authoritative conduct to save their lives, they might well give up their lives in order to achieve it" (*Analects* 15.9/42/21). When extended to governing people, this could be used to justify denying people security and material needs—in the extreme, even at the cost of their lives—for the sake of their ethical advancement, precisely the kind of authoritarian conclusions for which Berlin criticizes positive freedom.

Xu Fuguan rejects such interpretations. He argues that even though Confucius emphasizes that in cultivating oneself, and in one's own action, one should put ethical considerations first, when it comes to governing, the people's security and material needs must come first. When asked what more a government could do when a state already has a teeming population (presumably because its government has been able to provide adequately for the people's security and material needs), Confucius' response is "to make them rich" and *then* "to educate them" (*Analects* 13.9). This approach also is evident in the discussions of authoritative government in the *Mencius*.[17] But does this difference not fly in the face of the Confucian dictum of "using what is near as analogy" in behaving ethically in relation to others? (*Analects* 6.30). When others coerce the sacrifice of security and material needs, it is not comparable to one sacrificing them oneself. It would not result in the coerced one's ethical progress—the end used to justify the means—since the coerced action, not having emerged from one's learning and reflecting, has no organic unity with one's own ends and the rest of one's experience.

Ethical progress, the result of personal cultivation, and therefore positive freedom, is something that each person must attain by herself (*zide* 自得). This is why Confucius considers "love of learning" so important and once condemned a lazy student—who obviously did not love learning enough or he would not be taking naps when he should be studying—for being "a piece of rotten wood which cannot be carved" (*Analects* 5.10). Ethical progress is something one aims at for oneself. Confucius praises those in ancient times who "study for their own sake," in contrast to those who "study for the sake of others" (*Analects* 14.24). Some translations substitute "others' praise" for "others." Confucius would not disapprove of praise, others' affirmation and admiration per se; what he would object to is praise that one does not deserve, because there has been no real ethical achievement through personal cultivation and contribution to the community.

Given the relational character of one's self, one's study when successful would benefit others, but it could only do so if the result of studying is *in* oneself, part of what one becomes and therefore how one relates to others. "An exemplary person steeps herself in the way because she wishes to attain it in herself (*zide* 自得). When she attains it in herself, she will be at ease in it; when she is at ease in it, she can draw deeply upon it; when she can draw deeply upon it, she finds its source wherever she turns" (*Mencius* 8.14/41/32). When the way is *in* oneself, it is constantly renewed, for it flows from and with one's experience; it becomes one's experience, made more coherent and more meaningful through personal cultivation.

One does not cultivate oneself in isolation, by being left alone. Personal cultivation takes place only in association, and its culmination can be achieved only in community. When it comes to concern for others' freedom, which is concern for others' cultivation, the Confucian attitude is not one of noninterference. Confucius not only "studies without respite," he also "instructs others without growing weary" (*Analects* 7.2, 7.34). One should interfere, help others achieve their freedom, by providing the positive conditions for ethical living, wherein positive freedom is realized. Like Dewey, who defends the need for political intervention in the economy for his times, Confucius believes that a good government should take positive action to ensure the people's livelihood, because he also recognizes that economic conditions are important for ethical living, especially when people are just starting to cultivate themselves. As Mencius puts it, "those with constant means of support will have constant hearts-and-minds [in treading the way], while those without constant means will not have constant hearts-and-minds. Lacking constant hearts-and-minds, they will go astray and get into excesses, stopping at nothing. To punish them when they have thus fallen foul of the law is to set a trap for the people" (*Mencius* 1.7/6/19, 5.3/26/11). Instead of setting traps, a good government should be paving the way for people's ethical life—it should be taking positive, noncoercive action to help the people become free.

Implicit in early Confucianism and explicit in Dewey's philosophy are positive conceptions of freedom that build on the inseparability of ethics and politics, which is integral to their respective visions of ethico-political order, and which does not lead to the authoritarian justification of "forcing people to be free." For Dewey, whether negative or positive freedom is a more appropriate goal for a society depends on its specific historical and cultural conditions. Contemporary Chinese scholars have argued for the necessity of incorporating negative freedom into a Confucian conception of freedom to meet the present cultural and historical needs of Chinese society. However, to think that one could simply combine the two misses the point of Berlin's distinction. The distinction is not absolute, but the relative emphasis on one or the other question—Who governs? What are the limits of government?—has important implications for ethical and political action.

Instead of saying that Confucian societies need both, we need to examine the specific conditions of each society and ask whether negative *or* positive freedom should be emphasized in the immediate situation, albeit the longer term ideal is positive freedom. However, even if our inquiry reveals a need to emphasize negative freedom, Confucian societies may not resolve the question of the limits to interference as Western societies have done. The latter's answers to that question mostly center around individual rights, and more recently some group rights, but it is doubtful if rights would ever gain that kind of prominence in a Confucian social order.

RIGHT TO SPEAK AND RIGHT SPEECH

The concept of rights is less central to Dewey's political philosophy than it is to most contemporary liberal theorists.[18] Though the 1908 *Ethics* makes considerable use of the concept, it all but disappears in the 1932 *Ethics*, even in the section "Liberty of Thought and Expression." It is possible that his critical view of the conception of "rights" in contemporary discourse leads him to drop the concept as being more misleading than helpful in discussions of freedom. This, along with his attitude of undogmatic flexibility regarding political forms that realize democracy, brings his philosophy closer to Confucianism, wherein even negative freedom may have to be protected by other means in addition to laws and rights. Some scholars argue against the strategy of introducing "rights" into Confucian discourse and suggest that the important functions served by rights could be served as well by other conceptual and practical means more conducive to Confucianism, and without the disadvantages of the Western concept of rights.[19] A more moderate approach is to recognize that while contemporary Confucian societies are likely to have to take rights more seriously, one would do well not to overlook other means that are available and may actually work better to protect negative freedom without obstructing positive freedom.

Insofar as Confucian societies should institute rights, Dewey's conception of rights would be more compatible with Confucianism than a conception of rights as antecedent possessions of autonomous individuals. A right exists when a natural or moral law, or a positive statute, protects a specific freedom. Dewey does not believe in natural laws; laws are made by human beings. He sees rights as originating in the need of a society to affirm and protect certain behavior: "a right is the individual power granted to a man by the power of the whole society, which stands behind and supports the law."[20] Unlike those who argue for the priority of rights, who see rights as "trumps," Dewey rejects the suggestion that individuals are in possession of political rights independent of and prior to social sanction and protection of certain goods through the device of law. "A right, though individual in residence, is social in origin and intent" (M5.394).

Rights that members of a society should have at any time change with experience, with the needs of individual members. Whatever these rights may be, they are never unlimited. "Absolute rights, if we mean by absolute those not relative to any social order and hence exempt from any social restrictions, there are none" (M5.395). Every right carries with it an obligation to exercise it within limits set by society. Rights, for Dewey, are not as sharply differentiated from interests as many Western advocates would have it. This brings him closer to Chinese thinking on rights. The Chinese term for "rights," *quanli* 權利, may also be understood as the "balancing of interests."[21] The sociality and flexibility of Dewey's conception of rights render it more useful as a possible political form to protect negative freedom in a Confucian society.

The right to free speech is central to the whole group of rights secured in theory to individuals in a democratic social organization (L7.358). At its lowest level, the right to free speech has been defended as a "safety valve": allowing the discontented to express their dissatisfaction in words forestalls more disastrous explosions. While not denying this function, Dewey sees the need to protect freedom of speech in more positive terms. "Except for those who are most completely hardened in their own opinion and conceit, public expression gives opportunity for growth; it calls out the ideas and experiences of others and enables one to learn" (L7.361). Without freedom of speech and other forms of personal expression, there is no freedom of thought, as Dewey insists on an organic relation between thought and its manifestation. Freedom of expression must be legally protected because, in the words of Oliver Wendell Holmes Jr., "the ultimate good desired is better reached by free trade in ideas . . . the best test of truth is the power of the thought to get itself accepted in the market" where ideas are exchanged.[22] Dewey considers the right to free speech a minimum requirement for the "free circulation of intelligence," without which "there is no opportunity either for the formation of a common judgment and purpose or for the voluntary participation of individuals in the affairs of government" (L7.358).

For Dewey, all rights protected by the United States' Bill of Rights are guaranteed, because without them individuals are not free to develop, and society is deprived of what people might contribute. Personal growth drives social growth. The right to free speech is important not only for the individuals who enjoy it but also for the health of society and the development of its culture: no general culture has flourished without freedom of discussion, at least for a select group. Dewey resists the conception of rights as being merely individual claims, and he emphasizes rights' public functions. He argues that seeing rights as merely individual possessions, in opposition to the general welfare, puts them in greater danger of being sacrificed to the latter (L7.362). The right to free speech safeguards the freedom of intelligence—intelligence is not an individual possession but a social asset, the most important social asset. Freedom of speech "is the best method humanity has discovered for combining the conservation of attained values with progress toward new goods" (L7.361). If we recognize that the general welfare in any specific situation is not given and fixed—identified either as the status quo or a fixed revolutionary goal—but dependent on the situation, and can be determined only through intelligent public discussion and inquiry, then we would see the fallaciousness of arguing for suppression of the right to free speech for the sake of the general welfare in most cases (L11.47–48).

The right to free speech in the form of legal protection is, however, only a minimum that falls far short of a guaranteed freedom in thinking and speaking. Dewey points out that limitations of freedom of thought and speech are less flagrant, crude, and direct than popular opinion supposes; resorting to the law does not easily eliminate such limitations. An institution officially respecting the right to free expression may nevertheless be constrained by "a tradition of what is good form." The growth of administrative activity that is nothing more than "busy work," encroachment of narrow and overspecialized professionalism, and fear of the uncertain and unknown threatening the status quo could all limit free expression and contribute to a decline of intellectual freedom (L7.207–209).

Exercising the legal right to free speech in itself would not constitute real freedom if the words are no more than "cheap talk," without positive consequences, either because the speaker is not prepared to back it up with action, the words are simply ignored, or further consequences are deliberately prevented. Governments may seek public feedback with no intention of changing the policies, no matter what new information or consideration comes to light, or they may be too "blinkered" to see merit in any views other than their own. However, one should not be too quick in laying the blame on others when one's views are ignored; before one could justifiably demand that others listen and take one's views seriously, they should be worth listening to. As Dewey points out, "it is quite possible that in the long run, . . . the greatest foe to freedom of thought and expression, is not those who fear such freedom because of its effect upon their own standing and fortune, but the triviality and irrelevancy of the ideas that are entertained, and the futile and perhaps corrupting way in which they are expressed" (L11.253). The right to free speech should not be allowed to degenerate into a cheap safety valve, dissipating the energy required to overcome obstacles in a socially problematic situation.

Apart from not being exercised, or exercised with no effect or with negative effects, the right to free expression could be misused by minorities to the detriment of free thinking. In his social critiques, Dewey points out that ideas that were once means of social progress have been used to protect entrenched interests and to halt any further social advancement. In a relatively free society, propaganda is not a tool limited to the government. Dewey shows great concern over "agencies which skillfully manipulate and color the news and information, which circulate, and which artfully instill, under the guise of disinterested publicity, ideas favorable to hidden interests" (L7.360). In a 1935 article, "Unfree Press," he argues that abuses of the freedom of the press—irresponsible journalism, advertisers' covert control over what is printed, invasions of privacy under the guise of freedom, and reckless sensationalism—are not incidental but inherent to the country's economic organization (L11.269–73).

Too often, the media, by bombarding us with huge quantities of diverse and unrelated facts, isolated from more comprehensive and coherent interpretation of events and their relation to our daily lives, promote acquiescence and indifference rather than critical inquiry (L13.92–97). This increases the power of organized propaganda and mass prejudice over an unsuspecting audience. New communication technology, once seen as certain to advance the cause of democratic freedom, also has made it possible to create pseudo-public opinion and undermine democracy from within (L13.168).

Dewey's concern over how the right to free expression is exercised, its consequences, and the need for positive action to ensure its proper operation strikes a chord in Confucianism. We find Confucius stressing repeatedly the importance of being cautious in speech (*Analects* 1.14, 2.18, 19.25). He disapproves of those who are rash, who speak when they should not, more than he disapproves of those who hold back when they should speak—not because he considers the latter a lesser error, but because it occurs less frequently (*Analects* 16.6). Too often, those who speak are deficient in excellence and do not say anything worth listening to (*Analects* 14.4). Before speaking, one should consider carefully: the content (is it regarding appropriate conduct, and does it "hit the mark"?); the form (is it according to ritual practices?); the audience (is it someone with whom one could engage in appropriate discourse?); and the timing of one's speech.[23]

One should not speak without regard for consequences or engage in idle, empty talk—words should not be "wasted." Thinking, speaking, and acting are as integrally related for Confucius as they are for Dewey. Living up to one's word (*xin* 信) is of primary importance in ethical conduct in Confucianism. One's words should never exceed one's deeds.[24] "If one talks big with no sense of shame, it will be hard indeed to live up to one's word" (*Analects* 14.20). If one does not live up to one's word, one loses one's credibility and undermines others' trust in us. Through such abuse, one's words cease to be means with which one may shape the future as one loses control over their consequences. In such circumstances, words do not empower the speaker; they gain power over the speaker, who must suffer their consequences.

Words have power that may be used for good or bad purposes. Confucius himself does not aspire to eloquence and even wishes that he could accomplish his purposes without words altogether (*Analects* 14.32, 17.19). Being able to "dispute with a ready wit (*ning* 佞)" bears no necessary relation to ethical conduct (*Analects* 5.5). On the contrary, Confucius frequently condemns "glib talk," words that flatter, deceive, and mislead (*qiaoyan* 巧言) (*Analects* 1.3, 5.25, 11.25, 16.4). One should keep glib talkers (*ningren* 佞人) at a distance, for "clever words undermine excellence," and "glib-tongued talkers bring down states and families" (*Analects* 15.11, 15.27, 17.18). If speech, when irresponsible or malicious, could be so dangerous to social order and individual flourishing, then is it any wonder that Confucians have been traditionally more concerned with "speaking right" than with the right to speak?

When asked what his first priority would be if given the reins of government, Confucius' reply is "to insure that names are used properly (*zhengming* 正名)" (*Analects* 13.3). The way one uses *ming* is the way one speaks; "names" are the basic units of discourse guiding action. In ancient texts, "to name" is closely associated with "to command, to bring into existence (*ming* 命)." Speech is a social practice with consequences in the world of actions. The practice of *zhengming*, proper naming, should not be misunderstood as a recommendation for some kind of "linguistic totalitarianism." It is not about prescription of what one can say. It is a matter of transforming a discourse or practice from within, by working on the connection between one's own words and actions and thereby influencing how others connect them. The best place for doing this is a position wherein one's words and actions and their connections are highly visible, that is, a position of prominence, which in the Confucian context is the position of government.

Randall Peerenboom refers to the *zhengming* (he uses the traditional translation "rectification of names") passage as underlying the "rather bizarre importance attributed to language" in the People's Republic of China (PRC) government's unity of thought program. He draws on Chad Hansen's argument that most Chinese thinkers share a pragmatic theory of language rather than a realist or semantic theory of language to explain why "Chinese political and ethical thinking has focused on the appropriateness of social practices and the prescriptive role of language in establishing the proper social practices and ultimately sociopolitical order." This prescription may be done through persuasion or coercion, since doing what is right is "complying with prescriptive behavior."[25] If unity-of-thought programs in China today have proceeded along these lines, it is no wonder that they have been "quixotic"—they are a parody of Confucius' *zhengming* practice.

Peerenboom himself points out that in the above account, "the model of mind is behavioristic: the prescriptive *dao*/correct line conditions one's experiences and responses. One divides the world a certain way, and when one confronts a certain situation, one responds accordingly based on the programmed *dao*/correct line."[26] But why saddle Confucianism with a behavioristic psychology? The behavioristic model does not even gel with a pragmatic theory of language. Despite his adoption of Hansen's view, that "language is a social practice," Peerenboom's account does not grasp the "practice" character of *zhengming*. The "prescriptive *dao*/correct line" is an objectified theoretical construct that is imposed on the people by the government. The people are perceived as passive victims, objects upon which the government imposes its will. One must either be an autonomous subject, initiating actions in feats of *creatio ex nihilo*, or one is reduced to an automaton, determined by another's will. There is no middle ground in this "permanent dialectic between an organizing consciousness and automatic behaviors."[27] But, as Pierre Bourdieu points out, practice resides in the interstices between the purely subjective and the purely objectified.

If *zhengming* is to be successful, then the people and the government must be neither autonomous subjects nor automatons; they must be coparticipants. Confucius' proposed task is one of altering what Bourdieu terms the *habitus* in his *Logic of Practice*: "systems of durable, transposable dispositions, structured structures predisposed to function as structuring structures . . . principles which generate and organize practices and representations that can be objectively adapted to their outcomes without presupposing a conscious aiming at ends or an express mastery of the operations necessary in order to attain them. Objectively 'regulated' and 'regular' without being in any way the product of obedience to rules, they can be collectively orchestrated without being the product of the organizing action of a conductor."[28] Our use of *ming* 名 is such a habitus, through which we know the world, interpret our past, and envision our future—this habitus guides our actions in shaping the future.

Habitus is not something that can be altered overnight or by force. Confucius is well aware that the task of achieving ethico-political order takes a long time, even for good rulers (*Analects* 13.10–12). The only way to alter habitus is to alter the historically and socially situated conditions that produce it. This cannot be imposed top-down unilaterally but requires the participation of all involved in the practice. The task of a good government is to direct, not determine, the interactions that modify and are modified by the use of those *ming* in need of adjustment. We will have a clearer picture of how the people participate even as the government directs the practice without their taking the opposing positions of objects and subject, respectively, when we discuss the nature of authority later. But first we must examine Confucian view on censorship and the possibility of a Confucian "right" to free speech.

The "glib talkers" Confucius detests do not succeed in their wiles because of any "right" to free speech; the problem they pose would not be solved by denying that right. They do not cause riots by speaking irresponsibly in public; they often have the ear of the powerful whom they instigate to act unethically. The most dangerous of glib talkers are the "sham ministers (*taichen* 態臣)" who, with "their ingenuity, sharpness, and eloquent powers, . . . are expert at currying favors with their superiors"—they bring destruction to the rulers who employ them and chaos to society (*Xunzi* 13/63/17). Xunzi advises rulers not to promote or honor such glib talkers but says nothing about denying them the freedom to speak (*Xunzi* 9/42/3, 12/60/12). But his attitude is a little different with those who "by hair-splitting with propositions and creating names on their own authority bring confusion to the use of names and cause the people to be suspicious and multiply argument and litigation among them." These are "great villains" "whose crimes equal those who forge credentials and tamper with weights and measures" (*Xunzi* 22/108/4). Xunzi is not adverse to punishing these great villains under the law, as he believes that "those who come forward with good intentions should be treated with ritual courtesy; those who come forward without good intentions should be punished" (*Xunzi* 9/35/10).

Does Confucius share Xunzi's attitude when it comes to protecting the people from the villainy of speech that would lead them astray? The chapter, "The Warning Vessel on the Right (*youzuo* 宥坐)," in the *Xunzi*, recounts a story of Confucius executing deputy Mao 少正卯, a "famous man of Lu." When asked the reason for his act, Confucius charged Mao with "five ways that are detestable," any one of which deserved punishment. Among these five is "defending false teachings with discrimination (*yanwei erbian* 言偽而辯)" (*Xunzi* 28/138/17). Xu Fuguan has defended Confucius against the charge of suppressing freedom of speech by arguing persuasively that this story is a relatively late (beginning of Eastern Han) invention of legalist inspiration.[29] Not only is the incident historically unlikely, but it also goes against Confucius' own teachings in the *Analects*. To resort to censorship as a coercive means of preventing others from misusing speech is a failure of ethical excellence and will not bring about a genuine social order. Confucius may detest and avoid glib talkers, but he did not recommend that they be prevented from speaking by force. Mencius, despite his occasionally venomous rhetoric against other schools of thought, did not persuade rulers to suppress these "teachings of beasts." Instead, he engaged them in disputes in order to expose them and dissuade others from following them (*Mencius* 6.9/34/30).

While Confucius does not advocate, not even implicitly, "a right to free speech" in the sense of legal protection of free speech, he assumes the existence of a certain amount of such freedom in both his teachings and actions and, more important, he recognizes the value of such freedom. Nor is he unique in this. The *Conversations of the States* recounts the story of how when King Li of Zhou suppressed the people's protests against his tyrannical rule, the Duke of Shao warned him that stopping the people's mouths is like "damming up a river" and is eventually more dangerous. This "safety-valve" defense of free speech is strengthened further in *Zuo's Commentary*, when free speech is viewed as a means for the people to participate in and to improve governing. When it was suggested that the village schools be destroyed because they had become the forum of discussions about the conduct of government, Zichan, an important official in the state of Zheng, responded, "Why do so? If people retire morning and evening, and pass their judgment on the conduct of the government, as being good or bad, I will do what they approve of, and I will alter what they condemn; they are my teachers."[30]

In the *Analects*, Confucius says that a ruler who finds pleasure in everyone agreeing with him will ruin the state (*Analects* 13.15). One has an ethical claim on others to allow one to speak out against any unethical conduct, and one owes it to others to speak out. Xunzi considers "those who remonstrate, wrangle, assist, and oppose . . . true ministers of the altars of soil and grain. They are real treasures to the country and its ruler" (*Xunzi* 13/64/5). For Mencius, "to take one's prince to task is respect; to discourse on the good to keep out heresies is reverence" (*Mencius* 7.1/36/8). He advocates that relatives of ruler as well as ministers should remonstrate with the ruler when he is in error, and if he refuses to listen to advice, then the ministers should resign, while the ruler's relatives may remove him from his position (*Mencius* 10.9/56/1). According to Confucius, to serve one's lord properly, one must "take a stand against him without duplicity" (*Analects* 14.22). Confucius praises those who suffer or even die as a result of remonstrating with their rulers as examples of "giving up life to achieve authoritative conduct (*shashen chengren* 殺身成仁)" (*Analects* 15.9, 18.1).

Other than praising those with the courage to speak and meet whatever consequences with equanimity, Confucius' other response to the danger of free speech is a recommendation of circumspection. "When the way prevails, be perilously high-minded in your speech and conduct; when it does not prevail, be perilously high-minded in your conduct, but be prudent in what you say" (*Analects* 14.3). He does not recommend that the freedom to speak be protected by law—he does not assert a right to free speech. This is not because he is in any way ambiguous in his attitude toward authoritarian repression, but because, in his historical context, such a move is a nonstarter. As Ching points out, in China, the law has been an arbitrary instrument in the hands of the rulers.[31] In the absence of effective control over a government by the people, there is no way to use the law to protect individuals' rights.

Rights or Rites?

Public codes of punishment first appeared in China in the sixth century B.C. According to *Zuo's Commentary*, publication of the codes, a decisive step in the bureaucratization of the states, was highly controversial. It was resisted on the grounds that publicly formulated laws would promote litigation and undermine personal relations.[32] Confucius claimed to be "no different from others when it comes to hearing litigation," but for him, "the point is to bring it about that there is no litigation" (*Analects* 12.13). Litigation appeals to the worst in human beings, inclining them toward selfishness by requiring them to think in terms of themselves as *opposed* to others, undermining trust, and reducing the chances of harmonious associations thereafter. Resolving disputes according to a fixed published code rewards clever disputation that exploits loopholes and the vagueness of written codes. As a result, "the people will avoid punishments but will be without a sense of shame" (*Analects* 2.3). Societies ruled by laws and little else seem to have realized Confucius' fears. "You eventually have libraries filled with laws, an army of lawyers, jails overflowing, and you will still be insecure in your streets. Eventually, even your political leaders will say, 'What I did was immoral, but it was not illegal.'"[33]

Unlike in Western polities, where political order is closely associated with the rule of law, for Confucius, the measure of a good government is how little it needs the law. Laws, for Confucians, do not have the kind of legitimacy and legitimating power that they have in Western traditions. In Confucianism, ritual practices provide the social constraints that possess legitimacy and legitimating power, that contribute to ethico-political order. "Are you capable of ruling the state through ritual practices and deference? Then what difficulties will you have? If you are incapable of ruling the state through ritual practices and deference, what have you to do with ritual practices?"[34] Confucius appeals not to laws but to ritual practices to constrain the ruler—"rulers should employ their ministers by observing ritual practices."[35]

According to De Bary, Lü Liu-liang (1629–1683) suggests that rite "as formal definition and concrete embodiment of principle, covers some of our rational, moral, and legal conception of 'rights.'" Hsiao Kung-chuan argues that the broader meaning of laws (*fa* 法) includes "the institutions by which government is instituted and civil order maintained." As the Zhou clan system degenerated, the government had to institute social constraints that were less dependent on personal relationships; "the newly developing institutions might still utilize the terminology associated with the old rites, though their content gradually became more inclusive than formerly, and their meaning came to be merged with that of law in the broader sense." Such interpretations tend to overlegalize ritual practices and extend the meaning of *fa* so far that Hansen could argue that it differs little from saying that the ancient Chinese do not have a concept of law.[36]

The farther back in time, the more misleading it is to view Chinese *fa* through the Western modern concept of "law." As Mark Edward Lewis points out, the administrative codes of the Warring States period, forerunners of imperial laws, were not tools of rational bureaucracy or brutal *realpolitik*; they were deeply embedded within the religious and ritual practices of the society from which they emerged. What makes laws anathema to Confucians is the shift of focus from transformative influence to enforcement through punishments to elicit desirable behavior. Historically, "the evolution of law in China may be described as the *devolution* of ritual (*li*) into law (*fa*), and of law into punishments."—a devolution of spontaneous performance to coerced compliance.[37] Laws and ritual practices are functional equivalents to the extent that they are both means to the goal of political order, but they are very different kinds of means with very different consequences. Ritual practice transforms and is transformed by the participants; its order is inclusive. Law separates those who comply from those who do not; its order is exclusive. The order achieved by ritual practices would be ethical as well as political; the order achieved by laws is merely political.

Some might dismiss the idea that ritual practices could achieve what laws could not as sheer naiveté. It could be argued that what is needed is a way for the people to control the ruler, whereas ritual practices do not give the people any real power over the ruler. Ritual practices, the argument might continue, will actually work better in a democracy, but they will not, on their own, bring about democracy. Only with democratic control over the government through rule of law would individuals' negative freedom be protected, and only then might they have some chance of achieving positive freedom through ritual practices. But laws are neither necessary nor sufficient for people to have control over the government. We see too many countries adopt legal systems similar in form to those of Western liberal democracies without really becoming democratic, because there is no effective mechanism to ensure accountability—people have no power to constrain the government's action. The problem of how people may acquire power within a polity is one that must be solved whether one chooses laws or rites as the major political forms.

Outside direct democracies, a democratic relationship between the government and the governed requires a means of communication for the governed to make their preferences known and for the government to persuade them to accept some alternative rather than another. Communication may be structured by laws or ritual practices. The latter, with its emphasis on harmony, has an advantage over the former, less immune to adversarial attitudes, in resolving problems to everyone's satisfaction (or as close as possible) rather than to only one party's satisfaction. Associations structured by laws usually produce win-lose or, worse, lose-lose outcomes; ritual practices offer a better chance of a win-win outcome. But what happens when communication breaks down and a powerful party insists on having things its way regardless of ritual practice? In the West, the law that protects the people against despotism works only when the people are (have been, and could be again) organized to give it power, to assert its authority over the ruler. There is no reason such organization could not also give ritual practice the power to withstand despotism. Ron Guey Chu has given some examples from the Ming dynasty of how imperial power has in fact been checked by individuals mobilized against emperors' arbitrary exercise of power in disputes over ritual matters.[38]

In a Confucian society, ritual practices, not laws alone, provide both the ethico-political impetus and the means to organize the people when the power of imperfect government has to be checked to protect the people's freedom. This is not to deny that laws could have a place in Confucian politics. Ames's argument, that law is "a necessary if subordinate aspect of proper government," is persuasive as long as one takes the necessity to be historical and contextual.[39] Given the historical context, laws in Confucius' China have been associated only with governmental control of the people, but if the people could organize to exercise power over the law and the government, then it is not incompatible with Confucianism to use the laws against recalcitrant governments that abuse their office. However, as with the government's power over the people, use of law is secondary to ritual practices in getting the government to behave appropriately—it should be used with great reluctance, with a view to minimizing its own use and returning to ritual practices.

Rights advocates are not only concerned about despotic governments, they also worry over the tyranny of the majority. Since the founding of the United States, both practitioners and theorists have concerned themselves with various means of curbing the power of the majority, with an entrenched constitution, separation of powers, and the Bill of Rights among them.[40] "A right is an antimajoritarian device that removes a given issue from the legislative arena and the will of the majority."[41] In this respect, Deweyan rights may not seem like rights at all. If rights are "social in origin and intent," how is it to be asserted against its very source, against that which sets its boundaries, that in the interest of which it is granted? Dewey's best defense lies in differentiating conflicts between individuals and groups within a society, on the one hand, from a conflict between individual and society per se, on the other hand. The former he recognizes as important problems, while the latter he regards as nonexistent (L7.324). Tyranny of the majority is an example of conflicts within society; the majority is not society. A Deweyan solution would, instead of favoring one over the other, first attempt to dissolve the conflict through inquiry, which hopefully would arrive at answers acceptable to both parties. Failing that, whether the majority or minority should prevail depends on the specific circumstances. He would not favor any extreme suppression of minorities (e.g., denying them the freedom to seek support for their cause through peaceful means), as it would have detrimental consequences on experimental attitudes and open inquiry.

One of the reasons Peerenboom cites for the Chinese thinking of rights as interests is that "they may not recognize a conflict between the interests of the individual and those of the majority."[42] A belief in harmony in itself would not lead to this if harmony is understood as a long-term ideal, and if there is an appreciation of its complexity and of the difficulty of achieving it. The root of the problem is the tendency to resort to stop-gap measures rather than to seek enduring solutions to conflicts. When Confucius says "there is no contention (*wuzheng* 無爭) among exemplary persons," his point is not that they never compete or disagree but rather "even in contesting, they are exemplary persons" (*Analects* 3.7). Conflicts are not to be suppressed or avoided at all costs; they should be handled in a civilized manner, according to ritual practices, guided by a longer-term ideal of building a harmonious community. In the same vein, even as he emphasizes the importance of the exemplary persons' persuasive skills, Xunzi stresses the need for tolerance and magnanimity toward those he fails to persuade, or who fail to live up to his own high standards: the art of accommodation (*jianshu* 兼術) is an accomplishment of a true king, the son of heaven (*Xunzi* 5/20/4). There is diversity in the harmony achieved (*Analects* 13.23).

The ways in which ritual practice builds community show that changes in ritual practices, in majority behavior, come about through creativity in individual performances and the accumulation of subsequent emulation. Though less noticeable, this recalls Dewey's claim that "every *new* idea, every conception of things differing from that authorized by current belief, must have its origin in an individual" (M9.305). "Cultural progress must always start from a minority" (L7.355). Ritual practices can be a means that Dewey believes a genuine democracy must have for a minority to become a majority (L7.362). One might project a greater concern for a minority than critics of Confucianism usually have recognized from Confucius' own situation: though he gained a considerable following even during his lifetime, he was still very much a minority. The history of Confucianism itself is a classic example of a minority becoming a majority through communication.

Confucians, like Dewey, would want to avoid making an absolute rule to favor the minority *or* the majority. In finding a solution, they would want to do what is most ethically appropriate to the situation. According to Mencius, Confucius "would not perpetrate even one wrongful deed or kill even one innocent man to gain the empire"—he would not condone a majority oppressing the minority.[43] A Confucian would appeal to ethical rather than legal constraints to protect individuals and minorities from the majority. Historically, concern over how the majority or the people would exercise its power in a political democracy leads, in early-twentieth-century Chinese thinkers such as Liang Ch'i-ch'ao, not to advocacy of constitutional limits on majoritarian rule but to a belief that the Chinese people are "not ready" for democracy and need "an autocracy that would rule in the public interest and gradually raise the level of popular education and civic consciousness until the conditions were ripe for a transition to constitutional monarchy."[44]

Liang's view is exploratory rather than dogmatic. He was well aware of the difficulties of realizing an open, enlightened autocracy (*kaiming zhuanzhi* 開明專制) dependent as it is on ethically excellent and competent people getting into government. When China became a republic, he called on people of talent not to hold back from participating in government simply because they viewed the republican system as unsuitable for China—in the end, whether a government works, regardless of its structure, depends on the people who participate in it. In attempting to marry Western thinking to Confucian values in the quest for a modern China, Liang Ch'i-ch'ao sometimes borrowed Western concepts, which he then injected with a Confucian meaning. The failure to realize the subtle shifts in meaning when Western concepts are used in Chinese contexts—thinking that Liang Ch'i-ch'ao meant the same thing as Western thinkers when he used a concept such as "enlightened despotism"—often is at the root of criticism that Confucianism is so inherently authoritarian that even the best efforts could not break it out of that mold.[45]

Confucianism values authority, but Confucian authority (even political authority) is not so wedded to coercion as some Western conceptions of political authority. This is revealed in what Andrew Nathan views as Liang Ch'i-ch'ao's failure to grasp central parts of Hobbes's and Rousseau's arguments—parts involving the necessarily coercive character of political authority.[46] But the problem, if it is one, is not a naïve inability to recognize social conflicts. Liang's understanding is representative of the Confucian understanding of ideal authority as noncoercive.

AUTHORITATIVE VERSUS AUTHORITARIAN

There are Western as well as Eastern traditions that deny any difference between power and authority, but for most, authority differs from power in its claim to legitimacy. One has power over another when one is able to determine another's action—when another actually follows one's directives. One has authority when one has a *right* to determine another's actions, when another *should* follow one's directives. How is power legitimized? The classic answer in Western political philosophy is that power is necessary to establish and sustain society, to provide the security required for human living. As Hobbes puts it, in the state of nature, there is war of all against all, and a person's life is "solitary, poor, nasty, brutish, and short."[47] Liberties are limited for the weak in such an existence, and even for the strong, their liberties are always at risk. By recognizing some power as legitimate, as authority, certain liberties become more secure, even though one may have to give up others.

A simple social contract to define and mutually respect the limits of individual liberties would not ensure the desired security, since human beings do not always act as they *ought* and are ever tempted to break their words if it is to their advantage to do so. It is the job of the authority to intervene on occasion, to force them to do what they ought to do, to maintain peace and order. Laws, which came to be viewed in the West as the chief instrument of political authority, are coercive by their very nature—their effectiveness depends on the use of force against those who transgress. This view of political authority being coercive underlies the perception of authority as being opposed to liberty, but it is by no means unanimous in the West. It misleads by focusing on instances when authority fails. When authority works, no force is required for a directive to be obeyed. Obedience is not necessarily motivated by fear of punishments; it need not be dependent on the threat of force.[48]

Establishing a structure of authority does not quite end the problem of associated living. As John Stuart Mill points out, those in authority use their power against their subjects no less than against external enemies.[49] Liberalism was born in the ensuing struggle between liberty and authority; finding the boundaries between liberty and authority is a preoccupation of Western political theory and practice (L13.82). A familiar solution is to base the legitimacy of authority on the consent of the governed, as in social contract theories. Limits to authority are built into the very legitimacy of authority in practice. In all societies, there are provisions for the exercise of authority according to law, or other social norms determined not by the one who has authority alone but by tradition and the community.

Acts of authority will not be justified and, consequently, not voluntarily obeyed if they are simply arbitrary and peremptory dictates of power. Even outside constitutional democracies, abuses over time undermine not only the personal authority of the one in power but the very authority of the position itself. To describe as "authoritarian" a regime that ignores all limits to authority, either in areas of its application or in the means employed to elicit compliance, is a misnomer. Its claims of authority are invalidated by the very manner in which it exercises its power. The description of "authoritarian" is, however, also often used to criticize a regime in which the limits to authority are set differently from Western liberal democracies, so that the distribution of legitimized power, in the eyes of its liberal critics, unjustifiably favors authority at the expense of individual liberty.

My contention is that Confucianism is not authoritarian in the first sense. Being authoritarian in the second sense merely registers that Confucian societies are different from liberal democracies; it does not rule out the possibility of a reasonable balance between freedom and authority within Confucianism. I shall show that there is such a balance to be found in a conception of noncoercive authority, and that it is remarkably close to the balance that Dewey maintains between freedom and authority in his philosophy. For Dewey, "the real issue is not that of demarcating separate 'spheres' for authority and for freedom, for stability and for change, but that of effecting an interpenetration of the two" (L11.137). What is needed is a conception of authority that could direct the exercise of freedom to bring about an authoritative freedom.

A clarification of terminology is needed at this point. I use "authoritative" to describe ideal authority in Confucianism, but Dewey uses it as a general adjective for that which possesses or claims authority. To complicate our comparison further, he often uses it in a pejorative manner, to indicate an unjustified claim of *final* authority—for example, fixed principles are "authoritative rules," and traditional religion, the church in medieval times, has "authoritative norms" (M14.163; L16.338; L4.57). Bearing in mind this terminological difference, I shall show that the "authoritative" in Confucian thought differs from the pejoratively "authoritative" in Dewey's philosophy, and is comparable to "authoritative intelligence" in which Dewey locates legitimate power.

Ideal Confucian authority is noncoercive. Fingarette's discussion of authority-as-model portrayed in the *Analects* gives us a good starting point for understanding this noncoercive ideal of the authoritative. He distinguishes a consummate model from an instrumental model. The latter is copied or imitated for a purpose independent of the model. The former is a fulfillment of what it is a model of—a teacher, a human being—it "perfectly actualizes our ideal" of what a teacher, a human being, should be. In nonperfectionist language, one may say that a consummate model, the authoritative, shows us what it *means* to be a teacher, a human being, better than anyone else, sometimes even better than we had been able to imagine. The response called forth by the authority of a consummate model is not limited to the imitative; its more important aspect is correlative.[50]

Imitation is not the most important aspect of the response to the authoritative, and in some cases it may be usurpation, though to exclude it completely may go too far. A model teacher may inspire her students to become teachers—but only in the future. In the immediate relationship, what it brings about is a change in the students' behavior as a student. There is some imitation where there is an overlap in their activities—for example, how to write well or conduct an experiment—but even then, the model must be adapted to the unique individuality and situation of the student. Fingarette's illustration with music shows that a correlative response to the authoritative involves noncoerciveness of the power that calls forth the response and spontaneous participation on the part of all parties to the relation. "It is crucial to notice that it is not merely that we *need* no commands, arguments, or coercion—it is that none of these could *possibly* elicit *this* kind of response."[51] Fingarette exaggerates by excluding even noncoercive arguments from ideal authority. When one is persuaded by arguments, one's thinking affects one's feelings, and the results could be the kind of aesthetic response and spontaneous participation elicited by an authoritative model.

The teacher's authority is paradigmatic in Confucianism and closely associated with ideal political authority. "Good administration is not as efficacious as good education in winning the people—the former gains the people's wealth, the latter gains the people's hearts-and-minds" (*Mencius* 13.14/68/23). Xunzi considers both rulers and teachers the "root of order" (*Xunzi* 19/90/20). Sage-kings, Yao and Shun, "were the most expert in the whole world at teaching and transforming" (*Xunzi* 18/87/8). Sages make the best kings, because they are "teachers for hundreds of generations" (*Mencius* 14.15/74/18). What is the nature of the model teacher's authority? Confucius' favorite student, Yan Hui, gives us this description of Confucius as a teacher: "He is good at drawing me forward a step at a time; he broadens me with culture (*wen* 文) and disciplines my behavior with ritual practices" (*Analects* 9.11). Culture and ritual practices are not individual possessions; they are shaped by and in turn shape the entire community. They are both means of exercising authority and constraints on authority.

One becomes authoritative through fulfilling better than others the possibilities of the constraining forms and creating new possibilities; it is not an arbitrary disregard of all constraints. The authoritative is constrained by the community in terms of the latter's response to an act of authority. Unless it brings about spontaneous acceptance, emulation, and inspiration on the parts of others to cultivate themselves, an act fails to be authoritative. In an important sense, it is as much the receptivity and response of other people as one's abilities that make one authoritative.

Authority both enables and constrains. Its legitimacy rests ultimately on its contribution to personal cultivation. This applies to both parties in an authority relation. It is not a relation in which one party imposes her will on the other; rather, the ideal authority relation requires participation of both in shaping the means and ends to be shared, resulting in personal cultivation for both parties and contributing to communal harmony. The authority may be measured in terms of how much the constraints constituted by the action of the one in authority *enable* the action of the one under authority. The best method of teaching, according to Mencius, is "like that of timely rain, the second is by helping the student realize his excellence to the full, the third is by helping him develop his talents" (*Mencius* 13.40/72/8). These methods work by enabling a student to cultivate herself. They require the student's full participation rather than blind compliance.

Confucius requires that a student, "if shown one corner, return with the other three" (*Analects* 7.8). One corner is insufficient to determine the other three. This "under determination" aspect of authoritative direction is the key to an ideal authority that allows all parties in a relation to codetermine action and outcome. What a student contributes to the discourse could be something quite different and unexpected, from which the teacher also could learn something. This idea survives in later thinking. The *Shuowen* notes that the character for learning, *xue* (學), is the abbreviated form of *xiao* (斅), the character for teaching, "Thus it is said that teaching and studying reinforce each other."[52] In an ideal authority relation, both parties are transformed in the process; it is in this mutual transformation that a situation wherein ends initially conflict might become one wherein harmony is achieved.

Tradition, embodied in culture and ritual practices, is critical to Confucian authority. In apparent contrast, Dewey calls for the replacement of "the authority of tradition" with "the authority of science" in one of his lectures in China. However, the tradition to which Dewey is referring is a "restrictive and enslaving" one which, strictly speaking, is no longer tradition but "a fixed and absolute convention."[53] It is not the tradition that sustains the authoritative in Confucian thinking. Dewey's "authority of tradition" gives some people control over the behavior of others according to fixed rules often based on supposedly absolute truths, an eternal, unchanging order to which the only alternative is destructive disorder. When situations are determined by an appeal to such authorities, inquiry is precluded (L7.328). "Wherever external authority reigns, thinking is suspected and obnoxious" (M12.160). It leads to a "thralldom to rules," a slothful dependence on others' ideas, and an unthinking acceptance of unquestioned and unexamined rules.

Dewey is especially scathing about appeals to external authority in education, which turn education into "the art of taking advantage of the helplessness of the young" (M14.47). For example, when a teacher sets himself up as an authority, "he offers himself as the organ of a whole school, of a *finished* classic tradition and arrogates to himself the prestige that comes from what he is the spokesman for. Suppression of the emotional and intellectual integrity of pupils is the result; their freedom is suppressed and the growth of their own personalities stunted" (L2.58). This bears no resemblance to the Confucian model teacher.

Contrary to the beliefs of those who blame Dewey for the ill effects of America's progressive education movement, Dewey does not advocate "permissiveness" and "bedlam in the classroom" by rejecting authority totally in favor of unlimited freedom for pupils. It is not discipline per se that he objects to but the kind of discipline that imposes external controls on a pupil's action according to some fixed mold regardless of the pupil's individuality, instead of rechanneling her energies in directions more conducive to her growth. In education, as in the wider society, "when external authority is rejected, it does not follow that all authority should be rejected, but rather that there is [a] need to search for a more effective source of authority" (L13.8). For Dewey, power is legitimate, insofar as it is located in the method of organized intelligence, which he also refers to as the "scientific" or "experimental" method.

The experimental method turns education into a cooperative activity in which teacher and pupil participate, each in her or his own manner, to develop reflective habits and powers of judgment. Teachers direct without completely controlling students. According to Dewey's "general principle of social control of individuals without the violation of freedom," the control to be achieved is one required by the situation to solve the common problem and is shared by all concerned according to the relevance of their abilities to the problem (L13.33). When the control is exercised through the teacher's authority, she acts as a representative of students' common interest in solving the problem at hand. One's authority in a situation is derived from one's greater contribution to the process of solving problems through organized intelligence, to the increase in organized intelligence as a community possession, and to the development of others' powers of acting intelligently.

Other than the requirement of participation from all parties in an authority relation, Dewey's conception of authority as legitimate, effective power located in organized intelligence resembles Confucian ideal authority in the way that the authoritative enables even as it constrains action and in the communal constraints on the exercise of authority. A teacher does not teach by simply leaving her pupils to do what they will; otherwise, their reactions would likely be "casual, sporadic, and ultimately fatiguing, accompanied by nervous strain" (L2.59). She discharges her responsibilities by exercising her authority in directing her pupils' learning processes, ensuring that these would themselves be processes of organized intelligence.

Students learn by using the resources of the past to achieve a better understanding and control over their own experience. The resources of the past, being applied in a process of organized intelligence no less than in the Confucian educative process, both constrain and enable action. They constrain by circumscribing the possibilities of the situation; they enable action by freeing energies that would otherwise be expanded on ascertaining those possibilities to make the most of them, or to create new possibilities. Authority is indispensable in directing and supporting individuals; without it, freedom becomes a disorganized explosion of power rather than a deployment of purposive energies. The method of organized intelligence achieves a balance between freedom and authority and between stability and change, which is conducive to growth, while Confucian authority is organically united with personal creativity in personal cultivation.

Although Dewey advocates challenging the authority of custom enforced by external control with the authority of knowledge and thought, the latter is not independent of the community and the past. Just as the Confucian teacher becomes authoritative through embodiment of the tradition, the Deweyan teacher, with her "greater experience and background," has authority acquired through past participation in processes of organized intelligence. Both tradition and organized intelligence are products of communal activities. Knowledge, what is workable or not workable, is the outcome of past communal activities; it cannot be arbitrarily determined by the teacher. New claims of knowledge become authorized only when affirmed by the experience of the relevant community (L11.142). Organized intelligence, in authorizing the teacher—or anyone else—also imposes communally constituted constraints.

In Confucianism, the communal constraints work over the long term, through the day-to-day participation of the community in the culture and ritual practices, responding to the transformative influence of the authoritative enlivening the cultural and ritual forms through personal creativity. While such a process is more likely to achieve and maintain an organic union of authority and freedom, it becomes problematic in times of rapid change. In contrast, the communal constraints on authority in Dewey's philosophy are found in the process of open inquiry, in the verbal communication of claims to be verified and results of inquiry. These constraints are likely to be more effective in the short run, but the desired balance between freedom and authority runs the risk of penetrating no deeper into experience than the level of verbal discourse. A more satisfactory outcome may require a combination of both approaches.

Ideal Confucian authority and Deweyan authority differ from the external authority embodied in the oppressive institutions against which liberals revolt. Dewey argues that to reject authority entirely is to endorse that mistaken conception of authority "as inherently external to individuality, and inherently hostile to freedom and social changes that the overt expression and use of that freedom would bring to pass" (L11.132). A total rejection of authority due to its being presented as purely restrictive leaves the exercise of freedom without direction. While this may result in chaos, the greater danger lies in driving people into the arms of the real enemies of freedom for whom authority is external and ultimately coercive, because some form of guidance is required for desires and purposes, and few could tolerate chaos for any long period of time. "The need for authority is a constant need of man. For it is the need for principles that are both stable enough and flexible enough to give direction to the processes of living in its vicissitudes and uncertainties" (L11.454). The only long-term answer to authoritarianism, in Dewey's view, lies in "the development of scientific method" that guards against the inherent dogmatism and absolutism of the authoritarian by insisting on the fallibility of all authority (L17.443). An authority remains legitimate only insofar as the experience of those under its direction presents no evidence that questions it and requires a reexamination of its claims (L7.330).

At first glance, such explicit acknowledgment of fallibility seems to be absent in Confucian authority. While one might introduce an assumption of fallibility into current and lesser authorities—such as in the Confucian practice of remonstration (*jian* 諫)—it is difficult to envisage the authority of Confucius, or that of the legendary sage-kings, ever being challenged in the way Dewey believes authority should be challenged in scientific inquiry, at least periodically. But it would be a mistake to treat their authority as dogmatic and absolute, stifling all individuality. Verification in experience is still present, though it works differently.

Mark Edward Lewis argues persuasively that figures of authority such as Yao, Shun, and Confucius are "inventions of the texts." The enunciatory structure of early texts along with Confucius' pedagogy of giving one step and demanding the rest from the students imply that "their reinterpretations or extensions of the words of the master were implicitly there from the beginning."[54] In subsequent reading of the texts, reinterpretations and extensions remain necessary, and both students and readers reinterpret and extend the master's words in the context of personal experience. Figures of authority in the Confucian tradition are constructions that are reconstructed with every appeal to them. When authority ceases to facilitate people's interactions with one another and with their environment, prevailing constructions need to be reconstructed to reconstitute the problematic situations that arise. When reconstruction does not take place, or fails, the problems are not solved but increase in number and magnitude. It is in the reconstruction that we must look for verification and validation of authority through experience.

COERCION AND AUTHORITY IN IMPERFECT SITUATIONS

The authoritative in Confucianism limits its means to those that are not coercive. Coercion is a failure of authority as the authoritative. As the ideal, it is something to be pursued; it does not describe the conditions we start with, the status quo. In less than ideal situations, a complete, simplistic rejection of force, of coercion, could have worse consequences than a judicious use of coercive means. According to Dewey's distinction, force is power as energy when it is harnessed to accomplish ends; it is violence when it frustrates one's ends, and it is consequently destructive and wasteful; and it is coercion—something between energy and violence—when organized to accomplish some ends with as much efficiency as possible under imperfect conditions, where a conflict of ends results in some waste and frustration of some more limited, or less important, ends (M10.211–15). For Dewey, what is to be rejected is violence. The use of coercion can be justified—it does not in itself invalidate the legitimacy of authority.

Law, for example, has authority, even though it is coercive. Not just any coercion but socially efficient, intelligently applied coercion is justified. "Force is efficient socially not when imposed upon a scene from without, but when it is an organization of the forces *in* the scene" (M10.215). Coercion should be employed only to rechannel forces that might otherwise break into violence. "The state, as governmental coercive power," remains a key player in all societies in the foreseeable future (L13.128). The kinds of social and economic reforms that Dewey considers necessary for freedom to become a reality for more people than the small minority controlling the economic and cultural resources would require coercive intervention by the state. *Liberalism and Social Action* goes so far as to argue, reluctantly, that it is justifiable to coerce a minority "when society, through an authorized majority, has entered upon the path of social experimentation leading to great social change, and a minority refuses by force to permit the method of intelligent action to go into effect" (L1.61).

The ends served will determine the legitimacy of coercion as a part of authority. Dewey distinguishes his position from the usual argument that "the end justifies the means." The means used will determine the end actually reached. The end justifies the means only when the consequences match the desired end, and no unintentional consequences detract from the desirability of the action. The desirability of consequences of coercive means is assessed based on its contribution to growth, both personal and communal.

We can see in Confucianism a similar restriction of the use of coercion by the ends served. The legitimacy of Confucian authority rests on the achievement of communal harmony through personal cultivation. An act is authoritative for one under authority only if it contributes to one's personal cultivation. For the one in authority, an act is authoritative if it contributes to one's own personal cultivation; this would not, however, justify egoistic acts that oppress others.[55] Since a Confucian person is a focus of a field of relations, personal cultivation means cultivating others, including cultivating their freedom. An ideal is regulative for imperfect situations. Any use of coercion should therefore facilitate the achievement of communal harmony through personal cultivation; it should at least not prevent or reduce the chances of achieving that end.

Coercion cannot bring about another's personal cultivation. This means that even in imperfect conditions, the only legitimate use of coercive authority would be to bring about external conditions—physical security and material welfare—which are required for personal cultivation rather than personal cultivation itself. Such acts of authority would moreover be limited by the consideration of not injuring the people's capacity for personal cultivation. Social welfare policies that could actually discourage its beneficiaries from becoming economically productive or educational policies that encourage mediocrity rather than excellence in the mistaken attempt to give everyone the same education are injurious in this sense.

The Confucian approach to coercive authority may be seen in the distinction between a true king and a hegemon (*wangba zhi bie* 王霸之別). This distinction increases in importance in the later dynasties as Confucians became more critical of the way imperial power was exercised. According to Mencius, "One who uses force to borrow the authoritative (*jiaren* 假仁) is a hegemon; hegemony requires a large state [by implication, military and economic strength]; one who is authoritative through ethical excellence (*de* 德) is a true king; his state need not be large."[56]

Mencius is extremely critical of hegemons, claiming that Confucius' students would not deign to discuss them let alone be compared to their minions (*Mencius* 1.7/3/22, 3.1/14/11). When authority is coercive, "the people do not submit willingly; they do so because they are not strong enough. When people submit to the transforming influence of excellence, they do so sincerely, with admiration in their hearts, like the seventy students' submission to Confucius" (*Mencius* 3.3/17/17). But hegemons are not the worst rulers. They impose coercive rule with due regard to ethical ends, and their people often live well, at least materially. Mencius considers them inadequate, because they, unlike true kings, fail to make the people "expansive": the people do not "move daily toward goodness without realizing who it is that brings this about" (*Mencius* 12.7/64/23, 13.13/68/19). Hegemons' coercive authority is legitimate to the extent that it creates the external conditions for personal cultivation; its inadequacy lies in failing to foster the internal conditions for personal cultivation through transformative exemplification.[57]

Scholars often emphasize differences rather than similarities between Confucius' and Mencius' views on hegemony. Benjamin Schwartz attributes to Confucius an "ambiguous attitude to hegemony." There is, in fact, no ambiguity. Confucius praises Guan Zhong for not resorting to arms in making Duke Huan a hegemon (*Analects* 14.16). The hegemon may elicit submission through intimidation, but coercion is justified by its prevention of the violence of continued warfare, or by its provision of sufficient security and peace for the people to continue their valued cultural practices. Huang Junjie sees Confucius as positing a developmental process between hegemony and true kingship, in contrast to Mencius, who insists on a "difference in substance" between the two that makes them mutually exclusive.[58] Though Mencius condemns hegemons for only "borrowing the authoritative," he also suggests that "if a man borrows a thing and keeps it for long enough, how can one be sure that it would not become truly his?" (*Mencius* 13.30/70/15). In a continued effort to appear authoritative, a hegemon might become truly authoritative, that is, a true king. It seems that Mencius' distinction between hegemony and true kingship does not preclude the possibility of a developmental process connecting the two.

According to John Knoblock, Xunzi holds a more favorable view of hegemons later in his career, as expressed in "The Ways of True Kings and Hegemons," in contrast to his earlier position in the chapter, "On Confucius," which is considered characteristically Confucian in condemning the way of the hegemons.[59] This overlooks important elements of qualified approval of hegemons in the Confucian tradition, including Mencian teaching, before Xunzi. The change in Xunzi's position is due to a change in his conception of hegemons rather than to a change in the kinds of political behavior condemned.

Although "On Confucius" and "The Ways of True Kings and Hegemons" both compare hegemons unfavorably with true kings for "not rooting their practice in proper educative governing, nor developing fully the highest and most noble, nor ordering cultural patterns, nor winning the hearts-and-minds of the people," and instead "preferring strategies and tactics," the latter chapter emphasizes that hegemons are able to reduce disorder by gaining the trust of the people—they do not stray completely from the way of good government (*Xunzi* 7/25/18; 11/50/7). "When the rules and edicts of government have been set forth, then although they might see opportunity for profit or danger of loss, they would not deceive their people. When agreements had already been settled, then although they might see opportunity for profit or danger of loss, they would not deceive their allies" (*Xunzi* 11/50/5). This differs starkly from the earlier characterization of hegemons as "the kind of men who would deceive the hearts-and-minds as a means of triumph, cloaking their belligerence in a show of deference, relying on authoritative appearance while treading the path of selfish gain" (*Xunzi* 7/25/20).

The "hegemonic" behavior of the earlier chapter is in fact the behavior contrasted with both the ways of hegemons and true kings in the latter chapter and condemned as "the way of expediency and opportunism by which states would perish." "In domestic affairs [those who rule by expediency and opportunism, *not* hegemons] do not shrink from treacherously deceiving their people out of a hankering for minor profits. In external affairs they do not shrink from treacherously deceiving their allies in their hankering for great profits" (*Xunzi* 11/50/10). In the chapter "On the Regulations of a King"—associated with a later stage of Xunzi's career than both "On Confucius" and "The Ways of True

Kings and Hegemons"—the comparison is again tripartite, with the hegemons occupying a middle position.[60] A true king is described as one who "tries to win people," in contrast to a hegemon, who "tries to win allies" (*Xunzi* 9/36/22). The hegemon does not resort to underhanded methods to achieve his goal; rather, he brings security and material welfare to his people and wins the friendship of feudal lords, because he treats them with respect and refrains from annexing their lands. The way of governing that is ruinous seeks power by trying to capture lands and thereby making enemies of the feudal lords. Though there is greater refinement in the distinctions among different ways of governing, winning, and using power, the *Xunzi* agrees with the *Analects* and the *Mencius* in condemning the use of coercion, unless it contributes to communal order through the people's personal cultivation.

Xunzi's views on authority often are misunderstood, because scholars tend to see him through his legalist students' perspectives. Xunzi's condemnation of deception, along with the use of coercion, is significant, because legalists advocate both overt coercion and the covert use of power to deceive and manipulate as a means for a ruler to retain and increase his power. For the legalists, staying in power is the raison d'être of governing; there is no difference between authority and power. Scholars such as Xu Fuguan who are anxious to defend Confucianism from charges of authoritarian tendencies often emphasize a sharp distinction between Confucian and legalist doctrines and attribute the authoritarian excesses of imperial power to the latter. In contrast, François Jullien is among those who see "an ideological compromise . . . between the two rival factions, providing the basis for the entire subsequent tradition."[61]

While Jullien's account shows how, in Chinese traditions, power is not mechanical and usually works nonobtrusively, an outcome of the configuration of situations rather than willful agency, he obscures an important distinction between different traditions regarding what is considered the "best" use of power. Confucian ethical excellence (*de* 德) cannot be subsumed under "a logic of manipulation" along with a legalist conception of power (*shi* 勢).[62] While there may be many individuals in or out of political office whose behavior is a mixture of legalist tactics and Confucian rhetoric, Confucian thinking and practice, I would contend, subject power to ethical evaluation.

Just because power does not function blatantly, with openly articulated means and ends, does not mean that it is necessarily manipulative. The concept of manipulation implies an agonistic context in which the manipulator achieves her ends—which are in conflict with those of the manipulated—by deceiving the manipulated into believing that the latter is achieving her own ends. It is not a legitimate exercise of power by Confucian standards, because the deception makes it impossible to achieve a harmony of ends through mutual transformation, through the personal cultivation of both parties to the relation. Such an act injures the manipulated by preventing and reducing her capacity for personal cultivation in which she must know what she is about, in which her knowledge of how each part fits into the whole of experience is integral to its progress. It also injures the manipulator who, through her deception, undermines trust. Trust should not be understood as a subjective state, or it would be undermined only if the manipulation is found out; trust has to do with whether one can be relied on to act in the interests of others, to contribute to their personal cultivation. Being manipulative makes one unworthy of trust and obstructs one's own personal cultivation, as trustworthiness (*xin* 信) is a key ethical attribute. Without trust, community, the concomitant of personal cultivation, is impossible.

Maintaining the philosophical distinction between Confucianism and legalism is especially important in view of their historical coexistence. The Han rulers inherited the legalist centralized state machinery created by the First Emperor of Qin, but popular sentiments against the Qin reign and the legalist thought underpinning it, the people's preference for Confucianism, and the assistance of Confucians in the founding of the Han dynasty ensured the "triumph" of Confucianism over legalism, at least on the surface. Scholars have pointed out that Han Wudi, who has been credited with instituting Confucianism as the state orthodoxy, was almost as thoroughly a legalist monarch as the First Emperor had been.[63] However, Confucianism was not merely used cynically to "whitewash" the legalist practice of Chinese rulers; the rulers recognized the need for a civil administration, and the Confucians were best placed to fulfill that function.

Confucians who recognized the tension between their philosophical commitment and the legalist state faced the dilemma that Confucius previously had faced: should one serve a regime that is not wholly committed to the Confucian way? For most, the answer was positive, but only up to a point. They did not support the state at all costs. Many tried hard to turn the ruler in the direction of good government, sometimes at the risk of their careers and even their lives. While their collective efforts never quite achieved the Confucian ideal government, it is likely that Confucian influence in government contributed considerably to the welfare of the people, and at times it curbed some of the excesses of despotism.[64] The gains were not without costs. The worst is perhaps the constant risk of de facto powers misappropriating Confucianism as a tool of oppression, but the distortion can be exposed for what it is so that Confucianism may be rescued from authoritarianism.

Chapter 6

Cultivating Democracy

RECONSTRUCTING CONFUCIANISM AND DEMOCRACY

Rather than the end of history in capitulation to Western liberal democracy, or the clash of Western and Confucian civilizations, I argue that Confucian societies are capable of an alternative future as Confucian democracies, different perhaps from Western liberal democracies but no less capable of living in peace with other civilizations. Contrary to skeptics such as Samuel Huntington, I contend that not only is a Confucian democracy not a contradiction in terms, but that it in many ways might compete with Western liberal models as an alternative ideal. Societies dominated by Confucianism in East Asia might have been resistant to democracy in the past, but the fault might not lie entirely with their Confucian culture. Philosophical and cultural resources within Confucianism could foster democracy, as understood by John Dewey. It would not be the liberal democracy that currently exists in the United States and Western Europe but a democracy based on a conception of individuals as inherently social, on a commitment to building a harmonious community in which every member contributes, participates, and benefits according to his or her abilities and needs.

Building such a Confucian democracy precludes liberal neutrality that excludes questions regarding conceptions of the good life from the political arena. Both political life and ethical life suffer as a result of the exclusion of substantive value discourse from politics. In many societies today, shared values seldom guide political action except in the form of all too often unreasoning and fanatical partisan ideology. The political rhetoric of the day is not, nor can it ever be, in any sense "value free." Where values are acknowledged as important, what results often is not "discourse"—earnest efforts to exchange views aimed at resolving conflicts—but shouting matches, where neither side is listening, and the "victor" is decided by who shouts the loudest and is most adept at manipulating public opinion in the partisan struggle for power. The failure of communication is astounding and immensely frustrating in the face of modern communication technology that advances by leaps and bounds.

In a Confucian ethico-political order, as in a Deweyan democracy, questions about conceptions of the good that should guide social and political actions are resolved in cooperative inquiry and institutionalized in ritual practices, in which all of those who are affected or who have something to contribute will speak out, listen, and understand. While it is the responsibility of everybody, including the government *qua* government, to inquire into conceptions of the good, no one conception should be imposed by any one group within society on the rest. Common goods must be constructed through ritual practice and cooperative inquiry in which each person participates according to his or her capacities. Such a community would be a democracy, with government of the people, by the people, and for the people. Freedom would be balanced with authority, so that everyone would have the best chance of personal fulfillment within a flourishing community. Stability and continuity in functioning interpersonal relations would be balanced with diversity and the capacity for change through individual creativity.

In exploring the possibility of a Confucian democracy, I have reconstructed a Confucianism that opposes authoritarianism, that is at odds with the state orthodoxy of imperial China, which so often passes for Confucianism. While remaining as close to the texts as possible, I have interpreted early Confucianism in light of what I consider the needs of East Asian societies in their current historical contexts. In this regard, Dewey's pragmatism proves illuminating. His understanding of what government by the people means, what democratic participation requires, and how cooperative inquiry should proceed facilitates the reconstruction of Confucianism in support of democracy.

Confucianism often has taken social and political structures for granted, believing that it is sufficient to transform people through Confucian education, and that good people will constitute a good community, no matter what social or political structures exist. It can learn from Dewey's philosophy, that organization involving structures that distribute power and resources is important to the outcome of social and political processes. Without effective organization, a public remains inchoate, and a society will not move toward democracy as a way of life. However, what kind of organization, what kind of social and political structures are required for a Confucian democracy, remains a question that must be answered within the specific context of each Confucian society.

While I have focused on the reconstruction of Confucianism for Confucian democracy, the exercise implicitly involves interpreting Dewey's philosophy in a new context. Consequently, it also profits our understanding of Dewey's task of fostering democracy as a way of life. Though he insists on flexibility of political forms and the necessity to pay as much attention to the content that affects the functioning of political forms, Dewey has been rather vague about the cultural processes that give content to political forms. In this regard, Confucianism, which traditionally has been more concerned with cultural processes than with political forms, offers new possibilities for accomplishing Dewey's task.

Robert Cummings Neville has offered illustrative cases from Boston society to show how Confucianism can relate to modern American society as critic and cultural creator through ritual practices.[1] The key elements of cultural processes required to give content to formal democracy, to transform merely political democracy to cultural and moral democracy, are practices that allow requests and concerns to be communicated swiftly and smoothly, so that public matters can be handled effectively and efficiently, practices of deference to excellence that do not merely reinforce authority structures but illuminate positions of authority and their occupants for critical scrutiny. In a Confucian democracy, these would be accomplished through fiduciary ritual practices that would temper the antagonism that undermines trust and communal feelings in many late modern capitalist societies.

By elucidating the nature of Confucian and Deweyan democracy, I have argued that not only are they coincident in many respects but also, more important, they are worthy ethico-political ideals. The main argument for a Confucian democracy is that it is the best way to ensure government for the people in the long run. If we understand government for the people, as we should, as not merely providing material welfare but contributing to personal fulfillment in a flourishing community, then government by the people is an indispensable, constitutive means of government for the people. Neither Deweyan nor Confucian democracy is a reality yet. What passes for democracy today is "government *by* a few, approved by a large number (not always a majority), *for* one or another coalition of special interests."[2] In response to critics of existing democracy, such as Walter Lippmann and Reinhold Niebuhr, Dewey points out that what is the case now need not always be so, and that the belief in democracy is a faith in the possibilities of human experience, in the abilities of the people to govern themselves when appropriate conditions are provided.

DEMOCRACY AND THE *REALPOLITIK* OF STABILITY

Those who believe that authoritarian forms of Confucianism account for the stability and economic success of East Asian societies in recent decades will ask, "Why risk losing the good life the people already enjoy today for a faith

whose outcome is so uncertain?" Their argument becomes even more persuasive when what Asian societies are being urged to do to democratize is adopt
the current political forms of Western democracies to institute the political
democracy that they, like Dewey, find quite uninspiring. There is no guarantee that one could move from this kind of political democracy to the more
worthy ideal of democracy as a culture. To some Asian critics of democracy,
instead of being a precondition for ideal democracy, political democracy will
more likely destabilize and damage Asian economic prosperity.

One may suspect that the "stability-economic prosperity" argument is no
more than an excuse for governing parties to protect their own interests in
monopolizing power by maintaining a tight control over their societies. But
for such an excuse to work over a significant period of time, not only must
governments maintain their performance in benefiting enough people to continue to secure their legitimacy, they also must persuade enough people that
the authoritarian way is the only, or at least the best, way to achieve stability
and economic prosperity. The political upheavals in the Philippines and in
Indonesia in the last two decades illustrate how legitimacy is undermined when
economic development runs aground, and large sections of a population find
their livelihoods at risk. But the road to democracy is long and arduous. Other
Asian societies will not willingly follow the same path. Not only is it too
painful for too many people, it is not at all certain that democracy lies at the
end of that road—perhaps not even political democracy, let alone an ideal
democracy of any kind.

It would be better to persuade Asians that an authoritarian government
is neither the only nor the best way to a stable and an economically prosper-
ous society, even in Asia. There is no guarantee that an authoritarian government will act in the interests of the people. Experience has instead proven over
and over again Lord Acton's maxim that "power corrupts, and absolute power
corrupts absolutely." Moreover, by denying the people participation in directing their society, an authoritarian government weakens their moral fiber. A
child who has never been given any responsibility will never learn to act
responsibly; people who have been led to believe that "the government knows
best" will tend to behave like immature, spoiled brats. No matter how good a
government is, if the majority of people lack a sense of responsibility toward
their own society, then it is doubtful whether stability and prosperity could
continue for long. Personal fulfillment in a flourishing community certainly
will be impossible in such a society. As James Tiles points out, "persuade
enough people that it is not their responsibility, their role, their place to contribute to the determination of policy by interpreting events and prevailing
values, and the result will be a structure of power which is the antithesis of
community—one which realizes the values of a privileged few and limits the
possibilities of the rest."[3]

If we wish to aid democratization in Asia, to offer democracy as a faith is not enough; we must allay some of the fears that Asians have about democracy. We must show that the risk of destabilization and economic loss could be minimized in an experiment for democracy. Arguments about the desirability of democracy as an ideal would be more persuasive if we could first persuade people that the risk of an authoritarian government turning against its people is greater and worse than the risk of democratization undermining stability and economic progress in their society. The risk of destabilization is greatest when a country introduces Western democratic political forms without considering how these forms would interact with indigenous cultures. In a country with deep ethnic or religious schisms, political democracy could entrench and escalate conflict. Where the people have no experience of responsible citizenship, their participation in formal democracy might be ineffectual at best, damaging at worst.

To minimize the risks involved in the process of democratization, we turn to Dewey's idea of democracy as a culture—a set of practices, attitudes, and expectations pervading every aspect of human interaction. Instead of changing governmental forms overnight and expecting a miracle, it would be more prudent to adopt a "bottom-up" approach, to gradually transform the culture. Practices that would prepare people for democracy could be introduced at various levels gradually in social environments and organizations where the effects of any mistakes and failures—and there are bound to be quite a few along the way—would not bring the country crashing down. Over time, the spread of such practices would foster attitudes and expectations for democracy; it would equip people with the skills for responsible participation and give them reasons to believe that the open discussions and disagreements could be part of a cooperative process to solve a shared problem instead of always bringing unproductive chaos.

Through the experience of democracy within limited social contexts, wherein people of different ethnic origins and religions could interact, people could learn that diversity and loyalty to one's own commitments need not preclude cooperation with others; that it is possible to construct shared interests without losing one's identity. Learning to build consensus through cooperative inquiry in more limited contexts first will foster trust and prevent ethnic and religious differences from undermining democratization at the national level.

Departing from the usual state- and elite-focused analyses of China, Kate Zhou argues persuasively that "The farmers of China are changing China this time around—not the leaders, not the bureaucrats, not the cadres, not the intellectuals but farmers themselves." Though the farmer's movement that she examines is basically a disorganized economic movement, it has widespread and important social and political implications. Under those economic reforms, China has become a more open class society, but it is still not democratic. Zhou herself sees farmers as "radical individualists by default" who prefer a "libertarian state" rather than a democratic one. In a survey of some cultural requisites for democracy, Andrew Nathan and Shi Tianjian discern patterns in the data suggesting difficulties if the Chinese political system begins to democratize.[4] They suggest a top-down approach: "A democratic regime could speed the pace of cultural change by actively inculcating the popular attitudes it needs to survive." Possible, but unlikely, given the character of the current political leadership. The driving force for democratization probably will have to come from the lower levels of society. The rural population makes up nearly 80 per cent of the people who should be governing a democratic China. However daunting a task, cultural transformation of the rural population is necessary in any move toward democracy. As Zhou puts it, "The sun rising in the villages is the future of China."[5]

Zhou argues that "Chinese farmers in Communist China are not reactionary, passive, anti-capitalist, or anti-modern." One also may argue that they are not anti-democratic, even though they have not, so far, actively sought democracy. Farmers were able to improve their economic situation, because they were able to slough off the constraints of central planning and party mismanagement of resources. Their enrichment goes hand in hand with a reduction in state and party control, that is, an increase in their freedom of action, at least in the economic sphere. The experience nurtures democratic culture, as it is an exercise in individual and cooperative problem solving and decision making. Even though the farmers' movement has not openly challenged the state authorities in any organized fashion and is characterized by individuals exploiting loopholes in the system and the corruptibility of party cadres to gain their own ends, the practice of regaining control even in a limited area would reduce their willingness to accept oppressive control in other areas. The farmers' economic activism eventually could lead to political activism and economic liberalization to democratization.[6]

The primary focus of a "bottom-up" democratization process will not be political institutions, or ideology. As a farmer of Tongxin village puts it, "Only the cadres pay attention to political lines; the farmers are only interested in what works."[7] Many Chinese probably share this practical attitude. For democracy to gain a foothold in the development of Chinese society, it must be perceived as being relevant to the ordinary Chinese's daily life. This is best done by understanding democracy as a culture, as a better way of life, where each individual has more say in how she lives her life, where everybody has a better chance of living a fulfilling life in a flourishing community. The process of change must start at the level of how the ordinary person solves the problems she faces in cooperation with those around her.

Political institutions are not, however, insignificant. As long as some kind of structure is necessary to organize collective life, even though there could be a great variety in terms of the fluidity of what constitutes "structure," then democratization in China requires political institutional reform. And as long as the existing political institutions remain unchanged, democracy as culture will not be complete; along the way, these institutions also obstruct democratic enculturation to various extents. This is likely to be the most difficult part of democratization in China. As Zhou points out, the success of the farmers' movement is due largely to the fact that it presented no focus for governmental attack, both ideological or in the form of leading individuals. They had no specific ideological agenda that threatened the political monopoly of the Communist Party. It would be much more difficult to change political institutions in the same way.

But political institutions also could be changed in a gradual, bottom-up manner that is relatively less threatening to those in power at the top level. Taiwan is such a case of political democratization that has adopted a gradual, "bottom-up" approach. Ambrose King observes that even while its government was "authoritarian," Taiwan experimented with democracy at the level of local representative institutions from the 1950s. The people's participation in this limited local-level democracy over a few decades contributes to the viability of its national democracy, when the country eventually democratized its national governmental system in the 1980s. Apart from its economic development, the nearly half-century-long practice of elections at the local and provincial levels that have institutionalized the values and "rules of the game" of democratic participation and competition has brought about cultural changes that make the more comprehensive change in political forms viable. As Dankwart Rustow notes, "habituation" is an important source of democratic cultural change.[8] One could extend King's and Rustow's argument about political culture and political democracy from a Deweyan perspective. Introducing democracy as a culture gradually should not only be a matter of moving from local elections to national elections, but democratic practices should be encouraged and democratic habits formed in all arenas—the family, the workplace, temples and mosques, and politics.

De Bary considers the question of civil society a crucial issue in discussing Asian communitarianism if we want to avoid authoritarian conclusions. There is an increasing interest in the development of civil societies in relation to democratization in Asia. Many scholars have borrowed the concept in their studies of China, though not without some reservations.[9] The concept is incompatible with Confucianism, insofar as it implies a concept of autonomous rather than social individuals, a radical separation of the private and public, and an irreconcilable antagonism toward the state. But the concept of civil society, like democracy, is contested and flexible enough to be reconstructed for use in Confucian and other contexts.[10] It could be useful in exploring "bottom-up" approaches to democratization in East Asia.

By suggesting a peaceful, "bottom-up" approach to democratization, I do not mean that it could be done peacefully without at least the acquiescence, if not the active encouragement and support, of the government. The farmers in the PRC were able to change the rural economy, despite the bureaucracy and political leaders, because the latter were preoccupied with other problems. Actual economic success led to an after-the-fact endorsement from the Chinese state, which has been attempting to improve China's economy. It remains to be seen whether the political leaders would recognize the need for political reform, and whether they could be persuaded that democratization would not necessarily lead to a total collapse of the regime, provided that the Communist Party itself adapted successfully to the new world. After all, Communist parties elsewhere in the world have survived, and they even gain power in relatively democratic political systems.

King stresses that, in Taiwan's case, the Kuomintang's ideological commitment to the eventual introduction of constitutional democracy—arising from Sun Yat-sen's "Three People's doctrines" of "nationalism (*minzu* 民族), democracy/people's rights (*minquan* 民權), and people's livelihood (*minsheng* 民生)"—and the support of its powerful leader, Jiang Jingguo, for political reform in the 1980s were critical to the country's transition to political democracy. A "bottom-up" approach does not preclude "democratic engineering from above." Larry Diamond argues that "the most favorable development for democratization is a firm and forceful commitment to the process on the part of a country's leadership."[11] In the absence of such a commitment, an authoritarian government could place countless obstacles to prevent the growth of a democratic culture.

It is important to stress that the instant overhaul of political systems, any more than the violent overthrow of a government, is usually not the best way to democratize. In their zeal to spread the gospel of liberal democracy, some Westerners, and at times Asian liberal Democrats themselves, often push for too much too soon. The results of such impatience often are disastrous. However, the plea for patience and caution does not mean that one should be forever waiting for a "better opportunity," only to end up doing nothing. In any situation, there is always something, however small, that can be done to move a culture closer to democracy. Democratization is likely to be one of incremental progress, with periodic setbacks rather than overnight successes. Recognizing that experiments for democracy can be carried out in a gradual process, in fits and starts, beginning with more limited arenas than national politics, undermines the argument that it is too dangerous to experiment with democracy, as the cost could be the entire country's stability and economic prosperity. Governments that reject even limited democratic experiments are exposed as authoritarians working for themselves rather than for the people.

There is no magic formula for democratization. Dependence on any single means is unlikely to be successful; organizing as many means as available—whether educational, economic, or political—into a complex, well-coordinated strategy is more likely to succeed, but it is extremely difficult. Even though obstruction by recalcitrant authoritarian forces in some circumstances may require drastic action that could be considered "revolutionary," democracy can never be achieved overnight. As a culture, Confucian democracy will require painstaking, long-term cultivation, involving everybody. Even with the best efforts, there will never be any guarantee of success. The best that we can do is weight the chances in its favor.

Notes

CHAPTER 1

1. Fukuyama (1989, 4); criticisms by Samuel Huntington, Timothy Fuller, David Satter, and others and Fukuyama's response in no. 17 (1989) and no. 18 (1990) of the *National Interest*.

2. Fukuyama (1989, 11–18).

3. Fukuyama (1989, 17; 1992, 242–44; 1995, 21).

4. Fukuyama (1989, 13).

5. Kahn (1979, 121–23, 329–83). Besides South Korea, Japan, Taiwan, Hong Kong, and Singapore, Southeast Asian countries in which the Chinese minorities dominate the business sectors—for example, Malaysia, Indonesia, and Thailand—also have done relatively well. Within the United States, relatively speaking, the Chinese Americans also have fared better economically than other minority ethnic groups (Chan 1993, 39).

6. Zakaria (1994, 125); see also Mahbubani (1995). Most scholars agree that East Asian economic dynamism cannot be explained solely by cultural factors, even though these play a significant role (Tai 1989; Chan 1993; Berger and Hsiao 1988).

7. Mahbubani (1995, 102; 1992, 6–7); French (1996); Bell (1995, 34); Berger and Hsiao (1988, 4). It must, however, be noted that representatives of this school of thought demurred from talking about "models" for others, as it would be contradictory to the stand they take to pretend any kind of universalist claim (Kausikan 1998, 19–20). Short of universality, however, a model may simply be a set of useful guidelines that could be adapted according to different circumstances.

8. For studies supporting such general similarities, see Hitchcock (1994, esp. 38–41); Emmerson (1996, 3); report of the survey of the values of Asian executives conducted by Wirthlin Worldwide in the *Wall Street Journal*, 5 March 1996, p. 1.

9. Bauer (1995, 2).

10. Rosemont (1997, 68–69; 1998); Rorty (1991, 1993); Rawls (1993, 14, and Lecture III "Political Constructivism").

11. American Anthropological Association (1947); de Bary (1998b, 54); Onuma (1996).

12. Huntington (1993, 22).

13. See criticisms by Fouard Ajami (1993), Robert Bartley (1993), and Liu Binyan (1993) in *Foreign Affairs* 75:4 (1993); see also Rashid (1997).

14. A form of cultural détente is Huntington's (1996b, 41–46) proposed strategy for the West.

15. Howell (1997); Hall and Ames (1999, 89–97). This is not a new suggestion. During the Enlightenment, many European intellectuals were interested in the Chinese civilization and advocated learning from it (Ching and Oxtoby 1992); Jensen (1997, 77–134); Clarke (1997, 37–53).

16. The danger is not limited to non-Western countries. Western countries might make the same mistake if they feel threatened by the "clash of civilizations" scenario and react defensively (Smith 1997).

17. Sen (1996); Chan (1996; 1998, 32–34); Kausikan (1998, 24); Jones (1994, 19). Confucian culture is only one among many Asian cultures, and when the discussion moves from one to the other, there is no intention of reducing Asian to Confucian; instead, it is a move from the more general to the more specific, from a wider to a narrower field, when it is not clear that an argument could apply to the wider field.

18. Huntington (1996a, 15, 18, 21).

19. Pye (1985, 55–89; 1996).

20. Munro (1979, 40); Edwards (1986, 44); see also Kent (1993, 30–31).

21. Yu Ying-shih (1997, 208). Borrowing Rawls's framework of *Political Liberalism*, Yu argues that Confucianism may exist as one among several comprehensive doctrines within a liberal democracy.

22. Wu (1922, 15).

23. The slogan actually was coined by Hu Shih in his preface to Wu Yu's work (Wu 1922, 7).

24. Nussbaum (1997).

25. Weber (1951); Tu (1991).

26. Tu (1984, 90).

27. An approach that Amartya Sen (1996, 3) advocates. See also Chan (1998); de Bary (1998b); Hall and Ames (1999).

28. Chang et al. (1958); Tu (1986); Liu (1992).

29. Li (1999, ch. 7, emphasis added).

30. Parekh (1993, 172); Dunn (1992, vi); Bell (1995, 30).

31. Beetham (1993, 60); Dunn (1979, 11); see also Parekh (1993, 165).

32. Held (1993, 14); Zakaria (1997, 23–24); see also Bell et al. (1995).

33. Zolo (1992, 170).

34. Barber (1984, 1989); Dahl (1989, 1992); Gould (1988); Gutmann (1987); Okin (1989).

35. Bell (1995).

36. Sandel (1996, 3).

37. Rawls (1971, 1993); Dworkin (1977, 1978); Feinberg (1988); Raz (1986); Nozick (1974).

38. Chan (1998, 33).

39. Walzer (1989, 6, 22); Unger (1983, 41); Gutmann (1985, 320). Buchanan is probably not alone in excluding Walzer as a communitarian, despite some similarities between his theory and communitarianism (Buchanan 1989, 852n).

40. Delaney (1994, viii); Buchanan (1989, 882).

41. Tam (1998, 29); Etzioni (1993, 15).

42. Tam (1998, 21–23).

43. Gaus (1983).

44. Hall and Ames (1999).

45. Keenan (1977, 34).

46. Foreword to Barry Keenan's *The Dewey Experiment in China*, in Keenan (1977, v).

47. Cai (1968, 782–83), quoted and translated in Keenan (1977, 10).

CHAPTER 2

1. Parekh (1993, 157–58); see also Allen (1997, xi).

2. *De vera Religione*, XXXIX.72, translated in Taylor (1989, 129).

3. Psychoanalysis is an example of this emphasis; modern psychology has been called "the Science of Selves."

4. Romans 7:19, quoted in *Confessions*, VII, xxi.27, in Taylor (1989, 138).

5. *De Civitate Dei*, XIX.26, translated in Taylor (1989, 136). Following Augustine, many Christian theologians have presented self-inquiry as leading to an inquiry about God, and knowledge of God as being necessary for self-knowledge.

6. Taylor (1989, 188).

7. Kant (1948, 1993); Murdoch (1970, 80).

8. Sandel (1982).

9. Rawls (1971, 179).

10. Sandel (1982, 79).

11. Ibid., 132.

12. Rawls (1971, 520).

13. Ibid., 561.

14. Sandel (1982, 179).

15. Ibid., 189.

16. Rawls (1971, 191, 448).

17. Sandel (1982, 181).

18. M14.60. Citations from Dewey's works are from the *Collected Works of John Dewey*, edited by Jo Ann Boydston. An initial, indicating *Early Works* (E), *Middle Works* (M), or *Later Works* (L), is followed by the volume and page number.

19. Schilpp (1951, 586).

20. Taylor (1989).

21. *Concise Oxford Dictionary* definition. "There has been a tendency in recent philosophy to use the word 'person' for the most general category encompassing human beings" (Harré 1987, 99). I shall not take up the discussions regarding the possibility of nonhuman persons, though this is a popular topic in contemporary Western philosophical literature on the concept of persons.

22. Rorty (1990, 36).

23. Williams (1975).

24. Rucker (1980).

25. Elvin (1985, 170).

26. Taylor (1989, 375).

27. Tiles (1988, 232n).

28. Hollis (1977).

29. Mead (1934).

30. M14.16; see also Campbell (1995, 42).

31. Fingarette (1989, 198–99).

32. *Analects* 15.16. Unless otherwise stated, translations are from Ames and Rosemont (1998), with occasional modifications by the author.

33. Fingarette (1972, 28–36).

34. *Historical Records* (1964, 8: Biography of Lord Yin of Huai, 2624).

35. Some contemporary Western thinkers, for example, Ricoeur (1992), also take into account this inseparability of "inner" and "outer".

36. Hall and Ames (1998, 23–43); see also Hall and Ames (1987, 80–82); Ames (1994).

37. Ames (1993, 165); see also Tu (1994).

38. *Book of Rites* 43.1/164/25, translated in Hall and Ames (1999, 175).

39. M10.41; L1.235, 259; L12.88–89; L16.54–55, 68–69, 96. On the difference between Dewey's epistemology and the "spectator theory of knowledge," see Tiles (1988, 124–29); Rorty (1980).

40. Fingarette (1979, 131).

41. Kohn (1992).

42. *Analects* 12.1, translated in Lau (1979, 112).

43. The graph for *zi* begins as a pictogram showing a human nose; pointing to one's nose is a way of self-reference (Fazzioli 1986, 29; Wieger 1965, 325). It also is used as an emphatic pronoun: "I myself did it," in contrast to the reflexive use, "I did it to myself."

44. This implied sense of drawing boundaries is supported by the gloss of *ji* in the *Shuowen jiezi* as "having definite shape or form," and "the warp and weft of a loom" indicating an organized structure (*Shuowen* 1966, 748/14B:21a). See also Fazzioli (1986, 34); Wieger (1965, 217).

45. Boodberg (1953); Tu (1979, 18).

46. *Xunzi* 29/143/8. Unless otherwise stated, translations are adapted from Knoblock (1988–1994).

47. Elvin (1985, 159–62); for a translation of *lisao*, see Hawkes (1985, 67–95).

48. Henry Rosemont (1989) questions the use of the term *moral* in the Chinese context. Distinguishing between "morals" and "ethics," he argues that the concept clusters associated with "morals"—"freedom," "liberty," "autonomy," "individual," "utility," "principles," "rationality," "rational agent," "objective," "subjective," "choice," "duties," "rights" and "ought," prudential or obligatory—are absent in Confucian and other non-Western cultures, and that one would do better speaking instead of ethics as a more general evaluative discourse on human conduct. Rosemont's objection to "morals" is aimed at the mainstream concepts of moral laws and rights-based moral theories, but the concept cluster that bothers him could be used quite differently. Dewey (L7.9) uses the adjective "moral" generally, interchangeable with "ethical," rather than in the more specific way that Rosemont objects to. In the sense that Dewey uses it, "moral" is applicable to early Confucianism, even though I agree with Rosemont that, wherever possible, it is preferable to use "ethical."

49. Sandel (1982, 121).

50. Kymlicka (1989, 54).

51. Ibid., 61.

52. Kant (1948, 116). But Glenn Tinder, starting with a Kantian account of consciousness, nevertheless concludes that inquiry is inherently social (Tinder 1980, 18–30).

53. Rawls (1971, 412).

54. Rawls (1993, 50).

55. Schilpp (1951, 17; L1.170).

56. Allport (1951, 276).

57. Fingarette (1972, 18–36); cf. Fazzioli (1986, 60).

58. Fingarette (1972, 18).

59. Ibid., 21.

60. *Analects* 5.28, 6.3, 7.2, 7.34, 11.7.

61. The *Duan Yucai* 段玉裁 commentaries on the *Shuowen jiezi* associate *si* with *depth and thoroughness*, which might be taken as a reference to critical and evaluative thinking (*Shuowen* 1966, 506/10B:23b).

62. Bloom (1985, 299, 301).

63. Ibid., 294.

64. *Mencius* 8.30/44/19. Unless otherwise stated, translations are from Lau (1970), with occasional modifications by the author.

65. Fingarette (1979, 133).

66. The early graph combines "heart-and-mind" (*xin* 心) and "going to" (*zhi* 之) or "abiding in" (*zhi* 止).

67. Parekh (1993, 159).

68. *De* 德, *ren* 仁, *yi* 義, *li* 禮, and *zhi* 智 in the Confucian ethical lexicon also may serve as critieria in different circumstances, though *dao* may be seen as the most comprehensive notion and could be seen to include all of the others. In any case, what is said about *dao* in the discussion that follows applies equally to the other ethical notions.

69. Fingarette (1979, 135); Munro (1985, 4–6).

70. Tu (1985, 83).

71. Fingarette (1979, 137).

72. Munro (1985, 3–8).

73. Rawls (1993, 323).

74. Hegel (1942, 58ff., 70ff., 156ff., 186).

75. Rawls (1993, 41, 285–86; 1971, 264).

76. Gaus (1983, 68); Wolff (1977, 190). Rawls himself denies that his theory supposes that "society is an organic whole with a life of its own distinct from and superior to that of all its members in their relations with one another" (Rawls 1971, 264).

77. Hegel (1942, 290, 292).

78. Hegel (1975, 191–92); for a short but clear discussion of the debate on internal versus external relations and their implications, with an emphasis on the Hegelian position, see the exchange between Brand Blanshard and Errol Harris (Grier 1989, 3–27); see also Harris (1987).

79. Damico (1978, 40, 85).

80. Popper (1945, 2: 25–76); Berlin (1969, 41–117); cf. Avineri (1972); Taylor (1979).

81. Berlin (1969, 43–68).

82. Taylor (1979, 99, 122–23); Hegel (1955, 99, 105).

83. Schilpp (1951, 17); Berlin (1969, 47, 48fn).

84. Harris (1987, 37).

85. L1.64. Scholars today continue to understand social systems in this nontotalistic sense: "Social systems are open systems with fuzzy boundaries, because the system's structure is the regularity of interaction and that is a matter of degree. The regularity also is general but not universal, involving some order but not total order" (Mackin 1997, 50).

86. Munro (1985, 263); Kent (1993, 30–31); Edwards (1986, 44).

87. Munro (1985, 21, 17); see also Edwards (1986, 44).

88. Sartori (1984, 244–45). Dewey links the concept of organism to system (M2.178). Historically, organicism has been associated with general systems theory (Philips 1976, 46–79).

89. Tu (1985, 38–39).

90. Pasternak (1988, 659).

91. Munro (1985, 276).

92. Manfred Porkert (1974) discusses the differences in Chinese and Western views of the body from a medical point of view; see also John Hay's (1993) discussion of the differences in Western and Chinese body imagery.

93. The nonseparation of the human body from its environment is evident very early in *The Yellow Emperor's Classic of Internal Medicine* 黃帝內經, which is considered the earliest Chinese medical manual (Veith 1966, 105). The idea of "forming one body with the universe (*tianren heyi* 天人合一) is central to Song and Ming neo-Confucianism. Tu Wei-ming (1985, 35–50) argues that "the continuity of being is central to Chinese philosophy."

94. King (1985, 65).

95. *Conversations of the States* (1973, 114–15).

96. *Xunzi* 9/39/9–17. The term appears in many places in the *Xunzi*; in contrast, it appears only once without ethical connotations in the *Mencius* 14.19/74/31, where it refers to a group of "small men" in a quote from the *Book of Songs*.

97. Nakane (1973, 14).

98. Fei (1992, 62); King (1985, 61).

99. *Rites of Zhou* 4.0/53/5.

100. Fung (1939, 68); Li Zehou (1996, 14) shares this view to some extent, though he limits it to the Spring and Autumn period of China's history.

101. The state bureaucracy instituted administrative divisions of different population sizes over the next 2,000 years, but definitions of these divisions change frequently, and application also tends to be extremely flexible, even indiscriminate, at times.

102. Liang (1989, 3: 94).

103. Nivison (1996, 33) was describing *dao* in philosophical daoism rather than Confucianism, but the general idea could, arguably, be shared by both; Fingarette (1972, 20); Munro (1985, 262); cf. Hall and Ames (1995, 211–16, 244–52).

104. Mote (1971, 17); Bodde (1961); Birrell (1993, 18, 25); see also Yuan (1960, 30–34). The text that Birrell and Yuan cite as the earliest record of creation myth is "The Heavenly Questions" in *The Songs of Chu* 楚辭. This does not give an account of the birth of the cosmos; it is a sort of ritual catechism, beginning with a question about "the beginning of things in the remote past" (Hawkes 1985, 45–46).

105. Mote (1971, 20, emphasis added); Birrell (1993, 23–24); see also Loewe (1982, 63–64).

106. Needham (1956, 302); Hall and Ames (1995, 184).

107. Foreword to Birrell (1993, xi); see also Yuan (1960, 16–20).

CHAPTER 3

1. Wolff (1989, 13); Oppenheimer (1914, xxxi); Tönnies (1957, 34–35).

2. Gaus (1983, 15).

3. Crittenden (1992, 130–42).

4. Sennett (1977b, 308).

5. For the psychology of what such coordination would involve, see "The Reflex Arc Concept in Psychology" (E5.96–109).

6. Gaus (1983, 93).

7. Rorty (1989, 90); on narcissistic culture, see Sennett (1977a, 187–97; 1977b, 8, 238, 334).

8. It is uncertain if the works referred to are the ones that later became the classics central to Confucian education. There is probably a large overlap of content in the case of the *Book of Songs*. The date of origin of the extant *Book of Rites* is controversial, and probably not all chapters are of the same period. The text as we know it is probably compiled during the Han dynasty (Loewe 1993, 293–95).

9. *Analects* 15.20; see other similar uses of *ming* in *Analects* 4.5, 8.19.

10. Russell (1922, 40); Liang (1989, vol. 3, 30); Lin (1938, 180).

11. Mencius 1.7/5/7, author's translation.

12. *Analects* 1.2; see also *Mencius* 12.2/62/18.

13. *Analects* 12.1, 6.30; see also *Mencius* 7.3/36/16.

14. Roger Ames (1994, 206) points out that this metaphor seems especially apt, given the interesting cognate relations between the Chinese characters for ethical human relations (*lun* 倫) and a ripple (*lun* 淪).

15. For more detailed arguments for a less perniciously familistic interpretation of Confucian responses to the tension between family and wider social relations, see Tan (2002).

16. *Analects* 13.18; see also *Mencius* 13.35/71/17.

17. *Mencius* 8.29/44/10; in *Analects* 8.21, Confucius praised Yu for "living in humblest circumstances yet gave all of his strength to the construction of drain canals and irrigation ditches."

18. King and Bond (1985, 38–42).

19. *Analects* 15.12, author's translation; cf. "He who gives no thought to difficulties in the future is sure to be beset by worries much closer at hand" (Lau 1979, 134). Both the temporal and spatial interpretations of *yuan* 遠 (far) and *jin* 近 (near) work—the text is richer for its polysemy.

20. An exception is Thomas Alexander (1987), who argues that the aesthetic dimension of experience is central to Dewey's philosophy. Another who recently has paid attention to the artistic aspect of community building is Carolin Woolson (1998, 126–28), who focuses on social inquiry but mentions Dewey's conception of art contributing to a rethinking of community.

21. The contrasts being drawn here are polaristic rather than dualistic.

22. *Book of Rites* 32.9/143/30; Legge (1970, vol. 1: 396–97).

23. *Book of Rites* 43.1/164/28; Legge (1970, vol. 1: 359). The notion of peace (*ping* 平) and calm in the ideal of "bringing peace to all under heaven" is closely related to harmony (*he* 和). It often is portrayed as the state of mind or relations accompanying the achievement of harmony (*Zuo's Commentary*, Duke Zhao, twentieth year, Legge [1970, vol. 5: 679, 684]). In modern mandarin, the two characters together, *heping* 和平, translate "peace."

24. *Book of Rites* 32.6/143/8, author's translation; Legge (1970, vol. 1: 390) translates this as "the superior man cultivates a *friendly* harmony without being weak."

25. *Zuo's Commentary*, Duke Zhao, twentieth year, Legge (1970, vol. 5: 679, 684).

26. Cheng (1988, 234); Tang Yi-jie (1988, 321) translates *datong* as "the great harmony." Tu Wei-ming (1979, 29) seems to think that "great unity" and "great harmony" work equally well as a translation of *datong*. Others prefer translations such as "grand union" (Legge) or "grand unity" (de Bary, Wing-tsit Chan).

27. Duke Zhao, twentieth year, Legge (1970, vol. 5: 680, 684–85).

28. *Lü's Spring and Autumn Annals* 14.2/71/19, author's translation. The passage from the *Zuo's Commentary* mentioned earlier also uses gustatory harmony as a metaphor for social harmony.

29. For a discussion of the applicability of Deweyan aesthetics to the Chinese worldview through an exploration of Chinese art, see Tan (1999).

30. Schilpp (1951, 552).

31. Schilpp (1951, 371–89, 546). Benedetto Croce later took this up. The controversy has persisted. For an account of the "Pepper-Croce thesis," its wider implications for Dewey's philosophy, and a convincing defense of Dewey against the charge of being an organic idealist, see Alexander (1987, 1–13).

32. *Book of Rites* 32.1/142/24. The message therein is cosmic rather than merely social.

33. Tiles (1988, 227).

34. Cua (1979, 373–75).

35. *Analects* 1.12. According to D. C. Lau (1979, 249), Master You is a student of Confucius and occupied a special place in the Confucian school after Confucius' death. On his resemblance to Confucius, see also the *Book of Rites* 3.70/18/8.

36. Nivison (1996, 47, 67); Cua (1983, 13; 1985, 98).

37. The *Shuowen* glosses *li* as "treading, following, enacting" (*Shuowen* 1966, 2/1A: 4b).

38. *Book of Rites* 32.13/144/17; Tu (1989, 48); cf. "Honoring the dead with reverence is a way of celebrating our humanity" (Cua 1979, 387).

39. *Book of Rites* 32.13/144/21, author's translation.

40. See Cua (1979, 387) on Xunzi's view of the mourning and sacrificial rites; see Tu (1989, 41) on the importance of continuing one's parents' works in the Confucian view of filiality.

41. *Book of Rites* 32.1/142/22; Legge (1970, vol. 1, 384).

42. Fingarette (1972, 9–14).

43. Creel (1949, 83); Li (1996, 7).

44. Creel (1949, 143–44); Fingarette (1972, 57–70); Ching (1997, 69–74).

45. *Book of Rites* 19.3/99/21; see also Hall and Ames (1987, 259).

46. Hall and Ames (1987, 89–110).

47. *Mencius* 7.10/37/21, 11.10/59/25, 11.11/60/4.

48. *Xunzi* 19/90/4; "Hence the former kings reform the rites in order to attain meaning/appropriateness (*yi*)" (*Book of Rites* 9.36/64/11). In a more limited context of the father and son relationship, the *Book of Rites* 11.25/72/9 says that "When meaning/appropriateness (*yi*) arises, then rites work."

49. *Xunzi* 27/128/3; Cua (1985, 160–63; 1983, 12). There is some similarity between my account and Cua's understanding of *li* being as rule dependent and *yi* as being situation dependent, even though I would prefer to speak in terms of form and content, general meaning, and meaning specific to circumstances.

50. *Analects* 3.22, 14.16, 14.17; Shun Kwong-loi (1997, 57) points to examples in the *Mencius* of *yi* behavior that are not a matter of following *li*; whereas *li* could be overridden, *yi* could not.

51. On community as a "semiotic network," see Grange (1997, 193).

52. Dewey contrasts the thoughtful, the intelligent, and art with both the capricious and the routine (M9.153; L1.270).

53. *Book of Rites* 19.1/99/10; Li (1996, 15).

54. Tu (1979, 25).

55. "Diary of a Madman," in Lu (1990, 29–41); see also Wu (1922, 63–72).

56. Cheng (1930, 22B, 3a), "Surviving Works (*yishu* 遺書)." The character translated as "chastity (*jie* 節)" is closely connected to ritual practice: the function of ritual practice is to regulate (*jie* 節) conduct (*Book of Rites* 11.25/72/7).

57. Eldridge (1998, 41).

58. Saatkamp (1995, 94); see also Rorty (1991, 63–77); Rorty's introduction to vol. 8 of Dewey's *Later Works* (L8.ix–xvii); cf. Ratner's introduction in Dewey (1939); and Michael Eldridge (1998), who specifically focuses on Rorty's criticism in his arguments about the importance of intelligence, and following from that, the importance of the method of inquiry and of the scientific method in Dewey's philosophy as a whole.

59. Wu (1997, 74).

60. Wu (1997, 76–77) acknowledges this when he argues for a joining of the two kinds of pragmatism (American and Chinese) that he describes. It is telling that in searching for a description for "the community of spirited Pragmatism" that would result from such a fusion, he quotes from Dewey's *Essays in Experimental Logic* (1916, 103).

61. Hall and Ames (1999, 209).

62. Hall and Ames (1987, 50).

63. Ibid., 55.

64. Waley (1996, 107).

65. Lau (1979, 136); Legge (1970, vol. 1, 304).

66. For other examples of how an active understanding of *zhi* provides a better interpretation of the *Analects*, see Hall and Ames (1987, 52–56).

67. *Shuowen* (1966, 598/12A: 17a).

68. Chen (2000).

69. Ban (1952, 404, 528); see also Boltz (1982).

70. *Tang Yu zhi dao* 唐虞之道, strip 3 of the *Bamboo Text Discovered in the Chu Tomb at Guodian* 郭店楚墓竹簡, translated in Chen (2000, 417).

71. De Bary (1998a, 53–57). The other area in which de Bary discovers an unsuccessful attempt at civil society is the community compact (*xiangyue* 鄉約), which is a form of public instruction as well as local organization.

72. Lee (1994).

73. *Book of Rites* 32.3/142/31; Legge (1970, vol. 1, 388). This also is implied in Chen Ning's (2000) study of the early forms of the *sheng* graph.

74. Schwartz (1985, 68–71).

75. Devins and Douglas (1998, 3–4).

76. Lovejoy (1936): Lewis (1954, vol. 2, 383).

77. Keightley (1978, 221).

78. According to Keightley, "the Shang had not yet developed orderly and consistent religious explanations for such large and strategically capricious phenomena" (de Bary and Bloom 1999, vol. 1, 13) and there is no record of any Shang cosmogonic myth (Birrell 1993, 18).

79. On correlative thinking in Chinese thought, see Needham (1956, vol. 2, 253–345); Hall and Ames (1995, 12–33); Henderson (1984); Zhang (1959). On the linguistic logic that "divides down," see Graham (1986, 322–59; 1989, 262, 286, 389ff.); Hansen (1983).

80. Hall and Ames (1987, 204–208; 1998, 219–44); Xu (1969, 86–89, 99, 181); Tang (1991, vol. 4, 470–76); see also Xiong (1960, 22); Lao (1974, 131–33, 139–40).

81. Sigmund (1967, 138–42); Locke (1967, 348).

82. Locke (1967, 322); Rawls (1993, 34); see also Gutmann (1980, 1).

83. Munro (1969, 11–16, 49–83); Ching (1998, 72); Bloom (1998, 100–104).

84. For more details, see Shun (1997, 222–31).

85. *Mencius* 3.2/17/13, 11.7/58/28. On why *lei* is not equivalent to "a kind," as understood in the Western method of classification, see Hall and Ames (1995, 246–56).

86. Munro (1969, 11–16, 49–83); Irene Bloom (1998, 98) agrees, though she sees a strong egalitarian theme in the *Mencius*.

87. Berlin (1979, 90).

88. Locke (1967, 287); cf. Gutmann (1980); Rawls (1993, 34); Bedau (1967, 3–13).

89. Leys (1997, 81); Waley (1996, 110); Lau (1979, 138).

90. *Analects* 11.17. Confucius also obliquely criticizes Master Ji Kang for being rich at the expense of the people (12.18).

91. *Analects* 4.14, 13.2, 15.14; *Mencius* 3.4/17/22, 3.5/17/28.

92. Menzel (1963, 9–21, 28–33, 41–48).

93. Fan (1980, 24).

94. Hall and Ames (1999, 160; 1998, 268); cf. Tan (2001).

95. The *Luxuriant Dews of the Spring and Autumn Annals* 春秋繁露, henceforth referred to as "*Luxuriant Dews*," first mentions this only in passing without elaborat-

ing (10.1/46/23); the *Comprehensive Discourses in the White Tiger Hall* (Ban 1952, 559–64) provides the Confucian understanding of this idea. On the idea's deviation from early Confucianism, see Lin (1990); Ching (1997, 267); de Bary (1998a, 124–25).

96. Yu (1976, 43); *Historical Records* (1964, vol. 10, 3105–14, "Biography of Ji An 汲黯"); see also Creel (1949, 234); *Han Feizi* (1974, vol. 2, 207–208, author's translation).

97. On the superiority of *yang* and the inferiority of *yin*, see *Luxuriant Dews* 11.3/51/2, 11.4/52–23; on their complementarity, see Ban (1952, 560); de Bary (1998a, 125).

98. *Book of Rites* 12.41/78/4, 45.3/165/26.

99. Ching (1997, 266).

100. Li (1982, 3–6).

101. For translations of these women's instruction texts, see de Bary and Bloom (1999, 819–36).

102. de Bary and Bloom (1999, 826–27); *Book of Rites* (1992, 11.25/72/12); de Bary and Bloom (1999, 836).

103. Rosemont (1997); see also de Bary (1998a, 118–33).

104. Swann (1932, 84–85); Wawrytko (2000, 179).

105. Li (2000). See also Lai (2000).

106. Eisenstein (1983); Phillips (1987); Croll (1995, 178).

Chapter 4

1. For the relation between Dewey's political activism and his philosophy, see Westbrook (1991); Campbell (1995, 211–13); Eldridge (1998). Confucius' quest for political office is well known and found even in the shortest of biographies. For a more extended treatment, see Creel (1949).

2. Mill (1985, 135).

3. Sandel (1996, 4); Berlin (1991, 13; 1969, 167); Rawls (1993, 197–200).

4. Rawls (1993, 175).

5. Ibid., 137.

6. Immanuel Kant, "Idea for a Universal History with a Cosmopolitan Purpose," in Reiss (1970, 44).

7. Rawls (1993, 11, 258, 269, 271).

8. Ibid., 146, 246.

9. Ibid., xlix, emphasis added, 290, 370.

10. Ibid., 13–14, 420, emphasis added.

11. Ibid., 145, 148.

12. Ansen (1990).

13. Rawls (1993, 159).

14. Ibid., 258.

15. M14.28. Damico (1986) discusses this important sense of practicality in Dewey's philosophy.

16. L7.315; Addams (1902, 3). Significantly, Dewey replaces Addams's "individual morality" with "personal morality."

17. Xu (1959, 155–200).

18. *Analects* 2.3, 13.3, 12.13. While Confucius' preference for rituals instead of laws as a means of government is indisputable, this ideal should not be confused with how the law actually operated in China. Recent studies, such as those in the Stanford University Press series, *Law, Society, and Culture in China*, have shown that law has played a greater, more important role in Chinese societies than has hitherto been recognized; see also Liu (1998).

19. Manicas (1982, 411).

20. Manicas (1982). Dewey's comments about anarchists indicate that he is unaware of this affinity between his views and anarchism (L13.32).

21. Tiles (1992, vol. 2, 21).

22. Knowledge or wisdom (*zhi* 知) is closely associated with authoritative conduct/ person (*ren* 仁) (*Analects* 4.2, 6.23).

23. *Song History* (1977, 12728); Huang (1986, vol. 1, 464); Ching (1997, 5–8); cf. Chen (2000).

24. Chen (1995).

25. Xu (1959, 155–200); also Tu (1993, 1–28).

26. Li (1996, 284–88); Ching (1997, xv).

27. Chen Daqi (1964, 247–51) ranks the several types of personal achievement in the *Analects* hierarchically; cf. Hall's and Ames's (1987, 186) contrasting view of these as "different aspects of one organic process of personal growth."

28. Boodberg (1953, 321–22).

29. Hall and Ames (1987, 182–84).

30. *Analects* 11.24. Ability may be inadequate relative to a specific position. It is much more doubtful if Confucius believes that anyone is completely inadequate for any kind of political participation.

31. Liang (1996, 81; 1930, 38); Hsiao (1979, vol. 1, 103); Chan (1975); see also Cai (1996, 11).

32. *Analects* 4.5; cf. 14.6. Exemplary persons sometimes may fail to act authoritatively, but petty persons (the antithesis of exemplary persons) are never able to act authoritatively. In the later passage, the criterion (in terms of authoritative conduct) is less stringent, but the importance of authoritative conduct remains intact.

33. *Analects* 6.26; both authoritative person and exemplary person are not anxious (14.28, 9.29, 12.4), they are cautious in speech (1.14, 4.24, 12.3), respectful, reverent, and generous (5.16, 13.19, 17.6), love others (12.22, 17.4), and establish others in seeking to establish themselves (6.30, 14.42).

34. Twelfth year of Duke Zhao, Legge (1970, vol. 5, 641).

35. *Analects* 12.17. For other associations of "proper" with effective political engagement, see *Analects* 13.6, 13.13, 15.5.

36. *Mencius* 6.9/35/9; the "Great Learning" in *Book of Rites* 43.1/164/27; Hall and Ames (1998, 173–74); ethical use of *zheng* 正 in the "*zhongyong,*" *Book of Rites* 32.8/143/26, 32.30/147/11.

37. Lincoln (1953, vol. 7, 22); Dewey adopts this formulation of democracy (L17.473).

38. Chow (1960a, 59; 1960b, 302).

39. Yu (1997); Hu (1941, 1–12; 1953, 1960).

40. Hsiao (1975, 197–200); Sun (1950, vol. 5, 454).

41. King (1997).

42. Chang et al. (1958, 472, 476).

43. King (1993b, 5); Nathan (1985, 127–28, ix).

44. Liang (1996, 5; 1930, 10); Hsiao (1979, vol. 1, 161); Liu (1992, 17–40); also Li (1999, 169).

45. Harrison (1998, 867).

46. They were relying on the Jesuits for what China was like, and the latter were prone to emphasizing the good over the bad in their attempt to garner support for their mission in China, but the reports were not totally unfounded.

47. "The Songs of the Five Sons 五子之歌," *Book of Historical Documents*, in Legge (1970, vol. 3, 158–59). The dating of this text is complex. Some chapters are believed to be from the Zhou period. This chapter is considered a forged addition, probably from around the fourth century A.D. (Loewe 1993, 376–85). Unless otherwise stated, references to this text are from the twenty-eight "new text" chapters believed to be written mostly in the Zhou period and some during the Warring States period but no later than the Qin period.

48. Legge (1970, vol. 4, 273, 489); Loewe (1993, 415); Legge (1970, vol. 3, 454).

49. *Mencius* 1.3/2/3, 1.7/6/27, 13.22/69/20; *Analects* 13.9.

50. *Xunzi* 9/36/17, 9/40/1–16, 10/42/23, 13/63/20, 27/130/24.

51. *Mencius* 14.14/74/14, modified from Lau (1970, 196).

52. "The Announcement of the Duke of Shao 召誥" and "The Numerous Offi-cers 多士," *Book of Historical Documents*, in Legge (1970, vol. 3, 425, 430, 455). These are among the twelve chapters attributed to the reign of King Cheng (r. 1042/35–1006 B.C.) (Loewe 1993, 379).

53. Eno (1990, 99–130).

54. Ames and Rosemont (1998, 46–48); Couplet et al. (1687, 395); Mungello (1985, 44–90); Jensen (1997, 92–113). Ricci was careful in not actually identifying *tian* with "God" but instead using the term "*tianzhu* 天主," even though his use of the Chinese classics to support his case clearly associates *tianzhu* with *tian*. The appropri-ate term for "God" is the subject of a major controversy in the history of Christian mis-sions to China. See also Mungello (1994, 50–52, 129–45); a summary of the debate about *tian* can be found in Shun (1997, 206–10).

55. Hou et al. (1957, vol. 1, 153–54); Ren (1983, 194–95); Fung (1935, vol. 1, 82; 1952, vol. 1, 57; 1983, 152).

56. Eno (1990, 131); Edward Machle (1993, 21–27) gives a useful summary of the naturalistic interpretive tradition, including H. H. Dubs, Wing-tsit Chan, Hu Shih, and John Knoblock; Machle (1993, 167–78).

57. Xu (1969, 88); *Mencius* 14.24/75/24, 3.7/18/15, 11.16/61/3, 5.5/30/21, 13.1/67/15; see also *Analects* 3.24, 5.13, 7.23, 2.4, 16.8.

58. *Analects* 9.5, 11.9, 12.5; *Mencius* 2.14/12/25, 2.16/14/1, 9.6/49/11.

59. Roetz (1993, 194–97); Schwartz (1975); for Roetz (1993, 227), "the only point of transcendence" is to call the existing order into question; Mou Zongsan's (1968, vol. 1, 524–26) account deals with Song neo-Confucianism rather than with early Confu-cianism; see also Yang (1995, 237–38).

60. Liu (1972, 49). See also Tu (1992, 199–211); Yu (1992, 9–13, 22–23); Ching (1997, 100–101).

61. Hansen (2001); Roetz (1993, 228).

62. Hall and Ames (1987, 13).

63. Legge (1970, vol. 3, 223–29). Many scholars believe "Pan Geng" to be the earliest document in Chinese history, but it probably was written during the Zhou dynasty (Loewe 1993, 378); Legge (1970, vol. 3, 292, 75).

64. *Mencius* 2.8/11/15; Ambrose King (1993b, 9–10, 59–62) equates Mencian teaching on the relation between *tian* and the people with a form of government by "popular consent," though he stops short of calling it "government by the people"; Fung (1983, vol. 2, 64–69); Julia Ching (1997, 257–63) points out that Karl Marx is among those who hold this view, and her analysis of the peasant rebellions and the Commu-nist revolution in China indicates that she shares his view, if not the reasons for it; see also Liang (1989, vol. 2, 174–77).

65. Liang Ch'i-ch'ao (1996, 39) argues that the people in ancient China had a say in at least three kinds of questions: when the state faced a crisis, relocating the state,

and setting up a new ruler; Li Zehou (1996, 4) believes that the clan-based societies of ancient China are democratic; Seizaburo Sato (1997, 81) points out that a primitive society of hunters and gatherers could be democratic in terms of its legitimate members participating with a reasonable degree of equality in the decision-making process; cf. de Bary (1994, 11); Sun (1950, vol. 5, 454). Ching (1997, 268).

66. Chen (1964, 102).

67. Legge (1970, vol. 3, 387).

68. Eno (1990, 24).

69. If we are dealing with people only *qua* people, this argument is of course common in theories such as those about false consciousness and those about people's *real* interests as distinct from what they perceive to be their interests.

70. "The Announcement about Drunkenness 酒誥," *Book of Historical Documents*, author's translation; cf. Legge (1970, vol. 3, 409).

71. *Analects* 6.23; *Xunzi* (1996, 9/36/7, 31/147/6); Rorty (1980).

72. Nathan (1985, 128–29).

73. Lippmann (1927, 38, 77, 71, 147).

74. Ibid., 69, 62, 126, 65, 70, 155; see also Lippmann (1965, 250–251).

75. Ibid., 39.

76. Westbrook (1991, 316).

77. Lippmann (1927, 148).

78. McDermott's introduction to volume 11 of Dewey's *Later Works* (L11.xxxii).

79. Niebuhr (1932, xx).

80. Ibid., 2–3, 40, 93, 140.

81. Ibid., 47, 94.

82. Ibid., 197, 21, 22; see other descriptions of Niebuhr's (1932, 164, 234) modest goal.

83. Westbrook (1991, 526).

84. Niebuhr (1932, 35); an example of Niebuhr's (1932, 212) "strawman" attacks is his criticisms of Dewey's education theory, quoting not from Dewey but from Harold Rugg, who distorts Dewey's concept of "intelligence" into some kind of technical expertise in planning and administration.

85. Niebuhr (1932, 199, 221).

86. Niebuhr (1932, 255). Niebuhr's liberal theism may not be too distant from Dewey's natural piety. See Westbrook's (1991, 528) discussion of "the affinities between Niebuhr's theology and Dewey's metaphysics."

87. James (1979, 79).

88. *Shuowen* (1966, 380/8A: 24b); Hall and Ames (1987, 140–41).

89. *Analects* 16.2. *shuren* 庶人 rather than *min* 民 are actually the people in question, but most translators take it to mean "the common people," or commoners.

90. *Luxuriant Dews* 10.1/44/29; Hall and Ames (1987, 139–46).

CHAPTER 5

1. Berlin (1969, 171).

2. L11.250. This account of negative freedom appears frequently in Dewey's work (L3.97; L11.6–16, 247–50, 282–84).

3. Berlin (1969, 122).

4. Ibid., 138.

5. Ibid., 132.

6. M12.10; see also M9.311; L8.186; L11.220.

7. Bode (1938, 98).

8. For an argument of how suffering aids ethical progress in Confucian context, see Tu (1993, 45–56).

9. M14.214. By "objective," Dewey means intersubjectively valid alternatives, alternatives that we have reasons to believe are practical within the given environment, as opposed to purely subjective, imaginary alternatives.

10. Xu (1988, 292) traces its earliest known appearance to the *Han History*, "Chronicles of the Five Practices"; Ching (1998, 73).

11. Zhang (1946, 118, 120, author's translation). Usually "it," in "getting it in, by, or for oneself," refers to the way (*dao*), and attaining *dao* in Confucianism amounts to the same thing as self-realization; de Bary (1983, 1991a).

12. Zhang (1946, 118–53).

13. Xu (1988, 292); He (1991, 95–118).

14. Xu (1988, 198–220, 291); Mou (1973, 212–14); Tang (1991, vol. 5, 329–87); Chang (1981, 248; 1988, 6); He (1991, 110–12).

15. Berlin (1969, 135–41).

16. *Analects* 8.9; see also *Xunzi* 23/116/17.

17. *Mencius* 1.3/2/3, 1.7/6/27, 11.10/59/25, 13.22/69/20.

18. Joseph Betz (1978) argues that there is an implicit reconstruction of the concept in the 1908 *Ethics* and Dewey's lectures in China. Without rejecting that argument, which is useful for a review of rights thinking in the Western context, I think a different lesson could nevertheless be drawn for the Confucian context from Dewey's latter abandonment of the term as a key philosophical tool.

19. Rosemont (1989, 1998).

20. Dewey (1973, 147–48).

21. Randall Peerenboom (1995) also argues persuasively that the different perceptions of contemporary America and China on the distinction between rights and interests are at the root of their talking past each other in discussions on rights.

22. *Abrams v. United States* (1919) Holmes (1992, 320, quoted in L7.358).

23. *Analects* 11.4, 12.1, 14.13, 15.8, 15.17.

24. *Analects* 1.7, 2.13, 4.22, 4.24, 12.3, 14.27, 15.6.

25. Peerenboom (1998, 246).

26. Ibid., 247.

27. Bourdieu (1990, 80).

28. Ibid., 53.

29. "The formation and development of a historical fiction: On Confucius' executing Deputy Mao 一個歷史故事的形成及其演進：論孔子誅少正卯" in Xu (1988, 269–88).

30. *Conversations of the States* 131–90; Legge (1970, vol. 5, 565–66). Confucius admired Zichan for being kind and good, an exemplary person (*Analects* 5.16, 14.9).

31. Ching (1998, 74); see also Hall and Ames (1999, 216).

32. Duke Zhao sixth year and twenty-ninth year, Legge (1970, vol. 5, 609–10, 732).

33. Hansen (1994, 463); see also Fei Xiaotong's (1992, 105–107) description of the effect of introducing laws into a rural society ruled by rituals.

34. *Analects* 4.13; see also *Analects* 2.1, 2.3, 12.19, 15.5.

35. *Analects* 3.19; see also *Mencius* 8.3/41/4.

36. De Bary (1991b, 67); Hsiao (1979, vol. 1, 194–95); cf. Hansen (1994, 459). Hansen defines "law" as "universal propositions (sentences) with either descriptive or prescriptive necessity (causation or obligation)."

37. Lewis (1999, 18); Ching (1998, 74).

38. Chu (1998).

39. Ames (1983, 115–25); see also Hsiao (1979, vol. 1, 114).

40. De Tocqueville (2000). Apart from institutional/procedural means, there has been a concern with culture and character, the "habits of the heart" of the people in relation to sustaining American democracy (Bellah et al. 1985). Dewey also is concerned with both sets of variables.

41. Peerenboom (1995, 364).

42. Peerenboom (1995, 377); Andrew Nathan (1985, 57) shares this view.

43. *Mencius* 3.2/17/5; see also *Xunzi* 11/49/16.

44. Nathan (1985, 61).

45. Even finding a candidate for a figurehead monarch is fraught with difficulties in China's situation (Liang 1997, 374–79); Liang (1997, 380–82); Nathan (1985, 45–63) translates *kaiming zhuanzhi* 開明專制 as "enlightened despotism," and no doubt the Chinese term was used to translate "enlightened despotism," but I have rendered it differently as "*open* and enlightened autocracy," which I believe is closer to its less pejorative meaning in the Chinese context. The shifts in translation bring to light the important shifts in meaning when Western concepts are used in a Chinese context. John Fairbank (1983, 739) makes a similar argument: "To say that liberalism rests on individualism under the supremacy of law is more sensible and gratifying than to say, as one does in Chinese, that the doctrine of spontaneous license (*ziyou zhuyi* 自由主義) rests on the doctrine of self-centeredness (*geren zhuyi* 個人主義) under the supremacy of administrative regulations (*falu* 法律)."

46. Nathan (1985, 52–54).

47. Hobbes (1968, 186).

48. Joseph Raz (1985) argues that authority is better understood through its ideal functioning and sees authority as a kind of normative power that changes the reasons for action; see also Weber (1978, 946–47).

49. Mill (1985, 126–27).

50. Fingarette (1981, 33–34); on emulation that is not mere imitation, see *Analects* 6.30, 15.36.

51. Fingarette (1981, 36). Emphasis in original.

52. *Shuowen* (1966, 128/3B: 41a), translated in Hall and Ames (1987, 339).

53. Dewey (1973, 164–72); in "Individuality and Experience," Dewey differentiates this from tradition that is "enhancing and liberating" (L2.57–58); see also distinction of "tradition" as a process and a thing (M7.356).

54. Lewis (1999, 85).

55. Fingarette (1981, 43) considers this a possibility outside of the Confucian contexts, unless we believe, with little justification, that human nature is more inclined toward the virtuous than the vicious. I agree with him regarding the possibility, but I see it not as a question of whether human nature is good or bad but as a question of its sociality, and to what extent egoistic ends are moral or legitimate.

56. *Mencius* 3.3/17/16. To "borrow" probably refers to acquiring a false reputation, or to bringing about results that are only superficially similar to the results of the truly authoritative.

57. The terms *internal* and *external* are used in the sense of "internal relations" and "external relations," discussed in chapter 3; they do not invoke an "inner/outer" psychology.

58. Tang (1991, vol. 14, 255); Zeng (1989, 145–46); Schwartz (1985, 304); Huang (1995, 86–88).

59. Knoblock (1990, vol. 2, 139); see also Zeng (1989, 145–47).

60. See the introduction to Knoblock's translation (1988) for the dating of the chapters that does not follow the order arranged by the Han scholar, Liu Xiang 劉向.

61. Jullien (1995, 67).

62. Ibid., 59–71.

63. Fairbank and Reischauer (1989, 68); Creel (1949, 234).

64. Fairbank and Reischauer (1989, 69); Hall and Ames (1999, 154); Xu (1959, 155–200).

CHAPTER 6

1. Neville (2000, 15–21).

2. Tiles (1997, 120).

3. Ibid., 123.

4. Zhou (1996, 1, 245); Nathan and Shi Tianjian (1993, 114).

5. Zhou (1996, 245).

6. Ibid., 14; for a similar argument regarding economic reform and democratization that does not, however, focus on the farmers' role, see Perry and Fuller (1991).

7. Zhou (1996, 7).

8. King (1993a, 157); Rustow (1970, 358–61).

9. De Bary (1998a); Strand (1990); Solinger (1991); Rowe (1993); cf. Chamberlain (1993).

10. Tan (2003).

11. Sun (1937); King (1993b, 149–51); Diamond (1989, 151).

References

Addams, Jane. 1902. *Democracy and Social Ethics*. London: Macmillan.

Ajami, Fouard. 1993. "The Summoning." *Foreign Affairs* 75:4: 2–9.

Alexander, Thomas. 1987. *Dewey's Theory of Art, Experience, and Nature*. Albany: State University of New York Press.

Allen, Douglas, ed. 1997. *Culture and Self*. Boulder: Westview Press.

Allport, Gordon W. 1951. "Dewey's Individual and Social Psychology." Pp. 265–90 in *The Philosophy of John Dewey*, ed. Paul A. Schilpp. New York: Tudor.

American Anthropological Association. 1947. "Statement on Human Rights." *American Anthropologist* 49: 539–43.

Ames, Roger T. 1983. *The Art of Rulership*. Honolulu: University of Hawaii Press.

———. 1993. "The Meaning of Body in Classical Chinese Philosophy." Pp. 157–77 in *Self As Body in Asian Theory and Practice*, ed. Thomas Kasulis, Wimal Dissanayake, and Roger T. Ames. Albany: State University of New York Press.

———. 1994. "The Focus-Field Self in Early Confucianism." Pp. 185–212 in *Self As Person in Asian Theory and Practice*, ed. Thomas Kasulis, Wimal Dissanayake, and Roger Ames. Albany: State University of New York Press.

———. 1998. *The Analects of Confucius*. Translated by Roger T. Ames and Henry Rosemont Jr. New York: Ballantine.

Ansen, Alan. 1990. *The Table Talk of W. H. Auden*. Edited by Nicholas Jenkins. Ontario: Ontario Review Press.

Avineri, Shlomo. 1972. *Hegel's Theory of the Modern State*. Cambridge: Cambridge University Press.

Ban Gu 班固. 1952. *Comprehensive Discourses in the White Tiger Hall* 白虎通德論. Translated by Tjan Tjoe Som. Leiden: E. J. Brill.

Barber, Benjamin. 1984. *Strong Democracy: Participatory Politics for a New Age*. Berkeley: University of California Press.

Bartley, Robert L. 1993. "The Case for Optimism: the West Should Believe in itself." *Foreign Affairs* 75:4: 15–18.

Bauer, Joanne. 1995. "International Human Rights and Asian Commitment." *Human Rights Dialogue* 3: 1–4.

Bedau, Hugo. 1967. "Concepts of Equality." Pp. 3–27 in *Equality*, ed. J. Roland Pennock and John W. Chapman. New York: Atherton.

Beetham, David. 1993. "Liberal Democracy and the Limits of Democratization." Pp. 55–73 in *Prospects for Democracy*, ed. David Held. Stanford: Stanford University Press.

Bell, Daniel. 1995. "Democracy in Confucian Societies: The Challenge of Justification." Pp. 17–40 in *Towards Illiberal Democracy in Pacific Asia*, ed. Daniel Bell et al. New York: St. Martin's Press.

Bell, Daniel et al., eds. 1995. *Towards Illiberal Democracy in Pacific Asia*. New York: St. Martin's Press.

Bellah, Robert et al. 1985. *Habits of the Heart*. New York: Harper and Row.

Berger, Peter L., and Hsin-Huang Michael Hsiao, eds. 1988. *In Search of An East Asian Development Model*. New Brunswick: Transaction Books.

Berlin, Isaiah. 1969. *Four Essays on Liberty*. New York: Oxford University Press.

———. 1979. *Concepts and Categories*. Edited by Henry Hardy. New York: Viking.

———. 1991. *The Crooked Timber of Humanity*. New York: Knopf.

Betz, Joseph. 1978. "John Dewey on Human Rights." Pp. 173–93 in *John Dewey*, vol. 3, ed. James E. Tiles. New York: Routledge.

Birrell, Anne. 1993. *Chinese Mythology: An Introduction*. Baltimore: Johns Hopkins University Press.

Bloom, Irene. 1985. "On the Matter of the Mind: The Metaphysical Basis of the Expanded Self." Pp. 293–330 in *Individualism and Holism*, ed. Donald J. Munro. Ann Arbor: Center for Chinese Studies, University of Michigan.

———. 1998. "Fundamental Institutions and Consensus Statements: Mencian Confucianism and Human Rights." Pp. 94–116 in *Confucianism and Human Rights*, ed. William de Bary and Tu Wei-ming. New York: Columbia University Press.

Bockover, Mary I., ed. 1989. *Rules, Rituals, and Responsibility*. La Salle: Open Court Press.

Bodde, Derk. 1961. "Myths of Ancient China." Pp. 369–408 in *Mythologies of the Ancient World*, ed. S. N. Kramer. New York: Doubleday, Anchor Books.

Bode, Boyd H. 1938. *Progressive Education at the Crossroads*. New York: Newson.

Boltz, William G. 1982. "The Religious and the Philosophical Significance of the *Hsiang Erh Lao Tzu* in the Light of the Ma-Wang-Tui Silk Manuscripts." *Bulletin of the School of Oriental and African Studies* 45: 101–2.

Bontekoe, Ron, and Marietta Stephaniants, eds. 1997. *Justice and Democracy.* Honolulu: University of Hawaii Press.

Boodberg, Peter. 1953. "The Semasiology of Some Primary Confucian Concepts." *Philosophy East and West* 2: 317–32.

Book of Change 易經. *A Concordance to the I-Ching.* 1966. Harvard-Yenching Institute Sinological Index Series. Taipei: Chinese Material and Research Aids Center reprint.

Book of Rites 禮記. *A Concordance to the Liji.* 1992. ICS Ancient Chinese Text Concordance Series. Edited by. D. C. Lau and Chen Fong Ching. Hong Kong: Commercial Press.

Bourdieu, Pierre. 1990. *Logic of Practice.* Translated by Richard Nice. Stanford: Stanford University Press.

Buchanan, Allen E. 1989. "Assessing the Communitarian Critique of Liberalism." *Ethics* 99: 852–82.

Cai Yuanpei 蔡元培. 1968. *Complete Works* 蔡元培先生全集. Taipei: Commercial Press.

———. 1996. *History of Ethical Theories in China* 中國倫理學史. Beijing: Oriental Books.

Campbell, James. 1995. *Understanding John Dewey.* La Salle: Open Court Press.

Chamberlain, Heath B. 1993. "On the Search for Civil Society in China." *Modern China* 19:2: 199–215.

Chan, Joseph. 1996. "The Task for Asians: To Discover Their Own Political Morality for Human Rights." *Human Rights Dialogue* 4: 5–6.

———. 1998. "Asian Values and Human Rights: An Alternative View." Pp. 28–41 in *Democracy in East Asia*, ed. Larry Diamond and Marc F. Plattner. Baltimore: Johns Hopkins University Press.

Chan, Steve. 1993. *East Asian Dynamism.* San Francisco: Westview Press.

Chan, Wing-tsit. 1975. "Chinese and Western Interpretations of *Jen.*" *Journal of Chinese Philosophy* 2:2: 107–29.

Chang, Carsun. 1981. "Philosophical Foundations of Democratic Politics 民主政治的哲學基礎." Pp. 245–50 in *Collected Essays on Chinese, Western, and Indian Philosophies* 中西印哲學文集, ed. Chen Wenxi 陳文熙. Taipei: Student Books.

———. 1988. *An Overview of Socialist Thought and Movement* 社會主義思想運動概觀. Taipei: Daoxiang.

Chang, Carsun et al. 1958. "A Manifesto for a Reappraisal of Sinology and Reconstruction of Chinese Culture." Pp. 455–83 in *The Development of Neo-Confucian Thought*, ed. Carsun Chang. New York: Bookman.

Chen, Daqi 陳大齊. 1964. *Teachings of Confucius* 孔子學説. Taipei: Zhongzheng.

Chen, Ning. 2000. "The Etymology of *Sheng* (Sage) and Its Confucian Conception in Early China." *Journal of Chinese Philosophy* 27:4: 409–427.

Chen, Xiyuan 陳熙遠. 1995. "The Sage-King Model and the Actual Content of the Confucian 'Inner-Sage-Outer-King' 聖王典範與儒家內聖外王的實質內涵." Pp. 23–67 in *Historical Development of Mencius' Thought* 孟子思想的歷史發展, ed. Huang Junjie 黃俊傑. Taipei: Central Research Institute.

Cheng, Chung-ying. 1988. "On Harmony As Transformation: Paradigms from the *I Ching*." Pp. 225–47 in *Harmony and Strife*, ed. Liu Shu-Hsien and Robert Allison. Hong Kong: Chinese University Press.

Cheng Yi 程頤. 1930. *Complete Works of the Two Chengs* 二程全書. Shanghai: Zhonghua.

Ching, Julia. 1997. *Mysticism and Kingship in China*. New York: Cambridge University Press.

———. 1998. "Human Rights: A Valid Chinese Concept?" Pp. 67–82 in *Confucianism and Human Rights*, ed. de Bary and Tu. New York: Columbia University Press.

Ching, Julia, and Willard Oxtoby. 1992. *Moral Enlightenment: Leibniz and Wolff on China*. Steyler Verlag: Institut Monumenta Serica.

Chow, Tse-tsung. 1960a. *The May Fourth Movement: Intellectual Revolution in Modern China*. Stanford: Stanford University Press.

———. 1960b. "The Anti-Confucian Movement in Early Republican China." Pp. 288–312 in *The Confucian Persuasion*, ed. Arthur F. Wright. Stanford: Stanford University Press.

Chu, Ron Guey. 1998. "Rites and Rights in Ming China." Pp. 169–78 in *Confucianism and Human Rights*, ed. de Bary and Tu. New York: Columbia University Press.

Clarke, J. J. 1997. *Oriental Enlightenment: The Encounter between Asian and Western Thought*. New York: Routledge.

Classic of Filiality 孝經. *A Concordance to the Xiaojing*. 1992. Edited by D. C. Lau and Chen Fong Ching. Hong Kong: Commercial Press.

Conversations of the States 國語. *A Concordance to the Kuo-yu*. 1973. Taipei: Chinese Materials and Research Aids Service Center.

Couplet, Philippe et al. 1687. *Confucius Sinarum Philosophus*. Paris: Printed by Daniel Horthemels.

Creel, Herlee. 1949. *Confucius: The Man and the Myth*. New York: John Day.

Crittenden, Jack. 1992. *Beyond Individualism*. New York: Oxford University Press.

Croll, Elizabeth. 1995. *Changing Identities of Chinese Women*. Hong Kong: Hong Kong University Press.

Cua, A. S. 1979. "Dimensions of *Li* (Propriety): Reflections on an Aspect of Hsün Tzu's Ethics." *Philosophy East and West* 29:4: 373–94.

———. 1983. "Li and Moral Justification: A Study in the *Li Chi*." *Philosophy East and West* 33:1: 1–16.

———. 1985. *Ethical Argumentation*. Honolulu: University of Hawaii Press.

Dahl, Robert. 1989. *Democracy and Its Critics*. New Haven: Yale University Press.

———. 1992. "The Problem of Civic Competence." *Journal of Democracy* 3:4: 20.

Damico, Alfonso J. 1978. *Individuality and Community*. Gainesville: University Presses of Florida.

———. 1986. "Impractical America: Reconsideration of the Pragmatic Lesson." Pp. 267–86 in *John Dewey*, vol. 2, ed. James E. Tiles. New York: Routledge.

de Bary, Wm. Theodore. 1983. *The Liberal Tradition in China*. Hong Kong: Chinese University Press.

———. 1991a. *Learning for One's Self*. New York: Columbia University Press.

———. 1991b. *The Trouble with Confucianism*. Cambridge: Harvard University Press.

———. 1994. "A Round Table Discussion of *The Trouble with Confucianism* by Wm. Theodore de Bary." *China Review International* 1:1: 9–47.

———. 1998a. *Asian Values and Human Rights*. Cambridge: Harvard University Press.

———. 1998b. "Confucianism and Human Rights in China." Pp. 42–54 in *Democracy in East Asia*, ed. Diamond and Plattner. Baltimore: Johns Hopkins University Press.

de Bary, Wm. Theodore, and Irene Bloom, eds. 1999. *Sources of Chinese Tradition*. New York: Columbia University Press.

de Bary, Wm. Theodore, and Tu Wei-ming, eds. 1998. *Confucianism and Human Rights*. New York: Columbia University Press.

de Tocqueville, Alexis. 2000. *Democracy in America*. Translated by Henry Reeve. New York: Bantam Books.

Delaney, C. F., ed. 1994. *The Liberalism-Communitarianism Debate*. Lanham: Rowman and Littlefield.

Devins, Neal and Davison M. Donglas, eds. 1998. *Redefining Equality*. New York: Oxford University Press.

Dewey, John. 1916. *Essays in Experimental Logic*. Chicago: Chicago University Press.

———. 1939. *Intelligence in the Modern World*. Edited by Joseph Ratner. New York: Random House.

———. 1969–1972. *The Early Works, 1882–1898*. 5 vols. Edited by Jo Ann Boydston. Carbondale: Southern Illinois University Press.

———. 1973. *Lectures in China, 1919–1920*. Edited by Robert W. Clopton and Tsuin-chen Ou. Honolulu: University Press of Hawaii.

———. 1976–1983. *The Middle Works, 1899–1924*. 15 vols. Edited by Jo Ann Boydston. Carbondale: Southern Illinois University Press.

———. 1981–1991. *The Later Works, 1925–1953*. 17 vols. Edited by Jo Ann Boydston. Carbondale: Southern Illinois University Press.

Diamond, Larry. 1989. "Beyond Authoritarianism and Totalitarianism." *Washington Quarterly* 12:1: 141–68.

Diamond, Larry, and Marc F. Plattner, eds. 1998. *Democracy in East Asia*. Baltimore: Johns Hopkins University Press.

Dunn, John. 1979. *Western Political Theory in the Face of the Future*. Cambridge: Cambridge University Press.

———. 1992. *Democracy: The Unfinished Journey, 508 B.C. to A.D. 1993*. Oxford: Oxford University Press.

Dworkin, Ronald. 1977. *Taking Rights Seriously*. Cambridge: Harvard University Press.

———. 1978. "Liberalism." Pp. 114–43 in *Public and Private Morality*, ed. Stuart Hampshire. Cambridge: Cambridge University Press.

Edwards, R. Randle. 1986. "Civil and Social Rights: Theory and Practice in China Today." Pp. 41–75 in *Human Rights in Contemporary China*, ed. Randle R. Edwards, Louis Henkin, and Andrew Nathan. New York: Columbia University Press.

Eisenstein, Hester. 1983. *Contemporary Feminist Thought*. Boston: G. K. Hall.

Eldridge, Michael. 1998. *Transforming Experience*. Nashville: Vanderbilt University Press.

Elvin, Mark. 1985. "Between the Earth and Heaven: Conceptions of the Self in China." Pp. 156–89 in *The Category of the Person*, ed. Michael Carrithers, Steven Collins, and Steven Lukes. New York: Cambridge University Press.

Emmerson, Donald. 1996. "Do Asian Values Exist?" *Human Rights Dialogue* 5: 3.

Eno, Robert. 1990. *The Confucian Creation of Heaven: Philosophy and the Defense of Ritual Mastery*. Albany: State University of New York Press.

Erya 爾雅. *A Concordance to the Erya*. 1992. Edited by D. C. Lau and Chen Fong Ching. Hong Kong: Commercial.

Etzioni, Amitai. 1993. *The Spirit of Community*. New York: Simon and Schuster.

Fairbank, John K. 1983. "Review of Eugene Lubot's *Liberalism in an Illiberal Age*." *China Quarterly* 96:4: 734–40.

Fairbank, John K., and Edwin O. Reischauer. 1989. *China: Tradition and Transformation*. Rev. ed. Boston: Houghton Mifflin.

Fan Zhongyan 範仲淹. 1980. "On the Yue Yang Pavilion 岳陽樓記" Pp. 23–27 in *Selections of Song Literature* 宋文選, vol. 1, ed. Szechuan University, Chinese Department. Beijing: People's Literature Press.

Fazzioli, Edoardo. 1986. *Chinese Calligraphy: From Pictogram to Ideogram*. New York: Abbeville.

Fei, Xiaotong 費孝通. 1992. *From the Soil* 鄉土中國. Translated by Gary G. Hamilton and Wang Zheng. Berkeley: University of California Press.

Feinberg, Joel. 1988. *The Moral Limits of Criminal Law*. New York: Oxford University Press.

Fingarette, Herbert. 1972. *Confucius: The Secular As Sacred*. New York: Harper and Row.

———. 1979. The Problem of the Self in the Analects." *Philosophy East and West* 29:2: 129–40.

———. 1981. "How the *Analects* Portrays the Ideal of Efficacious Authority." *Journal of Chinese Philosophy* 8:1: 29–50.

———. 1989. "Comment and Response." Pp. 171–220 in *Rules, Rituals, and Responsibility*, ed. Mary I. Bockover. La Salle: Open Court Press.

French, Howard. 1996. "Africa Looks East for a New Model." *New York Times*, February 4.

Fukuyama, Francis. 1989. "The End of History?" *The National Interest* 16: 3–18.

———. 1992. *The End of History and the Last Man*. New York: Macmillan.

———. 1995. "Confucianism and Democracy." *Journal of Democracy* 6:2: 20–33.

Fuller, Timothy, David Satter et al. 1989. "More Responses to Fukuyama." *The National Interest* 17: 93–100.

Fung Yu-Lan 馮友蘭. 1935. *A History of Chinese Philosophy* 中國哲學史. 2 vols. Shanghai: Commercial.

———. 1939. *New Discussions of Current Affairs* 新事論. Hong Kong: Commercial Press.

———. 1952. *A History of Chinese Philosophy*. 2 vols. Translated by Derk Bodde. Princeton: Princeton University Press.

———. 1983. *New Edition of the History of Chinese Philosophy* 中國哲學史新編. Beijing: People's Press.

Gaus, Gerald F. 1983. *The Modern Liberal Theory of Man*. New York: St. Martin's Press.

Gould, Carol. 1988. *Rethinking Democracy*. Cambridge: Cambridge University Press.

Graham, Angus C. 1986. *Studies in Chinese Philosophy and Chinese Literature*. Singapore: Institute of East Asian Philosophies.

———. 1989. *Disputers of the Tao*. La Salle: Open Court Press.

Grange, Joseph. 1997. "Community, Environment, Metaphysics." *The Journal of Speculative Philosophy* 11:3: 190–201.

Grier, Philip, ed. 1989. *Dialectic and Contemporary Science: Essays in Honor of Errol Harris*. Lanham: University Press of America.

Gutmann, Amy. 1980. *Liberal Equality*. New York: Cambridge University Press.

———. 1985. "Communitarian Critiques of Liberalism." *Philosophy and Public Affairs* 14: 308–24.

———. 1987. *Democratic Education*. Princeton: Princeton University Press.

Hall, David, and Roger T. Ames. 1987. *Thinking through Confucius*. Albany: State University of New York Press.

———. 1995. *Anticipating China*. Albany: State University of New York Press.

———. 1998. *Thinking from the Han*. Albany: State University of New York Press.

———. 1999. *Democracy of the Dead*. La Salle: Open Court Press.

Han Feizi 韓非子. 1974. *Annotated Han Feizi* 韓非子集釋. 2 vols. Annotated by Chen Qiyou 陳奇猷. Hong Kong: Commercial Press.

Hansen, Chad. 1983. *Language and Logic in Ancient China*. Ann Arbor: University of Michigan Press.

———. 1994. "Fa (Standards: Laws) and Meaning Changes in Chinese Philosophy." *Philosophy East and West* 44:3: 435–88.

———. 2001. "Metaphysical and Moral Transcendence in Chinese Thought." Pp. 197–227 in *Two Roads to Wisdom?* ed. Bo Mou. La Salle: Open Court Press.

Harré, Rom. 1987. "Persons and Selves." Pp. 99–115 in *Persons and Personality*, ed. Arthur Peacocke and Grant Gillett. Oxford: Blackwell.

Harris, Errol. 1987. *Formal, Transcendental, and Dialectical Thinking*. Albany: State University of New York Press.

Harrison, Ross. 1998. "Democracy." Pp. 867–72 in *Routledge Encyclopedia of Philosophy*, vol. 2, ed. Edward Craig. New York: Routledge.

Hawkes, David, trans. 1985. *The Songs of the South*. Middlesex: Penguin.

Hay, John. 1993. "The Body As Microcosmic Source." Pp. 179–211 in *Self As Body in Asian Theory and Practice*, ed. Kasulis, Dissanayake, and Ames. Albany: State University of New York Press.

He Xinquan 何信全. 1991. "The Character and Problems of Contemporary New Confucian Conceptions of Freedom 當代新儒家自由觀念的性格及其問題." Pp. 95–118 in *Collected Essays on Contemporary New Confucianism* 當代新儒學論文集, vol. 3, ed. Liu Shuxian et al. Taipei: Wenjin.

Hegel, Georg Wilhelm Friedrich. 1942. *The Philosophy of Right*. Translated by T. M. Knox. Oxford: Clarendon Press.

———. 1955. *Die Vernunft in der Geschichte* (Reason in History). Edited by J. Hoffmeister. Hamburg: Felix Meiner Verlag.

———. 1975. *Lesser Logic*. Translated by William Wallace. Oxford: Clarendon Press.

Held, David, ed. 1993. *Prospects for Democracy: North, South, East, West*. Stanford: Stanford University Press.

Henderson, John B. 1984. *The Development and Decline of Chinese Cosmology*. New York: Columbia University Press.

Historical Records 史記. 1964. 10 vols. Shanghai: Zhonghua.

Hitchcock, David I. 1994. *Asian Values and the United States*. Washington, D.C.: Center for Strategic and International Studies.

Hobbes, Thomas. 1968. *Leviathan*. Edited by C. B. Macpherson. Baltimore: Penguin.

Hollis, Martin. 1977. "The Self in Action." Pp. 138–53 in *John Dewey*, vol. 1, ed. James E. Tiles. New York: Routledge.

Holmes, Oliver Wendell Jr. 1992. *The Essential Holmes*. Edited by Richard Posner. Chicago: University of Chicago Press.

Hou Wailu 侯外廬, Zhao Jibin 趙紀彬, and Du Guoxiang 杜國庠. 1957. *Comprehensive History of Chinese Thought* 中國思想通史. Beijing: People's Press.

Howell, David. 1997. "East Comes West." *Foreign Affairs* 76:2: 164.

Hsiao Kung-chuan 蕭公權. 1975. *A Modern China and a New World: K'ang Yu-wei, Reformer and Utopia, 1858–1927*. Seattle: University of Washington Press.

———. 1979. *A History of Chinese Political Thought*. 2 vols. Translated by Frederick Mote. Princeton: Princeton University Press.

Hu Shih 胡適. 1941. *Historical Foundations for a Democratic China*. Edmund J. James Lectures on Government, Second Series. Urbana: University of Illinois Press.

———. 1953. "The Natural Law in the Chinese Tradition." *Natural Law Institute Proceedings* 5: 119–53.

———. 1960. "The Chinese Tradition and Future." *Sino-American Conference on Intellectual Cooperation, Reports and Proceedings*. Seattle: University of Washington, 13–22.

Huang Junjie 黃俊傑. 1995. "Song Confucians' Debate over Mencius' Political Thought and the Debate's Implicit Problems 宋儒對於孟子政治思想的爭辦及其蘊涵的問題." Pp. 69–127 in *Historical Development of Mencius' Thought* 孟子思想的歷史發展, ed. Huang Junjie. Taipei: Central Research Institute.

Huang Zongxi 黃宗羲. 1986. *Records of Song and Yuan Scholars* 宋元學案. 4 vols. Shanghai: Zhonghua.

Huntington, Samuel P. 1993. "The Clash of Civilizations?" *Foreign Affairs* 72:3: 22–49.

———. 1996a. "Democracy's Third Wave." Pp. 3–25 in *The Global Resurgence of Democracy*, 2nd edition, ed. Larry Dimond and Marc F. Plattner. Baltimore: Johns Hopkins University Press.

———. 1996b. "The West Unique, Not Universal." *Foreign Affairs* 75:6: 28–46.

James, William. 1979. *The Will to Believe and Other Essays in Popular Philosophy*. Cambridge: Harvard University Press.

Jensen, Lionel M. 1997. *Manufacturing Confucianism*. Durham: Duke University Press.

Jones, Eric. 1994. "Asia's Fate: A Response to the Singapore School." *The National Interest* 35: 18–28.

Jullien, François. 1995. *The Propensity of Things*. Translated by Janet Lloyd. New York: Urzone.

Kahn, Herman. 1979. *World Economic Development 1979 and Beyond*. New York: Morrow Quill.

Kant, Immanuel. 1948. *Groundwork of the Metaphysics of Morals*. Pp. 53–123 in *The Moral Law*, translated by H. J. Paton. London: Hutchinson.

———. 1993. *Critique of Practical Reason*. Translated by Lewis White Beck. Upper Saddle River: Prentice Hall.

Kasulis, Thomas, Wimal Dissanayake, and Roger T. Ames, eds. 1993. *Self As Body in Asian Theory and Practice*. Albany: State University of New York Press.

Kausikan, Bilahari. 1998. "The 'Asian Values' Debate: A View from Singapore." Pp. 17–27 in *Democracy in East Asia*, ed. Diamond and Plattner. Baltimore: Johns Hopkins University Press.

Keenan, Barry. 1977. *The Dewey Experiment in China*. Cambridge: Council on East Asian Studies, Harvard University.

Keightley, David N. 1978. "The Religious Commitment: Shang Theology and the Genesis of Chinese Political Culture." *History of Religions* 17:3/4: 211–25.

Kent, Ann. 1993. *Between Freedom and Subsistence: China and Human Rights*. Hong Kong: Oxford University Press.

King, Ambrose Y. C. 金耀基. 1985. "The Individual and Group in Confucianism." Pp. 57–70 in *Individualism and Holism*, ed. Donald L. Munro. Ann Arbor: Center for Chinese Studies, University of Michigan.

———. 1993a. "A Non-Paradigmatic Search for Democracy in a Post-Confucian Culture: The Case of Taiwan, R.O.C." Pp. 139–61 in *Political Culture and Democracy in Developing Countries*, ed. Larry Diamond. Boulder: Lynne Rienner.

———. 1993b. *History of Chinese Thought on 'People as Basis'* 中國民本思想史. Taipei: Commercial Press.

———. 1997. "Confucianism, Modernity, and Asian Democracy." Pp. 163–79 in *Justice and Democracy*, ed. Ron Bontekoe and Marietta Stephaniants. Honolulu: University of Hawaii Press.

King, Ambrose Y. C., and Michael Bond. 1985. "The Confucian Paradigm of Man: A Sociological View." Pp. 29–45 in *Chinese Culture and Mental Health*, ed. Wen-shing Tseng and David Wu. Orlando: Academic Press.

Knoblock, John. 1988–1994. *Xunzi*. 3 vols. Stanford: Stanford University Press.

Kohn, Livia. 1992. "Selfhood and Spontaneity in Ancient Chinese Thought." Pp. 123–38 in *Selves, People, and Persons: What Does It Mean to Be a Self?* ed. Leroy Rouner. Notre Dame: University of Notre Dame Press.

Kymlicka, Will. 1989. *Liberalism, Community, and Culture*. Oxford: Clarendon Press.

Lai, Karyn, ed. 2000. *Feminism and Chinese Philosophy*. Special issue of *Journal of Chinese Philosophy* 27:2: 127–249.

Lao Siguang 勞思光. 1974. *History of Chinese Philosophy* 中國哲學史. Hong Kong: Chinese University of Hong Kong Press.

Lau, D. C., trans. 1970. *Mencius*. Middlesex: Penguin.

————, trans. 1979. *Confucius: The Analects.* Middlesex: Penguin.

Lee, Thomas H. C. 1994. "Academies: Official Sponsorship and Suppression." Pp. 117–43 in *Imperial Rulership and Cultural Change in Traditional China*, ed. Frederick P. Brandauer and Chun-Chieh Huang. Seattle: University of Washington Press.

Legge, James. 1970. *The Chinese Classics.* 5 vols. Hong Kong: Hong Kong University Press.

Lewis, Ewart. 1954. *Medieval Political Ideas.* 2 vols. New York: Knopf.

Lewis, Mark Edward. 1999. *Writing and Authority in Early China.* Albany: State University of New York Press.

Leys, Simon, trans. 1997. *The Analects of Confucius.* London: Norton.

Li Chenyang. 1999. *The Tao Encounters the West.* Albany: State University of New York Press.

————, ed. 2000. *The Sage and the Second Sex.* La Salle: Open Court Press.

Li Yu-ning. 1982. *Historical Roots of Changes in Women's Status in Modern China.* St. John's Papers in Asian Studies 29. Jamaica: St. John's University, Center of Asian Studies.

Li Zehou 李澤厚. 1996. *History of Ancient Chinese Thought* 中國古代思想史論. Taipei: Sanmin.

Liang Ch'i-ch'ao 梁啓超. (1930). *History of Chinese Political Thought.* Translated by L. T. Chen. New York: Harcourt Brace.

————. 1996. *History of Pre-Qin Political Thought* 先秦政治思想史. Beijing: Oriental.

————. 1997. *Collected Essays* 梁啓超文集. Beijing: Yanshan.

Liang Shuming 梁漱溟. 1989. *Complete Works* 梁漱溟全集. 8 vols. Shandong: People's Press.

Lin Lihsueh. 1990. "The Relationship between Ruler and Minister in the Theory of the 'Three Mainstays.'" *Journal of Chinese Philosophy* 17: 4: 439–71.

Lin Yutang. 1938. *My Country and My People.* New York: Halcyon House.

Lincoln, Abraham. 1953. *The Collected Works of Abraham Lincoln.* 9 vols. Edited by Roy P. Basler. New Brunswick: Rutgers University Press.

Lippmann, Walter. 1927. *The Phantom Public.* New York: Harcourt Brace.

————. 1965. *Public Opinion.* New York: Free Press.

Liu Binyan. 1993. "Civilization Grafting: No Culture is an Island." *Foreign Affairs* 75: 4: 19–21.

Liu Shu-hsien 劉述先. 1972. "The Confucian Approach to the Problem of Transcendence and Immanence." *Philosophy East and West* 22:1: 45–52.

————. 1992. *Confucianism and Modernization* 儒家思想與現代化. Edited by Jing Haifeng 景海峰. Beijing: Chinese Broadcasting and TV Publishing House.

Liu Shu-Hsien, and Robert Allison, eds. 1988. *Harmony and Strife.* Hong Kong: Chinese University Press.

Liu Yong Ping. 1998. *Origins of Chinese Law*. Hong Kong: Oxford University Press.

Locke, John. 1967. *Two Treatises of Government*. Edited by Peter Laslett. Cambridge: Cambridge University Press.

Loewe, Michael. 1982. *Chinese Ideas of Life and Death*. London: George Allen and Unwin.

———, ed. 1993. *Early Chinese Texts: A Bibliographical Guide*. Berkeley: University of California Press.

Lovejoy, Arthur O. 1936. *The Great Chain of Being*. Cambridge: Harvard University Press.

Lu Xun 魯迅. 1990. *Diary of a Madman and Other Stories*. Translated by William A. Lyell. Honolulu: University of Hawaii Press.

Luxuriant Dews of the Spring and Autumn Annals 春秋繁露. *A Concordance to the Chunqiu Fanlu*. 1994. Edited by D. C. Lau and Chen Fong Ching. Hong Kong: Commercial Press.

Lü's Spring and Autumn Annals 呂氏春秋. A Concordance to the *Lüshi chunqiu*. 1994. Edited by D. C. Lau and Chen Fong Ching. Hong Kong: Commercial Press.

Machle, Edward J. 1993. *Nature and Heaven in the Xunzi: A Study of Tianlun*. Albany: State University of New York Press.

Mackin, James A. Jr. 1997. *Community over Chaos*. Tuscaloosa: University of Alabama Press.

Mahbubani, Kishore. 1992. "The West and the Rest." *The National Interest* 28: 3–12.

———. 1995. "The Pacific Way." *Foreign Affairs* 74:1: 100–11.

Manicas, Peter. 1982. "John Dewey: Anarchism and the Political State." Pp. 407–29 in *John Dewey*, vol. 2, ed. James E. Tiles. New York: Routledge.

Mead, George Herbert. 1934. *Mind, Self, and Society from the Standpoint of a Social Behaviorist*. Edited by Charles Morris. Chicago: University of Chicago Press.

Mencius 孟子. *A Concordance to the Mengzi*. 1995. Edited by D. C. Lau and Chen Fong Ching. Hong Kong: Commercial Press.

Menzel, Johanna M., ed. 1963. *The Chinese Civil Service*. Boston: D. C. Heath and Co.

Mill, John Stuart. 1985. *Utilitarianism, including On Liberty, Essays on Bentham, and Selections from the Writings of Jeremy Bentham and John Austin*. Edited by Mary Warnock. Glasgow: Fontana.

Mote, Frederick W. 1971. *Intellectual Foundations of China*. New York: Knopf.

Mou Zongsan 牟宗三. 1968. *Mind and Nature* 心體與性體. 3 vols. Taipei: Zhongzheng.

———. 1973. "The Idealist Basis of Liberalism 自由主義之理想主義的根據." Pp. 207–15 in *Learning on Life* 生命的學問. Taipei: Sanmin.

Mungello, D. E. 1985. *Curious Land: The Jesuit Accommodation and the Origins of Sinology*. Honolulu: University of Hawaii Press.

———. 1994. *The Chinese Rites Controversy: Its History and Meaning*. San Francisco: The Ricci Institute for Chinese-Western Cultural History.

Munro, Donald J. 1969. *The Concept of Man in Early China*. Stanford: Stanford University Press.

———. 1979. "The Shape of Chinese Values in the Eye of an American Philosopher." Pp. 39–56 in *The China Difference*, ed. Ross Terrill. New York: Harper and Row.

———, ed. 1985. *Individualism and Holism*. Ann Arbor: Center for Chinese Studies, University of Michigan.

Murdoch, Iris. 1970. *The Sovereignty of Good*. London: Routledge.

Nakane, Chie. 1973. *Japanese Society*. Middlesex: Penguin.

Nathan, Andrew J. 1985. *Chinese Democracy*. Berkeley: University of California Press.

Nathan, Andrew J., and Shi Tianjian. 1993. "Cultural Requisites for Democracy in China: Findings from a Survey." *Daedalus* 122:2: 95–123.

Needham, Joseph. 1956. *Science and Civilization in China*. Cambridge: Cambridge University Press.

Neville, Robert Cummings. 2000. *Boston Confucianism*. Albany: State University of New York Press.

Niebuhr, Reinhold. 1932. *Moral Man, Immoral Society*. New York: Charles Scribner's Sons.

Nivison, David S. 1996. *The Ways of Confucianism*. Edited by Bryan Van Norden. La Salle: Open Court Press.

Nozick, Robert. 1974. *Anarchy, State, and Utopia*. New York: Basic Books.

Nussbaum, Bruce. 1997. "Capital, Not Culture." *Foreign Affairs* 76:2: 165.

Okin, Susan Moller. 1989. *Justice, Gender, and the Family*. New York: Basic Books.

Onuma, Yasuaki. 1996. *In Quest of Intercivilizational Human Rights*. Center for Asian Pacific Affairs Occasional Paper No. 2. San Francisco: Center for Asian Pacific Affairs.

Oppenheimer, Franz. 1914. *The State*. Indianapolis: Bobbs-Merrill.

Parekh, Bhikhu. 1993. "The Cultural Particularity of Liberal Democracy." Pp. 156–75 in *Prospects for Democracy*, ed. David Held. Stanford: Stanford University Press.

Pasternak, Burton. 1988. "A Conversation with Fei Xiaotong." *Current Anthropology* 29:4: 637–62.

Peerenboom, Randall. 1995. "Rights, Interests, and the Interest in Rights in China." *Stanford Journal of International Law* 31: 359–86.

———. 1998. "Confucian Harmony and Freedom of Thought: The Right to Think versus Right Thinking." Pp. 234–60 in *Confucianism and Human Rights*, ed. de Bary and Tu. New York: Columbia University Press.

Pennock, J. Roland, and John W. Chapman, eds. 1967. *Equality*. Nomos Series, vol. IX. New York: Atherton.

Perry, Elizabeth J., and Ellen V. Fuller. 1991. "China's Long March to Democracy." *World Policy Journal* 8:4: 663–87.

Philips, Denis Charles. 1976. *Holistic Thought in Social Science*. Stanford: Stanford University Press.

Phillips, Anne, ed. 1987. *Feminism and Equality*. Oxford: Blackwell.

Popper, Karl. 1945. *The Open Society and Its Enemies*. 2 vols. London: Routledge.

Porkert, Manfred. 1974. *Theoretical Foundations of Chinese Medicine*. Cambridge: MIT Press.

Pye, Lucian W. 1985. *Asian Power and Politics: The Cultural Dimensions of Authority*. Cambridge: Harvard University Press.

———. 1996. "The State and Individual: An Overview Interpretation." Pp. 16–42 in *The Individual and State in China*, ed. Brian Hook. New York: Oxford University Press.

Rashid, Salin. 1997. *Clash of Civilizations?: Asian Responses*. Karachi: Oxford University Press.

Rawls, John. 1971. *A Theory of Justice*. Oxford: Oxford University Press.

———. 1993. *Political Liberalism*. New York: Columbia University Press.

Raz, Joseph. 1985. "The Justification of Authority." *Philosophy and Public Affairs* 14: 2–29.

———. 1986. *The Morality of Freedom*. Oxford: Oxford University Press.

Reiss, Hans, ed. 1970. *Kant: Political Writings*. Translated by H. B. Nisbet. Cambridge: Cambridge University Press.

Ren Jiyu 任繼愈. 1983. *Development of Chinese Philosophy: Pre-Qin* 中國哲學發展史：先秦. Beijing: People's Press.

Ricoeur, Paul. 1992. *One Self As Another*. Translated by Kathleen Blamey. Chicago: University of Chicago Press.

Rites of Zhou 周禮. *A Concordance to the Zhouli*. 1993. ICS Ancient Chinese Text Concordance Series. Edited by D. C. Lau and Chen Fong Ching. Hong Kong: Commercial Press.

Roetz, Heiner. 1993. *Confucian Ethics of the Axial Age*. Albany: State University of New York Press.

Rorty, Amélie Oksenberg. 1990. "Persons and *Personae*." Pp. 21–38 in *The Person and the Human Mind*, ed. Christopher Gill. Oxford: Clarendon Press.

Rorty, Richard. 1980. *Philosophy and the Mirror of Nature*. Oxford: Blackwell.

———. 1989. *Contingency, Irony, and Solidarity*. New York: Cambridge University Press.

———. 1991. *Objectivity, Relativism, and Truth*. New York: Cambridge University Press.

————. 1993. "Human Rights, Rationality, and Sentimentality." Pp. 111–34 in *On Human Rights*, ed. Stephen Shue and Susan Hurley. New York: Basic Books.

Rosemont, Henry. 1989. "Rights-Bearing Individuals and Role-Bearing Persons." Pp. 71–101 in *Rules, Rituals, and Responsibility*, ed. Mary I. Bockover. La Salle: Open Court Press.

————. 1997. "Classical Confucian and Contemporary Feminist Perspectives on the Self: Some Parallels and Their Implications." Pp. 63–82 in *Culture and self*, ed. Douglas Allen. Boulder: Westview Press.

————. 1998. "Human Rights: A Bill of Worries." Pp. 54–66 in *Confucianism and Human Rights*, ed. de Bary and Tu. New York: Columbia University Press.

Rowe, William T. 1993. "The Problem of 'Civil Society' in Late Imperial China." *Modern China* 19:2: 139–57.

Rucker, Darnell. 1980. "Selves into Persons: Another Legacy from John Dewey." Pp. 166–81 in *John Dewey*, vol. 1, ed. James E. Tiles. New York: Routledge.

Russell, Bertrand. 1922. *The Problem of China*. London: Allen and Unwin.

Rustow, Dankwart A. 1970. "Transitions to Democracy." *Comparative Politics* 2: 337–63.

Saatkamp, Herman J. Jr., ed. 1995. *Rorty and Pragmatism: The Philosopher Responds to His Critics*. Nashville: Vanderbilt University Press.

Sandel, Michael. 1982. *Liberalism and the Limits of Justice*. New York: Cambridge University Press.

————. 1996. *Democracy's Discontent: America in Search of a Public Philosophy*. Cambridge: Harvard University Press.

Sartori, Giovani, ed. 1984. *Social Science Concepts*. London: Sage.

Sato, Seizaburo. 1997. "Asia and Democracy." Pp. 81–92 in *Democracy in Asia*, ed. Michèle Schmiegelow. New York: St. Martin's Press.

Schilpp, Paul Arthur, ed. 1951. *The Philosophy of John Dewey*. New York: Tudor.

Schwartz, Benjamin. 1975. "Transcendence in Ancient China." *Daedalus* 104: 57–68.

————. 1985. *The World of Thought in Ancient China*. Cambridge: Harvard University Press.

Sen, Amartya. 1996. "Thinking about Human Rights and Asian Values." *Human Rights Dialogue* 4: 2–3.

Sennett, Richard. 1977a. "Destructive Gemeinschaft." Pp. 171–97 in *Beyond the Crisis*, ed. Norman Birnbaum. New York: Oxford University Press.

————. 1977b. *The Fall of Public Man*. New York: Knopf.

Shun, Kwong-loi. 1997. *Mencius and Early Chinese Thought*. Stanford: Stanford University Press.

Shuowen jiezi, annotated 說文解字注. 1966. Taipei: Yiwen.

Sigmund, Paul E. 1967. "Hierarchy, Equality, and Consent in Medieval Christian Thought." Pp. 134–53 in *Equality*, ed. Pennock and Chapman. New York: Atherton.

Smith, Tony. 1997. "Dangerous Conjecture." *Foreign Affairs* 76:2: 163–4.

Solinger, Dorothy J. 1991. *China's Transients and the State: A Form of Civil Society*. Hong Kong: Hong Kong Institute of Asia-Pacific Studies, the Chinese University of Hong Kong.

Song History 宋史. 1977. 20 vols. Beijing: Zhonghua.

Strand, David. 1990. "Protest in Beijing: Civil Society and the Public Sphere in China." *Problems of Communism* 39: 1–19.

Sun Yat-sen. 1937. *Three People's Principles* 三民主義. Shanghai: Sanmin.

———. 1950. *Complete Works of the Prime Minister* 總理全書. Taipei: Zhongyang Wenwu Gongying She.

Swann, Nancy Lee. 1932. *Pan Chao: Foremost Woman Scholar of China*. New York: Century.

Tai, Hung-chao, ed. 1989. *Confucianism and Economic Development: An Oriental Alternative?* Washington, D.C.: Washington Institute.

Tam, Henry. 1998. *Communitarianism: A New Agenda for Politics and Citizenship*. New York: New York University Press.

Tan Sor-hoon. 1999. "Experience As Art." *Asian Philosophy* 9:2: 107–22.

———. 2001. "Mentor or Friend? Confucius and Aristotle on Equality and Ethical Development in Friendship." *International Studies in Philosophy* 33:4: 99–121.

———. 2002. "Between Family and State: Relational Tension in Confucian Ethics." Pp. 169–88 in *Mencius: Contexts and Interpretations*, ed. Alan K. L. Chan. Honolulu: University of Hawaii Press.

———. 2003. "Can There Be a Confucian Civil Society?" In *The Moral Circle and the Self: Chinese and Western Approaches*, ed. K. C. Chong, S. H. Tan, and C. L. Ten. La Salle: Open Court Press.

Tang Junyi 唐君毅. 1991. *Complete Works* 唐君毅全集. 30 vols. Taipei: Student Press.

Tang Yi-jie. 1988. "The Problem of Harmonious Community in Ancient China." Pp. 321–4 in *Harmony and Strife*, ed. Liu and Allison. Hong Kong: Chinese University Press.

Taylor, Charles. 1979. *Hegel and Modern Society*. Cambridge: Cambridge University Press.

———. 1989. *Sources of the Self—The Making of Modern Identity*. Cambridge: Harvard University Press.

Tiles, James E. 1988. *Dewey*. New York: Routledge.

———, ed. 1992. *John Dewey: Critical Assessments*. 4 vols. New York: Routledge.

———. 1997. "Democracy As Culture." Pp. 119–31 in *Justice and Democracy*, ed. Bontekoe and Stephaniants. Honolulu: University of Hawaii Press.

Tinder, Glenn. 1980. *Community: Reflections on a Tragic Ideal.* Baton Rouge: Louisiana University Press.

Tönnies, Ferdinand. 1957. *Community and Society (Gemeinschaft und Gesellschaft).* Translated and edited by Charles P. Loomis. New York: Harper and Row.

Tu Wei-ming. 1979. *Humanity and Self-Cultivation.* Berkeley: Asian Humanities Press.

———. 1984. *Confucian Ethics Today: The Singapore Challenge.* Singapore: Curriculum Development Institute of Singapore.

———. 1985. *Confucian Thought: Selfhood As Creative Transformation.* Albany: State University of New York Press.

———. 1986. "Toward a Third Epoch of Confucian Humanism: A Background Understanding." Pp. 3–21 in *Confucianism: The Dynamics of Tradition*, ed. Irene Eber. New York: Macmillan.

———. 1989. *Centrality and Commonality.* Albany: State University of New York Press.

———. 1992. *The Modern Transformation of the Confucian Tradition* 儒家傳統的現代轉化. Beijing: Zhongguo Guangbai Dianshi.

———. 1993. *Way, Learning, and Politics: Essays on the Confucian Intellectual.* Albany: State University of New York Press.

———. 1994. "Embodying the Universe: A Note on Confucian Self-Realization." Pp. 177–86 in *Self As Person in Asian Theory and Practice*, ed. Ames, Dissanayake, and Kasulis. Albany: State University of New York Press.

———, ed. 1991. *The Triadic Chord: Confucian Ethics, Industrial East Asia, and Max Weber.* Singapore: Institute of East Asian Philosophies.

Unger, Roberto M. 1983. *The Critical Legal Studies Movement.* Cambridge: Harvard University Press.

Veith, Ilza, trans. 1966. *The Yellow Emperor's Classic of Internal Medicine* 黄帝內經. Berkeley: University of California Press.

Waley, Arthur, trans. 1996. *Confucius—The Analects.* Hertfordshire: Wordsworth.

Walzer, Michael. 1989. "The Communitarian Critique of Liberalism." *Political Theory* 18:1: 6–23.

Wawrytko, Sandra A. 2000. "Prudery and Pruprience: Historical Roots of the Confucian Conundrum Concerning Women, Sexuality, and Power." Pp. 163–98 in *The Sage and the second Sex*, ed. Li Chenyang. La Salle: Open Court Press.

Weber, Max. 1951. *The Religion of China: Confucianism and Taoism.* Translated by H. H. Gerth. New York: Free Press.

———. 1978. *Economy and Society.* Edited by G. Roth and C. Wittich. Berkeley: University of California Press.

Westbrook, Robert B. 1991. *John Dewey and American Democracy*. Ithaca: Cornell University Press.

Wieger, Leon. 1965. *Chinese Characters*. New York: Dover.

Williams, Bernard. 1975. "Self and the Future." Pp. 179–98 in *Personal Identity*, ed. John Perry. Berkeley: University of California Press.

Wolff, Robert Paul. 1977. *Understanding Rawls*. Princeton: Princeton University Press.

———. 1989. "Social Philosophy: The Agenda for the Nineties." *Journal of Social Philosophy* 20:1/2: 4–17.

Woolson, Carolin. 1998. "Dewey on the Question of Community and the Community in Question." *International Studies in Philosophy* 30:1: 121–30.

Wu Kuang-ming. 1997. "The Spirit of Pragmatism and the Pragmatic Spirit." Pp. 59–91 in *The Recovery of Philosophy in America*, ed. John Edwin Smith, Thomas P. Kasulis and Robert Cummings Neville. Albany: State University of New York Press.

Wu Yu 吳虞. 1922. *Collected Essays* 吳虞文錄. Shanghai: Oriental Press.

Xiong Shili 熊十力. 1960. *Guide to Key Elements in Reading the Classics* 讀經示要. Taipei: Guangwen.

Xu Fuguan 徐復觀. 1959. *Essays on the History of Chinese Thought* 中國思想史論集. Taiwan: Donghai University.

———. 1969. *History of Chinese Theories of Human Nature* 中國人性論史. Taipei: Commercial Press.

———. 1988. *Confucian Political Thought and Democracy, Freedom, and Human Rights* 儒家政治思想與民主自由人權. Taipei: Student Press.

Xunzi 荀子. *A Concordance to the Xunzi*. 1996. Edited by D. C. Lau and Chen Fong Ching. Hong Kong: Commercial Press.

Yang Zuhan 楊祖漢. 1995. "Contemporary Confucian Explication of Confucius' View of *Tian* 當代儒學對孔子天論的詮釋." Pp. 231–52 in *Collected Essays on Contemporary Confucianism: Tradition and Innovation* 當代儒學論集：傳統與創新, ed. Liu Shuxian. Taipei: Central Research Institute.

Yu Ying-shih 余英時. 1976. "Anti-Intellectualism and Chinese Political Thought 反智論與中國政治思想." Pp. 1–46 in *History and Thought* 歷史與思想. Taipei: Lianjing.

———. 1992. *The Path of Internal Transcendence* 內在超越之路. Beijing: Zhongguo Guangbai Dianshi.

———. 1997. "The Idea of Democracy and the Twilight of the Elite Culture in Modern China." Pp. 199–215 in *Justice and Democracy*, ed. Bontekoe and Stephaniants. Honolulu: University of Hawaii Press.

Yuan Ke 袁珂. 1960. *Ancient Chinese Myths* 中國古代神話. Beijing: Zhonghua.

Zakaria, Fareed. 1994. "Culture Is Destiny: A Conversation with Lee Kuan Yew." *Foreign Affairs* 73:2: 109–26.

————. 1997. "The Rise of Illiberal Democracy." *Foreign Affairs* 76:6: 22–43.

Zeng Chunhai 曾春海. 1989. *Essays on Confucian Philosophy* 儒家哲學論集. Taipei: Wenjin.

Zhang Dongsun 張東蓀. 1946. *Rational Nature and Democracy* 理性與民主. Taipei: Dragon Gate.

————. 1959. "A Chinese Philosopher's Theory of Knowledge." Pp. 299–324 in *Our Language and Our World*, ed. S. I. Hayakama. New York: Harper.

Zhou, Kate Xiao. 1996. *How the Farmers Changed China*. Boulder: Westview Press.

Zhuangzi 莊子 *A Concordance to Chuang Tzu*. 1956. Cambridge: Harvard University Press.

Zolo, Danilo. 1992. *Democracy and Complexity: A Realist Approach*. Translated by David McKie. University Park: Pennsylvania State University Press.

Index